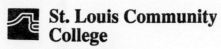

I HEARD IT THROUGH
THE GRAPEVINE

I HEARD IT THROUGH THE GRAPEVINE

Rumor in African-American Culture

PATRICIA A. TURNER

UNIVERSITY OF CALIFORNIA PRESS

BERKELEY   LOS ANGELES   LONDON

University of California Press
Berkeley and Los Angeles, California

University of California Press, Ltd.
London, England

©1993 by
The Regents of the University of California

Library of Congress Cataloging-in-Publication Data

Turner, Patricia, 1955–
    I heard it through the grapevine : rumor in African-American
culture / Patricia A. Turner.
        p.   cm.
    Includes bibliographical references and index.
    ISBN 0-520-08185-4 (acid-free paper)
    1. Afro-Americans—Folklore. 2. Urban folklore—United States.
3. Rumor—United States.   I. Title.
GR111.A47T87   1993
398'.08996073—dc20   93–17463
                                                              CIP

Printed in the United States of America
9 8 7 6 5 4 3 2 1

To the memory of my parents,
Issac Lloyd Turner and Sallie Beatrice Turner

Contents

Acknowledgments

My affection for folklore in general and contemporary legend studies in particular was born and nurtured at the University of California at Berkeley. One of the best things about folklore research is its inherently social nature. Student folklorists quickly learn how to establish collegial grapevines that allow for the sharing and swapping of versions and variants of raw material. My Berkeley professors, including Alan Dundes, Bengt af Klintberg, and Daniel F. Melia, graciously shared their expertise and time with me. The graduate student network I plugged into more than ten years ago still thrives, and Virginia Geddes, Elizabeth Radin Simons, Rosemary Levy-Zumwalt, Pamela Ow, and Florence Baer consistently send me leads and articles on issues relevant to this work.

My next stop was the University of Massachusetts at Boston, where I soon taught my colleagues and students to inform me of anything that sounded even remotely like a possible text. Mary Helen Washington, Lois Rudnick, Julie Winch, Frances Stubbs, and sister folklorist Eleanor Wachs enthusiastically supported my efforts. In addition, dozens of students, many of whom still drop me a line when they hear a new variant, contributed material; Wayne Miller, Lionel Rogers, Paula Carpenter, Marion O'Sullivan, Sheilah Mabry, and Rita Bourgeois were steadfast in their assistance. The William Monroe Trotter Institute for the Study of Black Culture, under the directorship of Wornie Reed, offered me financial and clerical support during the writing of early drafts of this manuscript. Eva Hendricks and Linda Kluz patiently assisted me in the clerical stages.

Folklorists at other campuses were extraordinarily generous with both their time and their data. Jan Harold Brunvand, Janet Langlois, and Gary Alan Fine freely shared versions of the items discussed in this book, as well as drafts of their own works in progress on rumor and contemporary legend. The entire membership of the Association of African and African American Folklorists offered me encouragement and commentary as I refined segments of this research. In particular, Adrienne Lanier Stewart, Gerald Davis, Trudier Harris, William Wiggins, and John Roberts kept those cards and clippings coming in to me.

Since my arrival at the University of California at Davis I have broken in a whole new crop of student and faculty compatriots. Jay Mechling, David Scofield Wilson, Simon Bronner (visiting professor in summer 1991), Jacob Olupona, and John Stewart have all made contributions. My Davis students soon got used to the ever-present tape recorder in my office and the data forms that I brought to all of my classes; Maya Hart, Terry Arnold, Denise Isom, Katrina Bell, Mia Patton, and Eric Cain deserve special mention. A U.C. Davis Faculty Development Award granted by the Office of the Provost allowed me to finish the final version of this manuscript. Aklil Bekele, Holly DeRemer, Carol Beck, and Gladys Bell assisted in the more tedious dimensions of the preparation of that version.

Benjamin Orlove, Judith Stacey, and Diane Wolf helped me find my way to the University of California Press, where editor Naomi Schneider took me and this project under her wing.

In the end, however, Mary Ellen Hanrahan and Dolores Beelard must be recognized as providing the most important professional help during the past several years. While I was working on this book, they were taking excellent, loving care of my young son, Daniel Turner Smith. Finally, I am grateful that Daniel and his father, Kevin Smith, took such good care of each other that my absences were rarely noted. Okay, guys, now I'm ready to go to Disneyland!

Preliminary research on the Church's chicken cycle, "Church's Fried Chicken and the Klan: A Rhetorical Analysis of Rumor in the Black Community," appeared in *Western Folklore* 46 (October 1987): 294–306, ©1987 The California Folklore Society; an essay study entitled "The Atlanta Child Murders: A Case Study of Folklore in the Black Community" appeared in *Creative Ethnicity: Symbols and Strategies of Contemporary Ethnic Life*, ed. Stephen Stern and John Allan Cicala (Logan: Utah State University Press, 1991), 75–86; a different version of Chapter 6 appeared as "Ambivalent Patrons: The Role of Rumor and Contemporary Legend in African American Consumer Decisions" in *Journal of American Folklore* 105 (Fall 1992): 424–41, ©1992 The American Folklore Society.

Preface

I remember the exact day and time that I began this book. I was teaching Introduction to Black Literature at the University of Massachusetts at Boston in February 1986. Like most folklorists, I rely on folk material for examples in even my nonfolklore courses. After telling the students about the popular contemporary legend known as the Kentucky Fried Rat, Wayne, an intelligent young African-American raised his hand to say, "Oh well, I guess that's like what they say about eating at Church's Chicken—you know the Klan owns it and they do something to the chicken so that when black men eat there they become sterile. Except that I guess it isn't really like the one about the Kentucky Fried Rat because it is true about Church's. I know because a friend of mine saw the story on '60 Minutes.'" Several other black students nodded in silent agreement; the white students looked at them in rapt disbelief, while the remaining black students seemed to be making a mental note not to eat at Church's. After class I sprinted to my office and began calling folklore colleagues. No professional folklorists (all white) had heard any version of the Church's text, but throughout the remainder of the day I was able to collect several variations from black students and black members of the university staff.

Several months later, as I was finishing an article on the Church's cycle, I found myself discussing it with another class. An African-American student raised her hand and said, "Well, if you don't believe that one, you probably don't believe that the FBI was responsible for the deaths of all those children in Atlanta. I heard that they were taking the bodies to the Centers for Disease Control in Atlanta to perform interferon experiments on them." As I began research on *that* story, also unknown to my white colleagues, I confirmed my earlier suspicions that these contemporary texts were not mere ephemera lacking in historical antecedents. Indeed, a provocative corpus of related material can be traced back to the early sixteenth century, when white Europeans began to have regular contact with sub-Saharan Africa. I realized that this discourse was sufficiently rich to explore in book-length form.

A white colleague familiar with my work on the Church's and Atlanta Child Killer stories then pointed out that the increasingly common claim that the AIDS virus was the product of an anti-black conspiracy fit the pattern of my research. And in early 1989 I was querying a black studies class about the Church's item when one student raised her hand and said, "I don't know about the Klan owning Church's, but I do know that they are supposed to own Troop clothing." Other African-American students expressed agreement, while white students sat perplexed by this unfamiliar news. With this text the students had a real advantage over me because I had never even heard of the popular line of clothing apparently marketed quite aggressively to young black consumers.

I was convinced that these items fit into the category dubbed by folklorists as "urban" or "contemporary legend." Interestingly enough, Jan Harold Brunvand, a prolific writer on urban legend, referred to such stories as "an integral part of *white* [emphasis added] Anglo-American culture and are told and believed by some of the most sophisticated 'folk' of modern society—young people, urbanites, and the well-educated."[1] The fact that no in-depth investigation of the texts that circulate among African-Americans has been conducted is not surprising. Most folklorists are white, and they have not discovered the black urban legend tradition. As later chapters in this book will demonstrate, the items under discussion circulate almost exclusively within the black community. Although some black verbal genres—songs, toasts, and other relatively structured folk expressions—call attention to them-

selves by their very form, making collection by white folklorists unproblematic, the formal dimensions of conversational
idioms are much more subtle and therefore more private.
Consequently, African-Americans are able to maintain more
control over their dissemination.

This book divides into two basic parts. In Chapters 1 and 2 I
discuss historical examples of "rumor" discourse and suggest
why many blacks have—for good reason—channeled beliefs
about race relations into familiar formulae, ones developed as
early as the time of first contact between sub-Saharan Africans
and European whites. Then in Chapters 3–7 I explore the
continuation of these issues in late-twentieth-century African-
American rumors and contemporary legends, using examples
collected in the field. Because I was able to monitor these
contemporary legends as they unfolded and played themselves out, rigorous analysis was possible.

What follows, then, is an examination of the themes common to these contemporary items and related historical ones,
and an explanation for their persistence. Concerns about conspiracy, contamination, cannibalism, and castration—perceived threats to individual black bodies, which are then
translated into animosity toward the race as a whole—run
through nearly four hundred years of black contemporary legend material and prove remarkably tenacious. I also note,
as appropriate, the existence of seemingly identical rumor/
contemporary legends in white society.

Because black history is relatively new as an academic subject, much of the history passed down by successive generations of African-Americans is in the form of folklore. Thus,
while one informant could offer no concrete information
about the Ku Klux Klan atrocities of 1868–72, he did know
from his grandparents that after the Civil War the white supremacist group had "burned and butchered black folk left
and right." He also knew from his parents that "they [the
KKK] got away with burning all these churches up and mutilating Civil Rights workers" during the 1950s and 1960s. It
therefore seemed entirely plausible to him that a modern Klan
might gain control over an athletic wear company in order
to exploit the generation of African-Americans to which he

belonged. Hence, in pondering the meanings and functions of these rumors and contemporary legends, I defend the somewhat controversial position that they do not necessarily reflect pathological preoccupations among African-Americans. Rather, I make the case that these rumors and contemporary legends often function as tools of resistance for many of the folk who share them.

Introduction

It seems from rumors I just can't get away
I'll bet there will be rumors floating around
on Judgment Day

Timex Social Club

When the Timex Social Club, a popular young singing group, lamented the pervasiveness of rumors in the mid-1980s, they meant those rumors that caused personal conflict within their own peer group: *Hear that one about Michael / some say he must be gay / I try to argue but they say / if he was straight he wouldn't move that way.* But these were not the only unverified orally transmitted stories circulating in African-American communities. In another type of rumor known primarily to African-Americans, the topic was not in-group discord, but rather conflict between the races.

In this century, only those stories that emerged during times of domestic or international crisis garnered serious interest. During World War II, rumor clinics were established in an effort to prevent potentially adverse hearsay of all sorts from gaining credibility. Many of the most widespread rumors reflected racial discord. While African-Americans heard that black soldiers were being singled out for particularly hazardous and even suicidal war assignments, whites heard that in the communities near armed forces training camps hundreds of white women were pregnant with black men's children. Racially based rumors did not vanish following the war, of course; in the absence of crisis, however, official concern with

1

them diminished. Only in the 1960s, when racial unrest escalated precipitously, did municipal and federal authorities again sit up and take notice. Rumor clinics and hotlines were reestablished to combat the proverbial grapevine, on which stories about acts of violence, both incidental and conspiratorial, abounded.[1]

After the crises of the sixties subsided, the clinics and hotlines closed down. Yet unconfirmed stories alleging bitter racial animosity still circulated within black communities. The following is a representative sampling of rumors known to many African-Americans from all over the United States during this era:

Text #1: Church's [fast food chicken franchise] is owned by the Ku Klux Klan [KKK], and they put something in it to make black men sterile.

Text #2: I remember hearing that the killings [of twenty-eight African-Americans] in Atlanta were related to genocide of the black race. The FBI [Federal Bureau of Investigation] was responsible and using the bodies for interferon research.

Text #3: I have heard that U.S. scientists created AIDS in a laboratory (possibly as a weapon to use against enemy in the event of war), and they needed to test the virus, so they go to Africa, as they [Africans] are expendable, introduce the disease, and then are unable to control its spread to Europeans and Americans.

Text #4: Troop [a popular brand of athletic wear] is owned by the Ku Klux Klan. They are using the money they make from the products to finance the lawsuit that they lost to the black woman whose son was killed by the Klan.

Text #5: Reebok is made in South Africa. All of the money they make off of those shoes goes to support whites in South Africa.

Text #6: The production and mass distribution of drugs is an attempt by the white man to keep blacks who are striving to better themselves from making it in the world. So many blacks take drugs in order to find release and escape from the problems they face in life. By taking drugs, blacks are killing themselves, and by selling them they are bringing about the imminent destruction of their race. Overall, the white man has conspired to wipe out the black population by using them [blacks] to destroy themselves.

Text #7: Tropical Fantasy [a fruit-flavored soft drink] is made by the KKK. There is a special ingredient in it that makes black men sterile.[2]

Many obvious and some not-so-obvious themes link these seven texts, of which I collected multiple versions from blacks—whites, for the most part, not being privy to them—during the mid-1980s and early 1990s. The overall theme is that organized anti-black conspiracies threaten the communal well-being and, in particular, the individual bodies of blacks. This concern predates the twentieth century. Indeed, a long list of similar sentiments can be compiled starting with the earliest contact between white Europeans and black Africans.

Before connecting these contemporary texts to possible historical antecedents, I need to issue a qualification. Tracing a rumor, legend, or indeed any primarily oral genre back to its earliest manifestations is always problematic. There is an obvious dilemma in trying to determine and, especially, document that certain information or misinformation was first circulated in the form of rumor or legend. In the first two chapters of this book, therefore, attention will be given to folk ideas that *most probably* circulated as rumor or legend, regardless of their precise mode of presentation. In any event, this study is less about rumor and legend analysis than it is about the pervasiveness of metaphors linking the fate of the black race to the fates of black bodies, metaphors in use since the very first contact between whites and blacks. It just so happens that, at least in this century, most of these metaphors have been rendered in the rumor/legend form; moreover, theory regarding this genre sheds light on the pre-twentieth-century material as well. Consequently, even the older material will be treated and referred to as rumor or legend.

Clarifying the often murky distinction between rumor and legend is equally problematic. Like other scholars engaged in textual analysis, folklorists frequently argue about how best to classify the material they collect. In the case of rumor and legend, the subtle nuances that distinguish one from the other are myriad. Yet in my research, both formats were clearly used to express a fairly specific body of African-American folk belief. As folklorist Patrick B. Mullen points out, the matter is further complicated by the fact that rumor has traditionally been studied by social scientists, while legend has fallen squarely within the disciplinary territory of folklorists.[3]

In their seminal book *The Psychology of Rumor*, Gordon W. Allport and Leo Postman define rumor as "a specific proposition for belief, passed along from person to person, usually by word of mouth, without secure standards of evidence being present."[4] For example, one of my informants claimed to have heard "something about AIDS being a product of a conspiracy." Such a comment fits the recognized criteria for rumor: it is a brief, oral, nonnarrative statement based on hearsay. Then consider the claim quoted above (text #3) that American scientists created AIDS in a laboratory and, to test the virus, introduced the disease in Africa, since Africans are "expendable"; in the end, however, they were unable to control its spread to Europeans and Americans. This comment does not quite conform to the definition of rumor. Containing several "propositions for belief," it has a strong narrative component; in fact, it falls into the often-problematic genre of legend or contemporary legend.

The standard, though often debated, folklore definition of legend is a narrative account set in the recent past and containing traditional motifs that is told as true. "Urban legend" is a more recent designation, referring to accounts incorporating modern motifs. The "urban" qualifier has occasionally caused misunderstanding, for it does not necessarily refer to nonrural events. Many people, for instance, know the notorious Kentucky Fried Rat story, an urban legend superficially similar to the Church's Chicken text. In most versions, a friend or relative of the narrator stops by a branch of the fast food franchise at night and orders a bucket of chicken to go. Taking a bite in the dark, the individual is disturbed to taste hair; when the lights are turned on in the car, a deep-fried rat is revealed. With its focus on a modern-day institution, this text is a classic "urban legend," even though many versions have been recorded in rural settings.[5] Taking this difficulty into consideration, most folklorists and social scientists now use the term *contemporary legend* to describe unsubstantiated narratives with traditional themes and modern motifs that circulate orally (and sometimes in print) in multiple versions and that are told as if they are true or at least plausible.

A brief examination of the AIDS text (#3) may help to illuminate the rumor/contemporary legend distinction. This informant's account contains some specifics, such as the involvement of U.S. scientists, a laboratory, and Africa. She tells it as a story with a beginning, a middle, and an end. The content and form clearly fit the contemporary legend designation. When I asked another informant what she had heard about the origin of AIDS, she responded, "I heard it was all some kind of conspiracy to kill black folk." Even after I questioned her for specifics, she could offer none of the concrete details that the informant for text #3 did. Yet I would argue that both sets of comments were influenced by the same concerns; thus the formal differences between the utterances are mitigated.

Allport and Postman, in fact, make the case that legends are often little more than solidified rumors.[6] This may well be true of many items in the African-American rumor/legend tradition. As we shall see, some racial conflicts have generated rumors, others have generated legends, and still others, the AIDS controversy being a good example, have generated both. Thus, in the course of my research I have found that theories about rumor formation and transmission usually help to explain contemporary legends, and theories about contemporary legend development lend themselves nicely to an understanding of rumor. As Mullen points out, "Since legends exhibit characteristics which are of interest to both rumor theorists and folklorists, the study of items in transmission should not be limited by terminology. The folklorist and social scientist should be aware of each other's work when they are dealing with similar phenomena."[7] In the remainder of this book, therefore, I will use the term *rumor* to refer to short, nonnarrative expressions of belief, *legend* to refer to the more traditionally grounded narratives of belief, and *contemporary legend* to refer to items containing particularly modern motifs.

In writing *I Heard It through the Grapevine*, I have struggled to make it a book that would be of interest to a wide range of scholars—those who earn their livings pondering the issues I discuss; at the same time, I want the book to be accessible to the informants who shared their texts with me—those who live these lives. I have thus tried to minimize attention to the theoretical underpinnings of my argument, such as psychoanalytic theory and reader-response criticism, which I trust scholars will recognize. My goal was a more rhetorical one: to uncover what determined the persuasiveness of these folklore cycles, what in the texts themselves or in the circumstances surrounding their dissemination gave them life and made African-Americans willing to incorporate them into their repertoires. Moreover, I wanted to know what value to place on the texts in terms of what they reveal about black worldview.

Some readers may be dismayed by the lack of solid statistical evidence I offer to support my claims that conspiracy and contamination motifs have been and continue to be strong in African-American folklore. Anyone wanting to know what proportion of the black population believes that John F. Kennedy was assassinated by the KKK or how many adolescents abandoned their Reeboks to support their brethren in South Africa will be disappointed. I possessed neither the training, time, nor resources to undertake a fully empirical study of these issues. In any event, I am not sure that valid answers to these kinds of questions are attainable.

Since I heard my first Church's text in 1986 I have been an almost-round-the-clock field-worker. At family and faculty parties, in university lecture halls and senior citizen centers, in correspondence with ministers and prisoners, while getting my hair cut or taking prepared childbirth classes, I have posed open-ended questions to those with whom I have had contact—for example, "Have you ever heard anything unusual about the ownership of any of these fast food places?" or "Do you think they'll ever really find out who killed Martin Luther King?" After establishing that an individual is willing to talk, I always identify myself and the scope of my project.

For the material quoted in this book, I used data forms or tape-recorded interviews accompanied by an informant's release.

During the past seven years I have held faculty positions at both an East Coast and a West Coast university. I have traveled extensively, and many colleagues in folklore have shared data from their own environs with me. Although most of my informants are African-American, I have conducted dozens of interviews with members of other ethnic groups as well. In order to maximize age, class, and occupational variety, I have also endeavored to collect beyond my students. The strongest insights, I believe, have come from sessions with informants I was able to interview repeatedly, though one-time sessions have also proved revealing, both of the contexts in which rumor flourishes and of the texts themselves. *I Heard It through The Grapevine* is built upon both kinds of interaction.

The writing of this book has spanned shifts in the accepted name not only for the texts under consideration here, but also for the folk who use the discourse. When I began conducting fieldwork in the mid-1980s, most informants identified themselves as black. By the early 1990s that label had shifted to African-American. However, Afro-American, West Indian, mixed race, and even Negro were terms offered by informants to identify their ethnicity. In my descriptions of specific informants, I use the label they use to describe themselves. In generalizations about Americans of African descent, I use African-American and black interchangeably.

Like most African-Americans, I am dismayed by essentialist generalizations that state, "African-Americans think . . ." or "Blacks in American society feel. . . ." Often I find that my own thoughts and feelings do not match such comments. I would thus not want the reader to assume that anything in this book represents "typical African-American thinking." Rather, the book takes seriously an under-studied folk tradition shared by many black Americans, a pattern of thought extant in African-American culture.

Chapter One

Cannibalism

"They doe eat each other alive"

Many modern American rumors, legends, and folk ideas about the origins and meaning of racial difference can be traced to the days of first contact between white English explorers and black sub-Saharan Africans. When the fully clothed Englishmen and the sparsely dressed Africans looked at each other, they came to the first of a long series of mutual misunderstandings—misunderstandings that may have permanently discolored their relationship. Each group needed to reconcile the foreign appearance and unfathomable actions of the other. And in trying to fit these unfamiliar "others" into their own worldview, both groups came to the same conclusion: these other people were cannibals.

Contemporary ethnographers would not endorse using the label *cannibal* or *man-eater* in a pejorative fashion. Ample evidence suggests that some form of cannibalism has been practiced in all corners of the world.[1] Today, moreover, we are taught to draw careful distinctions between peoples who practice ritual cannibalism—cultures for whom eating human flesh is an important component of their spiritual system—and peoples who practice gastronomic cannibalism—cultures for whom human flesh is simply part of their dietary regime. But the Englishmen and Africans of the sixteenth century entertained no such enlightened distinctions. To them, human-flesh eating was associated with barbaric and uncivilized behavior.

9

The etymology of the word *cannibal* dates back to this era when Europeans were discovering lands and peoples different from their own. Their misinterpretation was so fundamental that the word for "Carib" was changed to "Canib," and thus a new term for an alleged practice of southern Caribbean islanders entered the language. Some Shakespearean scholars claim that the otherworldly Caliban of *The Tempest* was so named after the newly encountered peoples with whom genuine European travelers were beginning to engage in one-sided trade relations.[2] Christopher Columbus himself reported to his Spanish brethren that the potential for enslaving these man-eating peoples should be explored.[3] Somewhat later, too, the enslavement of Africans was partly justified on the grounds that "man-eaters" deserved this fate.

Long before *cannibal* entered the dictionary, however, the intellectuals of the ancient world described Africans as man-eaters embracing horrific attributes. As early as A.D. 79, the Roman chronicler Pliny the Elder reported on Africans in a manner likely to generate fear, suspicion, and animosity in readers of his encyclopedia. "The Atlas tribe," he wrote, after describing the river Niger,

> have fallen below the level of human civilization, if we can believe what is said; for they do not address one another by any names, and when they behold the rising and setting sun, they utter awful curses against it as the cause of disaster to themselves and their fields, and when they are asleep they do not have dreams like the rest of mankind. The Cave-dwellers hollow out caverns, which are their dwellings; they live on the flesh of snakes, and they have no voice, but only making squeaking noises, being entirely devoid of intercourse by speech.

In conjunction with his description of the Nile, further, he enumerates "the Wild-beast-eaters, who live chiefly on the flesh of panthers and lions; the Eatalls, who devour everything; the Man-eaters, whose diet is human flesh; the Dog-milkers, who have dogs' heads; the Artabatitae, who have four legs and rove about like wild animals. . . ."[4] Thus in earliest times the precedent was already established for perceiving Africans as subhuman. When sixteenth-century Englishmen actually encountered sub-Saharan Africans, their observations echoed those of the ancients.

Written documents are replete with references supporting the conclusion that from at least the middle of the sixteenth century Africans and white Europeans both believed the other to be man-eaters. In discussing the outlook that developed during the era of the slave trade, the historian Basil Davidson notes: "Fear and ignorance quickened—on either side—into beliefs that were strange and strangely alike. There came into being a 'community of *legend*' [emphasis added]. Nothing shows this more than the currency of thought about man-eating."[5]

On the one hand, as travelers returned to England from their explorations of faraway worlds they found their countrymen eager to hear sensational details about the newly "discovered" nonwhite people. The historian Winthrop D. Jordan, in his study of the first contact between Africans and whites, refers to the common European belief that the black men "they doe eat" each other, "alive" in some places, but dead in others "as we wolde befe or mutton."[6] Thus the poorly substantiated notion that Africans indulged regularly in cannibalism was perpetuated; indeed, it still exists, even in academic circles.

On the other hand, the Africans believed equally that whites were cannibals (though again, and despite numerous and severe European atrocities against Africans, the evidence suggests that they stopped short of literally eating their captives). Several of the handful of firsthand African accounts of the slave trade were penned by black men from regions within the boundaries of modern-day Nigeria—significant trade areas during the slaving era. Probably the best known of these accounts was the earliest one, entitled *The Interesting Narrative of Olaudah Equiano, or Gustavus Vasa, the African* and first published in London in 1789. In his reminiscences of his kidnapping and journey to the New World, former slave Equiano recalls: "We thought . . . we should be eaten by these ugly men, as they appeared to us; and when soon after we were all put down under the deck again, there was much dread and trembling among us, and nothing but bitter cries to be heard all night from these apprehensions, insomuch that at last the white people got some old slaves from the land to pacify us."[7]

It was not just Equiano's fellow captives who feared that the whites intended them for consumption, however. Twenty-nine years after Equiano's capture, Ali Eisami, or William Harding as he came to be known, met a similar fate. Although Eisami was ultimately spared the horrors of New World slavery in favor of status as a recaptive in the Sierra Leone colony,[8] his comments about his initial fears of white men are germane. Eisami recalls being singled out by a white "reverend priest":

Having seen all of us, he came, took hold of my hand, and drew me into his house, and I did not fear him; but I heard inside the house that my people without were talking and saying, "The white man has taken Ali and put him into the house in order to slaughter him." So I looked at the white people and they looked at me. When the white man arose and went to the top of the house, I prepared myself, and thought, "If this white man takes a knife and I see it in his hand, I will [grab] hold [of] it."

According to the Africanist Philip D. Curtin, Eisami's fear of the white man's knife reflects his anxiety about being eaten by the Europeans.[9]

For Samuel Ajayi Crowther and his fellow prisoners, circumstantial evidence contributed to the idea that the whites would eat them. After being separated from members of their group, they encountered a number of huge hanging carcasses. The combination of the disappearance of their fellows and the sight of the corpses unsettled Crowther: "We soon came to a conclusion of what had become of them, when we saw parts of a hog hanging, the skin of which was white—a thing which we never saw before; for a hog was always roasting on fire, to clear it of the hair, in my country; and a number of cannonshots were arranged on the deck. The former we supposed to be the flesh, and the latter the heads of the individuals who had been killed for meat."[10]

The belief that some whites were cannibals could be fueled by the European captors themselves. While being transported on a Portuguese vessel, the slave Joseph Wright wrote, he and his fellow Africans noted an ominous ship on the horizon. "Next day we saw an English man of war coming. When the Portuguese saw this, it put them to disquietness and confusion. They then told us that these were the people which will eat us, if we suffered them to prize us."[11]

The reminiscences of slave traders likewise reflect the pervasiveness of the African belief that whites were cannibals. John Newton, the slave trader turned clergyman who is best known for composing "Amazing Grace," made several voyages transporting human cargo from Africa to the New World. Later, after finding his God, he reflected:

When a hundred and fifty or two hundred stout men, torn from their native land, many of whom never saw the sea, much less a ship, till a short space before they had embarked; who have, probably, the same natural prejudice against a black; and who often bring with them an apprehension they are bought to be eaten: I say, when thus circumstanced, it is not to be expected that they will tamely resign themselves to their situation.[12]

Similarly, the anthropologist Reay Tannahill refers to white explorer Mungo Park's surprise at the fate that captured Africans anticipated: "They viewed me at first with looks of horror, and repeatedly asked if my countrymen were cannibals."[13] The credence Africans gave to this rumor caused real problems for the slave traders, as the travel writer and historian James Pope-Hennessy describes: "The slaves from upcountry 'very innocently persuade one another that we buy them only to fatten them and afterwards eat them as a delicacy.' These rustic slaves had to be watched with particular care, as they were liable to plot rebellion, kill the Europeans, and try to put the ship ashore or swim from it."[14]

Amistad

An early-nineteenth-century incident involving the capture and subsequent trials of the blacks aboard the slave ship *Amistad* demonstrates well the emergence of New World cannibalism rumors among both whites and blacks. In 1839, the

Amistad, a Spanish slaver, had been transporting newly captured African slaves from Havana to Puerto Principe in Cuba
when its human cargo staged a "mutiny." The mutineers ordered one of their Spanish captors to sail the *Amistad* back to
Africa. Instead, hoping to call attention to the ship's plight,
the terrified navigator maintained an erratic course in the At-
lantic waters just off the eastern seaboard of the United States.
Attempting to return to Sierra Leone, not far from their Mende
homeland, the Africans were captured off New York's Long
Island Sound and transported to New Haven. For the next
three years their fate was debated from the District Court of
Connecticut all the way to the U.S. Supreme Court.

The leader of the mutiny was a man named Cinque, who
had been kidnapped near his Mende homeland in Sierra
Leone. Although he and the other prisoners had been subjected to all the horrors of the Middle Passage, they did not
attempt to seize control until after they had been transferred
from another ship to the *Amistad* in Havana. According to
their account of the takeover, a mulatto cook on the *Amistad*
had claimed that the white men intended to eat them. Their
throats would be slit, their bodies sectioned and salted, and
they would be consumed as dried meat. The cook lent credence to his claim by pointing to two barrels, one full and one
empty, allegedly reserved for the cured meat. Horrified by
this prospect, Cinque managed to unfasten his chains from
the wall. According to Kin-na, another of the captives, Cinque
convinced the rest to join him by pointing out, "If we do
nothing, we be killed. We may as well die in trying to be free
as to be killed and eaten."[15]

Following the eventual capture and incarceration of the
rebels, media reports of the incident—generally inaccurate
and exaggerated—captured public attention. One particularly tenacious story alleged that at least one of the African
rebels, a man named Konoma, was a cannibal, the evidence
being the pointy shape of his teeth. Although Konoma responded that in his homeland filed teeth were intended to
attract members of the opposite sex, he was persistently identified as a cannibal. The wealthy abolitionist Lewis Tappan,
a staunch problack advocate, found himself repeatedly having

to explain to antebellum white Americans that none of the *Amistad* Africans were cannibals.

In fact, cannibalism was as much a taboo for Konoma and Cinque's people as it was for the Spanish slavers.[16] Like many other societies, the Mende consider cannibals as threatening as witches, and individuals accused of cannibalism are executed. For Cinque and his companions, thus, the prospect of being eaten by the white men was the worst conceivable fate.

The expression *man-eater* is often used interchangeably with the word *cannibal*. The rumors that emerged in conjunction with the *Amistad* affair confirm that *men* were understood to be both the eaters and the eaten. The slave trade was a notoriously male-dominated enterprise. Slave ships were quite literally "manned," and most Africans had very little contact with white women. Male Africans also fetched a much higher price than females; as a result, far more male Africans were traded. The *Amistad* carried a few female children, but the bulk of the captives were forty-odd adult African men. Hence the emphasis in these slavery-era cannibalism rumors on black men as the specific target of white animosity, an emphasis that has persisted over the generations into the present day.

Given the differences between the Europeans and the Africans, it seems unlikely that the rumors which arose would be identical in origin and staying power. Why did cross-accusations about the eating of humans emerge, and why did they endure? Two kinds of evidence contribute to an item's plausibility. First, circumstantial evidence, such as Konoma's pointy filed teeth and the big boiling pots on the *Amistad*, was available to be misinterpreted by both sides. As these material clues mounted in number, people combined them with other extant information, sometimes true and sometimes false, about the other group's behavior. For example, news reports emphasized that Cinque and the others were almost completely unclothed at the time of their capture. This was an appalling and disturbing lack of modesty as far as white Americans were concerned. In their minds, it made sense that people who were ambivalent about clothing would be the kind to eat human flesh. From the point of view of the *Amistad* victims, conversely, the slave traders' dehumanizing treatment of them could easily be perceived as a precursor to cannibalism. After all, the rations on the ship had been quite meager, a fact that could be interpreted to mean that the whites were in need of additional foodstuffs. The second type of evidence is perhaps the most important; it has to do with subliminal associations—symbolism—and will be treated in depth below.

The misinterpretation of circumstantial evidence and of related information about the other group's habits triggered fundamental uncertainties and anxieties about methods and motives. "Discovering" each other forced the two cultures to rethink their view of the universe and of those with whom they shared it. For the whites, the fact of coexisting in the world violated their sense of divinely mandated propriety over other, "unchosen" peoples. In their quest for political, economic, and religious dominance, they established a power struggle that has lasted for centuries, in which the whites have been the oppressors, the blacks the oppressed. The initial brutality of the Europeans forced both parties into turmoil. For the enslavers, the dilemma was one of justification: on what grounds can a Christian people rationalize the destruction of another culture? For the enslaved, the question was more straightforward: why do these strangers keep coming back for more of us? That cannibalism was posited as a response on both sides can be explained in terms of the human psyche. It was a symbolically satisfactory explanation for the odd behavior of the "other" group, allowing justification for subjugation on the European side and explaining the irrational attack on their culture on the African side.

Circumstantial Evidence

It is possible to connect elements within a rumor or legend to historical events or circumstances that may well have precipitated their emergence in folkloric discourse. The idea that Africans were cannibalistic did not spring forth in a vacuum; its popularity in fifteenth-century Europe coincided squarely with the genesis of the African slave trade. The original Western traders who explored the African continent were shocked by the appearance and customs of dark-skinned peoples. Positing themselves as exemplifying the correct way to look and act, the Europeans, and particularly the English, declared dark-skinned, scantily clad, coarse-haired people who ate with their hands as unaccountably inferior beings. To accommodate the emergent conviction that they were in fact entitled to exploit the black "heathens," the Europeans exaggerated the physical, behavioral, and cultural gulf that existed between themselves and Africans.

The anthropologist Katherine George, writing in 1953, identified four beliefs, based partly in fact and partly in fiction, by which Western Europe rationalized its policies toward Africans and propelled the development of extreme ethnocentrism. For one thing, Europeans observed, and correctly, that West Africans were polytheistic, non-Christian peoples. They also identified minor physical differences, which, though accurate, were assessed with negative value: "The physical traits peculiar to the Negro, his thick lips and dark skin, are always thought ugly . . . the dark skin of the Negro becomes more than aesthetically displeasing: it becomes the symbol of a moral taint as well."[17] Finally, Europeans stated that Africans lacked material skills and mated with beasts, erroneous but nevertheless popular notions. Material skills different from those important to Europeans were simply not worth bothering about, in their view; then too, Europeans apparently believed Africans were so sexually permissive that black women mated freely with male "orang-outangs."[18]

The notion that Africans were cannibalistic fit neatly into this cluster of seemingly related truths and fictions. According to Jordan, the English considered African culture so inferior that it was supposed that blacks had more in common with the large beasts that inhabited the "dark continent" than with the white men and women of Europe.[19] The belief that such animals were man-eaters may have added credibility to the notion that these animal-like men were man-eaters as well.

Just as it is difficult to reconstruct a rumor conduit as it existed in the past, it is also hard to assess reports concerning an activity such as cannibalism. Nevertheless, while the extent of actual cannibalism among West African peoples may not be quantifiable, most contemporary scholars would agree that little evidence exists to support the popular notions of widespread, aggressive cannibalism attributed to blacks of this era. Summarizing the debate on real versus imagined African cannibalism, Jan Nederveen Pieterse writes:

In this way, or approximately so, most cannibal tales would have come into circulation, through the transmission of regional enemy images, collective intimidation and ethnological gossip. This is to discount cannibalism as an extreme measure in emergencies such as famines and disasters. A distinction must also be made for human sacrifices on ritual occasions (when the victims are not eaten) or occasions when a small part of the flesh of a slain enemy (particularly the head or the heart) is ritually eaten, to ingest its magical force. This is cannibalism not as a popular custom but as a form of warrior magic, and has little or nothing in common with cannibalism as popularly represented in the West.[20]

Certainly those explorers who described instances of the practice would not meet any contemporary standards for ethnography, even at an amateur level. As early as the 1680s, indeed, some European chroniclers began to question the charges made by their predecessors and colleagues. As Frenchman Jean Barbot put it, "Some Europeans would . . . persuade me that inland blacks of Whydah are maneaters and that at a town about a league above Savi, there is a market for slaves where, at the time of a violent famine, they sold them fatted up to be slaughtered like beasts and their quarters exposed in the shambles, to be eaten; but I will not answer for the truth of it."[21] In 1803, the Scottish physician Thomas Winterbottom conducted a careful review of the cannibalism claims of earlier visitors to Africa and compared them to his own experiences. His conclusion: "The Africans have been very unjustly branded with the title of anthropophagists."[22] Twentieth-century editors of Winterbottom's *Account of the Native Africans of Sierra Leone* maintain that Winterbottom's scrutiny of the cannibalism charges of his fellow travelers "entitle him to be taken seriously as a pioneer of African studies."[23] Discussing two reports in particular, Winterbottom asserts: "Notwithstanding both these authors are highly respectable, and worthy of the utmost credit in every instance where they have themselves seen, yet in the present instance, where ocular demonstration alone, not vague report, is to be depended on, we have no reason to believe that they were imposed upon, as they no where affirm that they were eye witnesses of the transaction."[24]

Like some twentieth-century anthropologists, Winterbottom was skeptical of assertions that *neighboring* Africans practiced cannibalism. He quotes one source in which this sentiment was clearly expressed: " 'But that other African nations are addicted to that unnatural practice I have not smallest doubt; because, from the concurrent and credible testimony of those who have been at Bonny, it is well known that a Bonny man kills and eats an Audony man, and an Audony man treats a Bonny man in the same way, whenever he has an opportunity.' " Winterbottom questioned such comments; they were, after all, little more than generalized, unvalidated statements of hearsay. Even when ostensibly firsthand evidence was offered, he disputed the traveler's ability to recognize cannibalism and its tools: "It may be alleged," he wrote, "that it would not be an easy matter for a common spectator to distinguish human *flesh* from beef or pork, and the bustle and confusion which must have attended the storming an enemy's camp, where this banquet was discovered, could not be favourable to such an investigation." In his concluding remarks, Winterbottom noted that while he believed the claims of cannibalism among Africans to be false, he found that "they make no scruple of accusing other nations at a distance, and whom they barely know by name, of cannibalism."[25]

Although some later explorer-ethnographers reinforced Winterbottom's and Barbot's view, the belief that Africans were not uniformly cannibalistic remained a minority one well into the twentieth century. Popularized accounts of African culture perpetuated the common view that cannibals lurked everywhere. Readers of John Gunther's best-selling *Inside Africa* (1955), for example, are assured that "cannibalism, we might add parenthetically, is now virtually extinct in

Bantu Africa. But I met a British judge who had sentenced a man in Uganda to death as recently as 1937 for boiling and eating a baby. Sometimes on long safaris Europeans change their porters every fifty miles or so, so that these can return to their homes without danger of ambush in hostile territory."[26] By claiming that cannibalism is "virtually extinct," of course, Gunther strongly suggests that it was once commonplace; and his unsubstantiated mention of the Ugandan baby-eating case seems dramatically gratuitous. Unfortunately, unvalidated assertions such as those contained in Gunther's book gain a certain respectability among lay readers.

Just as Winterbottom in the early 1800s criticized his fellow explorers' willingness to accept inconclusive evidence of cannibalism, so in 1979 did the anthropologist William Arens find wanting the unfounded assertions of his peers on the topic of cannibalism, even despite their professional training as observers. As we shall see, the symbolic appeal of cannibalism exerts an almost universal pull on the human psyche. "The most certain thing to be said," Arens maintains, "is that all cultures, subcultures, religious sects, secret societies and every other possible human association have been labeled anthropophagic by someone."[27] Accounts of African cannibalism, according to Arens, have all been based largely on hearsay (that is, rumor), on misunderstandings of ritual behavior and verbal folklore, and on a Western propensity to believe the worst about a culture as a prelude to exploitation.

It could be argued that the Africans inadvertently participated in the successful spreading of the cannibalism rumor among the whites. One of the accounts Winterbottom objected to claimed that while the Africans being described were not cannibals themselves, the chronicler accepted their testimony about the anthropophagic conduct of enemy groups. Arens observed this same tendency. Over the course of two centuries, it seems, European explorers uniformly assumed that although the particular African tribal group with whom they were trading did not intend to eat them, there were other, less friendly African peoples eager to add white men to their cuisine.

Archives and libraries are replete with journals, letters,

treatises, and other historical artifacts providing insight into
the minds of the white Europeans who instituted and maintained the African slave trade. Unfortunately, few documents
offer similar insight into the feelings of the Africans who were
being traded. Millions of Africans were brought to the New
World, but only a handful were eventually able to produce a
written record of their experiences and thoughts. Even so, the
probable source of the rumor that the *whites* were cannibals is
more easily explained. Having been forced to leave a familiar
environment and to board enormous seafaring vessels, the
Africans might certainly conclude that the fate awaiting them
was not the kind of servitude they would have experienced
as war booty in Africa. Massive-scale labor economies like the
ones they were destined for in the New World were uncommon in Africa. Slave traders, moreover, were notorious for
ignoring their prisoners' basic human needs, treating the Africans with an indifference incompatible with the proposition
that the white men wanted them for their strength as workers.
On many of the slavers, finally, the normally sparse rations
were often increased when the ships neared the New World,
the purpose being to fatten up the surviving slaves in order
to increase their value as potentially robust workers. From
the point of view of the Africans, the larger food allotments
were likely a source of dismay rather than pleasure. What else
could the white men want but to eat them?

Cannibalism is generally associated with the distant past:
most people believe it is something that *used to* happen, before modern times. If it does occur in the present, we argue,
then it is only in remote, "uncivilized" places or in the rare
context of survival episodes. In fact, however, rumors about
cross-racial cannibalism did not end with the cessation of the
slave trade. Despite the tremendous wealth of knowledge we
have about each other, the circumstances that influence relations between the two groups have changed only superficially, with an unfortunate legacy of mistrust and animosity—including, notably, stories of cannibalism—persisting
between Africans and Europeans.

Twentieth-century examples illustrate the durability of the
appeal of cannibalism rumors. Arens, for instance, during

fieldwork in Tanzania, soon met Africans who believed that whites sojourning in Africa were in need of or desired African blood or body parts. He repeats what is clearly a contemporary legend apparently quite popular during World War II: "A victim [African] would be rendered unconscious and then hung head down in order to let the blood from the slit jugular drain into a bucket. The fluid was then transported by a fire engine to an urban hospital, where it was converted into red capsules. These pills were taken on a regular basis by Europeans who . . . needed these potations to stay alive in Africa."[28] An informal survey of friends and colleagues who specialize in African history or anthropology turned up several similar stories about modern-day Africans who presume whites practice some form of cannibalism. From the point of view of the Africans, given the continued presence and, in many instances, power of whites in the continent, perhaps the only real difference between the era of slavery and the colonial/postcolonial times was that rather than being transported overseas to suffer, Africans were now the victims of white brutality on their own ground.

Whereas in earlier days the reports of a handful of explorers and travelers formed the basis of knowledge for those unable to travel to Africa, contemporary views of Africa are more likely to come from the visual media—television, film, and print. And in these modern portrayals of African life and culture, the stereotypes of semiclad, promiscuous savages remain very much in evidence. The many movies in the Tarzan series alone go far to perpetuate notions of uncivilized African behavior. Consider, too, how in many recent feature films set in Africa (*Gorillas in the Mist* and *Out of Africa*, for example), African animals are depicted much more sympathetically than African peoples. Bare-breasted African women appear often in family-oriented publications and TV documentaries. Cartoons, comic books, postcards, advertisements, and other forms of print ephemera have all included images of the well-meaning white missionary simmering in a large pot while exotically clad natives dance around the fire, as a prelude to eating him.[29]

As a result of these distorted portrayals, whites and even

blacks today are only marginally better informed about Africa than their ancestors were. And just as their ancestors presumed Africans to be cannibalistic, so do many modern men and women. According to Arens, his decision to write a book on cannibalism was inspired by his desire to answer more confidently his students' questions on the subject.

Symbolism

An item's capacity to trigger subliminal associations is the third and perhaps most important area of evidence that contributes to the rumor or legend's plausibility. Combining fundamental elements involving human bodies, death, eating, and ritual behavior, cannibalism stands out as one of the most symbolically laden concepts in the human cultural repertoire. Each of these components contributes to an individual's or a culture's worldview. When they coalesce into a single pattern, these elements offer insights into a given person's or people's attempt to develop a cogent sense of order. Keep in mind that the focus here is not on actual cannibalism, but on weakly substantiated beliefs that others, people outside the boundaries of a given group, are indulging in human-eating. Anthropologists such as Claude Lévi-Strauss and Mary Douglas have studied how social situations reflect individuals' anxieties about their own bodies.[30] Here I will extend their findings to explore how group conflict can foster anxiety about the motives of others regarding the bodies of an entire group. Typically, scholars focus on neighboring groups or minority sects within a dominant culture to examine cultural conflict. When two cultures as socially and physically remote as the West African and European are the point of discussion, the forces of intergroup conflict are, I believe, amplified.

The symbolic associations between the most basic activities of food consumption and procreation have long been recognized.[31] When two groups come into contact, there is typically extreme curiosity and speculation about these two essential bodily functions, with suspicion arising when sets of rules are found to differ. Ethnocentrically, people always assume that their own codes for natural behavior supersede those of others. The more unfamiliar the customs, the harsher the judgment will be. Moreover, the two groups will formulate opinions and theories not only about those customs they can observe, but also about those that they cannot. In this case, the more tension there is, the more farfetched the speculations are apt to be, with both groups assuming the worst.

Naturally, the disposition of the dead is of paramount interest when two groups meet. Causes of death, the handling of the corpse, and final disposal of the body will be probed. Since any one or all of these matters are likely be shrouded in secrecy, uninformed speculation often occurs. In the end, a fundamental question may emerge: If these people are willing to treat their bodies in such a way openly, what might they be doing in secret?

Two reasons can be offered for the frequency of cannibalism accusations. The first is psychoanalytic: wedding Freudian theory to conjectures about racism, for example, Joel Kovel observes that

scarcely anyone grows up without exposure to the myth of African cannibalism: grinning black devils with bones stuck through their nostrils dancing about the simmering pot containing the hapless missionary. What child has not contemplated this scene in one form or another? Now, we know that cannibalism is . . . a universal infantile wish arising in the oral sadistic phase of development (by virtue of which it becomes an element of the mass unconscious). . . . [32]

In an alternate point of view, William Arens maintains that because cannibalism is the worst fate in the minds of most of the world's peoples, when one group is dissatisfied with another's eating, copulation, and hygiene habits, cannibalism accusations circulate.[33] Attempting to impose order, we reconcile unfamiliar beliefs into an all-encompassing, and inevitably distorted, pattern of thought. "They" are so unlike us that they wantonly eat human bodies. Sexual promiscuity, moreover, is often implicit in the cannibalism charge. Eating humans becomes the ultimate act of human aggression and sexual domination.

The Europeans and Africans, of course, did not have equal access to information about each other. Whereas the Africans' experience was limited to contact with the traders who came on ships to their shores, the Europeans could observe black cultures in operation. Douglas maintains that anxieties about the body, particularly anything concerning its orifices, will mount when a group's boundaries with another group are weak.[34] By invading African communities and initiating a trade for humans, the Europeans were demonstrating just how weak those boundaries were. From the end of the fifteenth century until the eve of the twentieth, whites exhibited an insatiable appetite for Africans. Metaphors based on human consumption were inevitable; whites, after all, were large-scale consumers of African peoples. Consequently, whereas in reality the well-being of whole groups was in jeopardy, the African imagination sought order by focusing on individual fates: cultural cannibalism was translated into the more intelligible notion of individual cannibalism.

Blacks born into New World slavery recognized that their white masters and mistresses had no intention of actually eating them. Nevertheless, the metaphor of human consumption remained strong in the discourse. A passage from Frederick Douglass's autobiography eloquently attests to the fugitive slave's perspective on his status, speaking as well to the myriad ways in which the physical aspects of racial oppression were rendered:

The motto which I adopted when I started from slavery was this— "Trust no man!" I saw in every white man an enemy; and in almost every colored cause for distrust. It was a most painful situation; and, to understand it, one must needs experience it or imagine himself in similar circumstances. Let him be a fugitive slave in a strange land—a land given up to be the hunting-ground for slaveholders—whose inhabitants are legalized kidnappers—where he is every moment subjected to the terrible liability of being seized upon by his fellowmen, as the hideous crocodile seizes upon his prey!—I say, let him place himself in my situation—without home or friends—without money or credit—wanting shelter, and no one to give it—wanting bread, and no money to buy it,—and at the same time let him feel he is pursued by merciless menhunters, and in total darkness as to what to do, where to go, or where to stay—perfectly helpless both as to the means of defence and means of escape,—and in the midst of plenty, yet suffering the terrible gnawings of hunger,—in the midst of houses, yet having no home,—among fellow-men, yet feeling as if in the midst of wild beasts, whose greediness to swallow up the trembling and half-famished fugitive is only equalled by that with which the monsters of the deep swallow up the helpless fish upon which they subsist,—I say, let him be placed in this most trying situation,—the situation in which I was placed,—then and not till then, will he fully appreciate the hardships of, and know how to sympathize with the toil-worn and whip-scarred fugitive slave.[35]

This passage evokes literal and figurative images of the oppression experienced by Douglass. Like other slave narrators, he wants to inform the reader that the physical comforts free men and women take for granted are denied to slaves. Slaves can rely on no secure shelter or food source; slaves cannot protect their bodies from corporal punishment. In the world of fugitive slaves that Frederick Douglass reveals to his reading audience, the relationship between whites and blacks is characterized as the former group's need to maintain absolute control over the latter's body and the latter's desire to achieve complete physical autonomy. The passage is dominated by symbolic language that compares whites to carnivorous animals. Douglass's lexicon casts the various whites who pursue runaways as "crocodiles," "manhunters," "wild beasts," and "monsters of the deep." He then casts the fugitives as "prey" and as "helpless fish" trapped on a "hunting-ground." The threat implicit in the pursuit is that the fugitive will be "seized upon" and "swallowed up" by the aggressor. Although Douglass and his fellow slaves may have rejected their ancestors' idea that their oppressors intended actually to eat them, the cannibalism metaphor was still compelling as a way to characterize their plight.

Twentieth-century political relationships between Africa and the rest of the world reflected the tension of persistent global disharmony. The waning of slavery and colonization led to a new epoch defined largely by the struggle between the first and second worlds to carve the third world into morsels of either socialism or capitalism. African nations confronting the challenges of a return to autonomy were once again being torn apart in the high-stakes battles of nations far beyond their own borders. Here, too, the consumption metaphor is apt. Twentieth-century African independence required nations to choose between political philosophies established by the white world. It is not surprising that the modern-day African imagination sometimes translates the white world's preoccupation with its destiny into a belief that whites need African bodies or body parts to survive. After all, comprehending why the European superpowers feel compelled and entitled to interfere with the internal affairs of African nations was and is an often futile undertaking. But it can easily be boiled down to the precept that whites need black blood to survive.

That cannibalism can symbolize the most extreme dimensions of sexual aggression is evident in the persistence of African beliefs that whites are man-eaters. A feminine personality has long been attributed to sub-Saharan Africa. References to "mother" Africa abound in literary and historical discourse, and the use of feminine personal pronouns is commonplace in discussions of "her" culture. It does not really matter whether this attribution emerges from an internal understanding of the continent as female or whether it is an externally imposed construct; what matters is that an awareness of it is discernible in the African worldview. If Africa is woman, then the countries that have made her business their own for several centuries are masculine. By kidnapping her human resources, extracting mineral and other reserves from her land, and vying over her future direction, these countries effectively gang-raped her. After penetrating the most precious corners of the continent, they forced Africa into uncomfortable and often untenable positions. When she gathered the strength to fight them off, or they had exploited her until little of commercial value remained, they left her with the unwanted progeny of their one-sided union.

Vernacular or folk expressions that pair copulation with eating, and in some cases with flesh eating specifically, are common in most languages. The "Africa as woman" model draws attention to idioms that reflect an understanding of the female

as an inert, passive being for abuse or consumption. Women
are referred to, for example, as pieces of ass or meat. In American vernacular language, vaginal intercourse is described
with aggressive verbs such as pounding, humping, and bon-
ing. The female sex organ is referred to as her cherry, and an
assortment of oral sex acts are referred to as eating one's part-
ner. The abundance of metaphors connecting the act of sexual
intercourse with the act of eating lends credence to the theory
that in the minds of twentieth-century Africans victimized by
white nations struggling for control over African soil, the idea
that these whites might be secretly taking pills containing the
blood of murdered Africans was quite plausible.

The white Europeans, having explored the "dark" continent in order to maximize the potential for trade, had considerable access to information about African culture. As Jordan
has pointed out, the contact between the English and the sub-
Saharan Africans represented the meeting of the lightest-
skinned people in the world with the darkest.[36] And within
European languages and cultures, black is almost always the
color of evil. Black magic was the most sinister kind of sor-
cery; the black plague was the most threatening disease,
spreading as a fearful epidemic; the black sheep was the least
popular family member . . . and a whole culture of black people would be capable of the most hideous acts imaginable. In
addition to being fascinated with the African complexion, the
white explorers were nearly obsessed with African sexual
mores. Their accounts are replete with comments on the African's lack of Western modesty, the size of the male sexual
organ and of female breasts and buttocks, the fact that the
African lived in close proximity to animals whom the Europeans maintained the Africans resembled, and the acceptance
of polygamy as a satisfactory way of life. In these records,
human-eating is mentioned preeminently as an act of appalling conduct.

African traits, both genuine and fabricated, that captured
the interest of sixteenth-century whites continue to dominate
Western depictions of black men and women today. On stage,
screen, television, and in print, Africa's ostensibly exotic,
primitive dimensions still prevail. Popular-culture historian

Joseph Boskin, for instance, found that the image of human-eating Africans is plentiful in twentieth-century film.[37] Once again, the connections between sex and eating shed light on the tenacity of such beliefs. In contrast to African presumptions of white cannibalism, however, the white notion that Africans are cannibalistic seems to be based on individual rather than group behavior. Whereas the African belief in white cannibalism stems in part from a recognition that Western nations have violated Africans ones, the idea that Africans are cannibalistic no doubt stems from the notion that individual blacks possess heightened sexual prowess. The meeting of fair-skinned people with dark-skinned people, that is, also brought together a people with rigid prohibitions regarding sexual intercourse and a people with a much different attitude about sexuality. Based partly on fact and mostly on fiction, the belief that Africans countenance any kind of sexual conduct has retained popularity in the West. For some, a corollary exists that a people who place few restrictions on the basic human sexual drive would also place few restrictions on satisfying other human appetites. Thus, a people who would copulate with abandon would eat anything—even humans—with similar freedom.

Function

The cannibalism rumors on both sides sprang from circumstantial and psychological "evidence" about the other group. Yet although the rumors are similar, they did not serve identical purposes. As the relationship between the two groups evolved into one in which the whites exploited and abused the blacks, the ultimate function of the rumors was shaped. For the whites, the belief that blacks were cannibalistic became an important component of a complex network of rationales and justifications for the institution of slavery and the ultimate colonization of Africa. Since these beings were base enough to indulge in cannibalism, the reasoning went, they deserved to be forced to serve the Europeans. For the blacks, such as those in West Africa where labor economies were unknown, the rumor's function was more etiological: the slave traders kept coming back for more live bodies to satisfy their hunger for human flesh.

According to rumor specialists, it is this ability to explain bewildering changes in the world that leads to the emergence and perpetuation of rumors. As Gordon W. Allport and Leo Postman put it, "Rumor travels when events have importance in the lives of individuals and when the news received about them is either lacking or subjectively ambiguous. The ambiguity may arise from the fact that the news is not clearly reported or from the fact that conflicting versions of the news have reached the individual, or from his/her incapacity to comprehend the news s/he receives."[38] The "news" that the whites and blacks were receiving about each other during the slavery era was clearly lacking, ambiguous, and inaccurate. The cross-racial accusations of cannibalism filled in the blank spaces of incompletely rendered pictures of the other group.

The rumors also helped to dictate the direction of relations between the two groups. As Tamotsu Shibutani puts it, "Collective adjustments to crises are not just responses to events; they are also shaped in the *reactions of men to one another.* . . .* All those who are involved in the situation alter their perspectives in consultation with one another. It is through communication that new experiences and modes of action become shared." If rumors are considered to be "*modes of activity* used to influence the conduct of others," the cannibalism charges, both past and present, have a distinct rhetorical purpose.[39] After all, they swayed the Europeans into believing that Africans were capable of the most horrendous acts imaginable, a belief that in turn justified the perpetuation of slavery and colonization policies. In spite of abundant evidence that the original reports of human-eating Africans were overstated, if not wholly inaccurate, these misnomers have persisted and, more recently, have been used to sanction attempts by white nations to influence the affairs of African nations.

The belief that whites intended to eat them also influenced the conduct of the blacks; indeed, Cinque and his fellow *Amistad* rebels attacked and killed their captors only after being taunted by the possibility that their fate might be worse than death—that their captors in fact intended to eat them. The more up-to-date incarnations of this myth, in which whites require African blood in order to survive in Africa, continue to generate mistrust and apprehension with regard to outsiders.

Topsy/Eva Cycles

The cannibalism rumors are probably the first but certainly are not the last stories to circulate autonomously through white and black communities. In subsequent chapters attention will be given to more contemporary texts in which tellers of each race depict the other as the enemy. I refer to these dual-path texts as "Topsy/Eva cycles," after a popular folk doll purportedly inspired by the best-selling nineteenth-century antislavery novel *Uncle Tom's Cabin*. The book features two little girls: Little Eva is white, well-dressed, blond, and blue-eyed, while Topsy is black, poorly dressed, kinky-haired, dark-eyed. The novel and the stage shows inspired by it were immensely popular well into the twentieth century, and homemade Topsy/Eva dolls became common toys for little girls. Held one way, the doll resembled Eva, with neat, attractive hair and a cute dress; but when the doll was flipped upside down, little black Topsy appeared, with her pickaninny-style coiffure and unkempt clothes. A pantheon of symbols reflecting the popular stereotypes of the two cultures resides in one doll. The nearly identical rumors and contemporary legends that travel separately through black and white communities resemble the Topsy/Eva doll in that the same essential paradigm is shaped to fit the worldview of both groups.

Conclusion

When the belief that a given people eat the bodies of others is perpetuated, we can be sure that relations between the parties in question are, at the very least, strained. Coping with the tensions that result when one culture interferes with the well-being of another requires an enormous breadth of understanding. One way to make sense of large-scale uninvited domination is to reduce it to a more personal plane. Thus metaphors are generated that collapse the threat to the group into a threat to an individual. It is worth noting that the first accusations to emerge between Africans and the outside world were those concerning cannibalism. They are also the most extreme—none of the rumors discussed in subsequent chapters reflect a threat so ominous as human-eating. It is not surprising, moreover, that these stories emerged during the era of the slave trade, for as a rule the most damaging rumors and related folk ideas will arise when relations between two groups are at their most antagonistic. Given the longevity of these texts, we can see that undoing such notions is almost impossible. The following chapters will demonstrate that connecting the fate of blacks en masse to the fate of individual black bodies has remained a consistent pattern ever since the days when the European explorers found their way to sub-Saharan Africa.

Chapter Two

Corporal Control

"They want to beat us, burn us, whatever they can do"

> That destroyed the lice and the lice eggs. But it acquainted me with a terrible creature and it weren't the only creature I come to know that tried to eat the poor colored man up alive.
>
> Nate Shaw

Once they found themselves shackled by the chains of chattel slavery in the New World plantation fields and factories, displaced Africans no doubt began to realize that the whites who had sent for them were not cannibals. The slave traders' insatiable appetite for blacks was not stimulated by hunger for the flesh and blood of their bodies; rather, theirs was an economically rooted demand for the labor that could be extracted only from very-much-alive individuals. Given the horrendous conditions under which the slaves were forced to work, the fact that their white captors were not going to eat them was probably a small consolation. The rumors that the whites were genuine cannibals subsided, but the conviction that they harbored extreme malice toward blacks remained.

This chapter surveys a large corpus of rumor- and legendlike discourse, extending from the slavery era to the mid-

33

dle of the twentieth century, and traces the persistence of the metaphor linking racial aggression to attacks on individual black bodies. Because this material encompasses several crisis points of significance to African-Americans, a secondary aim of this chapter is to explore the folk interpretation developed by African-Americans about this nation's political and social culture. This topic is further developed in subsequent chapters, which examine the ways in which late-twentieth-century African-Americans still rely on folk knowledge and history passed down from these earlier times of crisis. Because of these models, the conflicting messages sent today by the dominant culture tend to be seen as very similar to ones issued in the past—a point that will emerge clearly in what follows. Another purpose here is to draw attention to those racially oriented rumors and legends that have elicited the most scholarly discourse—that is, those that have fueled measurable racial discord and violence.

Nineteenth-Century Sources

Just as Chapter 1 used the firsthand accounts of captured Africans to introduce cannibalism rumors, here the autobiographical accounts of individuals born into New World slavery will serve as source material, for they reveal most tellingly the kinds of concerns that likely developed after the demise of the cannibalism beliefs.

Two antebellum slave narratives—*Narrative of the Life of Frederick Douglass, an American Slave* and Harriet Jacobs's *Incidents in the Life of a Slave Girl*—will be used to argue that blacks continued, even after the Civil War, to strike metaphors linking white treatment of individual black bodies to the overall condition of the black race. These accounts are especially useful for several reasons. First, they represent both male and female perspectives. Second, although white ghost writers heavily edited and influenced many manuscripts in the slave narrative corpus, the authenticity of Jacobs's and Douglass's texts has been largely verified; therefore, we can be reasonably certain that their interpretations reflect those of individuals genuinely victimized by that peculiar institution.

At first glance, no rumors as striking and consistent as the cannibalism one can be culled from the antebellum slave narratives. In retrospect, of course, the cannibalism stories stand out because they proved ultimately to be untrue—at least in the literal sense. Nonetheless, several issues regarding blacks' belief about white malevolence become immediately apparent from material found in slave narratives. First, unlike the cannibalism texts, most of the rumors that circulated in America among the descendants of Africans proved to be true. Indeed, short of actually eating their bodies, whites did inflict just about every other injustice imaginable on their slaves. Second, the master class knowingly fueled the perpetuation of misinformation as a mechanism of slave control. The discussion that follows is thus not limited to rumors and contemporary legends per se, but rather examines the slave narratives to uncover how blacks articulated their concerns about the physical threats implicit in slavery. From there it is a short step to understanding the development of body-related rumors and legends in the aftermath of slavery and into the twentieth century.

Antebellum Animosity

Few settings could be more ripe for rumor formation than the antebellum South. In the decades before the Civil War, slave owners were engaged in a desperate battle to maintain the life-style to which they believed themselves divinely entitled. At the same time, antislavery forces in the free states were becoming increasingly well organized, and the nonslave black population was growing quite bold in its efforts to rescue and protect fugitives from the South. In the early 1830s, Great Britain had emancipated the slaves in its West Indian colonies. American slave owners had no choice but to confront a world that was finally questioning the legitimacy of the peculiar institution. While these developments were certainly good news for the slaves, they were bad news for the master class. But the master class was able to assert considerable control over the news that reached slaves' ears; for as long as possible, owners wanted to prevent their slaves from knowing that there were whites and nonslave blacks committed to dismantling slavery. By prohibiting slaves from learning how to read, by preventing loose-lipped whites and free blacks from having access to the slaves, and by deliberately spreading misinformation, the slaveholders endeavored to keep the "real" news from circulating in the slave quarters. Concurrently, they endeavored to dispel dissatisfaction by cultivating the idea that the world beyond the Mason-Dixon line was even more hostile than the world below it. With varying degrees of success, the slaves, as their narratives reveal, attempted to dispute the discourse being disseminated by their masters.

Abolitionists—the white reformers devoted to emancipating the slaves—were probably the first group of whites that black men and women could trust. Yet slaveholders, in addition to prohibiting their slaves from acquiring the skills that would allow them to read about antislavery activists, denounced the abolitionists, attempting to poison the minds of the slaves against these mysterious white people. When fugitive slave Henry Bibb ran away to Cincinnati, he immediately began looking for a certain "colored" man to help him reach Canada. That man referred him to an abolitionist society for assistance, however, and Bibb was so surprised that there were white people organized to assist fugitives, "I supposed they were a different race of people."[1] Prior to his escape, Bibb had not known that there were whites trying to help him. Proslavery whites threatened by the existence and policies of abolitionist whites had succeeded in keeping Bibb and most of his fellow slaves ignorant of the existence of well-meaning whites.

The planters used "disinformation" techniques to twist the facts and so discourage slaves from being seduced away by promises of a free life. When Bibb returned to his Kentucky master's home to rescue family members from slavery, for instance, he learned that the planters had "told the slaves to beware of abolitionists, that their object was to decoy off slaves and then sell them off to New Orleans." Bibb's more positive view of the North no doubt made its way into the slave information network.

William Wells Brown, also a fugitive slave, described his first encounters with northern whites by emphasizing how uncomfortable he felt in their presence: "The only fault I found with them was their being too kind. I had never had a white man to treat me as an equal, and the idea of a white lady waiting on me at the table was still worse! Though the table was loaded with the good things of this life, I could not eat. I thought if I could only be allowed the privilege of eating in the kitchen, I should be more than satisfied!"[2] Brown's owners, like Bibb's, had successfully convinced their slaves that all whites shared the proslavery position; from their mouths into the ears of their slaves went forth the message that no better life awaited black men and women than the one they were presently living in the South.

Yet keeping all of the slaves illiterate was hard work, and despite the planters' best efforts a few fortunate and resourceful blacks were able to learn to read and write. The slaveowners' anxiety about literate slaves is borne out in the cases of Frederick Douglass and Harriet Jacobs. Both could read and write, and both eventually made their way to freedom. Douglass mastered reading with the help of a "naive" white mistress and his own remarkable ingenuity. Before long, he later wrote, "I got one of our city papers, containing an account of the number of petitions from the North praying for the abolition of slavery in the District of Columbia, and of the slave trade between the States. From this time I understood the words *abolition* and *abolitionist*, and always drew near when that word was spoken, expecting to hear something of importance to myself and my fellow slaves."[3] Jacobs was taught to read and write by an aunt, and her status as a "reader" made her very much in demand around the slave quarters. Anxious to find out if what their masters were telling them was true, blacks pleaded with Jacobs to tell them what the newspapers said. She recalls,

They knew that I could read; and I was often asked if I had seen any thing in the newspapers about white folks over in the big north, who were trying to get their freedom for them. Some believe the abolitionists have already made them free, and that it is established by law, but that their masters prevent the law from going into effect. One woman begged me to get a newspaper and read it over. She said her husband told her that the black people had sent word to the queen of 'Merica that they were all slaves; that she didn't believe it, and went to Washington city to see the president about it. They quarrelled; she drew her sword upon him, and swore that he should help her to make them all free.[4]

The "queen goes to Washington city" narrative certainly sounds like an antebellum contemporary legend. Most probably the illiterate black woman, her husband, and their peers were weaving together threads of information that their masters had ineffectively censored. Although Jacobs offers no date for this incident, it may have occurred after 1830, when the British monarch emancipated that nation's New World slaves. The "news" that somewhere there were whites opposed to slavery was seeping into the slave quarters, and the planters could do little to keep it out. Such information surely invigorated the slaves privy to it.

Before the Civil War white southerners regularly grappled with the problem of runaways and potential violence among the slaves, developing a series of strategies designed to exert as much control as possible. To begin with, they established a surveillance system to minimize unauthorized slave mobility. Then they exploited slave folk beliefs, planting rumors so that blacks would assume the "paterollers" (patrols) possessed more power than they actually did. Terrorizing the slaves at night was an established mechanism for reinforcing the antebellum power structure.

Harriet Jacobs was still in the South in 1831 following Nat Turner's infamous rebellion. Although she was spared from the more brutal aspects of the white southerners' wrath in the weeks prior to Turner's capture, she recalled how devastating a time it was for the less fortunate blacks:

It was a grand opportunity for low whites, who had no negroes of their own to scourge. They exulted in such a chance to exercise a little brief authority, and show their subserviency to the slaveholders; not reflecting that the power which trampled on the colored people also kept themselves in poverty, ignorance, and moral degradation. Those who never witnessed such scenes can hardly believe what I know was inflicted at this time on innocent men, women, and children, against whom there was not the slightest ground for suspicion. Colored people and slaves who lived in remote parts of the town suffered in an especial manner. In some cases the searchers scattered powder and shot among their clothes, and then sent other parties to find them, and bring them forward as proof they were plotting insurrection. Every where men, women, and children were whipped until the blood stood in puddles at their feet. Some received five hundred lashes; others were tied hands and feet, and tortured with a bucking paddle, which blisters the skin terribly. The dwellings of the colored people, unless they happened to be protected by some influential white person who was nigh at hand, were robbed of clothing and every thing else the marauders thought worth carrying away. All day long these unfeeling wretches went round, like a troop of demons, terrifying and tormenting the helpless. At night, they formed themselves into patrol bands, and went wherever they chose among the colored people, acting out their brutal will.[5]

When Turner was finally run to ground, he was tried and hanged for his crimes. Instead of then affording his body a standard burial, however, his corpse was turned over to surgeons who dissected it. Eventually his body parts and products made from them were sold to whites.[6] Given the African-American respect for properly conducted funerals, this cavalier, contemptuous treatment of the dead man's remains no doubt served as particularly bitter evidence of what white people were willing to do to black peoples' bodies.

The random bands of poor white marauders were quickly institutionalized, becoming the models for patrol systems in which white southern planters shared the responsibility of monitoring slave traffic on the roads or hired poorer whites to do so.[7] One ex-slave defined them as follows: "Pattyrollers is a gang o' white men gittin together goin' thew the country catchin' slaves, an' whippin' an' beatin' 'em up if they have no 'remit.' "[8] These efforts were reinforced by attempts at mind control, in which slaveholders induced fears intended to keep the slaves from wanting to escape or rebel in the first place. Discussing the prevalence of such rumors at the beginning of the nineteenth century, Jacobs recalls: "Slaveholders pride themselves upon being honorable men; but if you were to hear the enormous lies they tell their slaves, you would have small respect for their veracity. I have spoken plain English. Pardon me. I cannot use a milder term. When they visit the north and return home, they tell their slaves of the runaways they have seen and describe them to be in the most deplorable condition." By perpetuating rumors that free blacks were an unhappy lot, the masters were able to deter some of their slaves from running away. According to Jacobs, their tales worked: "Many of the slaves believe such stories, and think it is not worth while to exchange slavery for such a hard kind of freedom."[9] And for those who did not subscribe to the planters' tainted version of free life, the presence of unpredictable paterollers was an additional deterrent to unsanctioned mobility.

Before the Civil War, the whites responsible for keeping blacks in their appointed environs were limited as to the range of punishments they could mete out to wandering slaves. Hence, slave owners embraced any mode of intimidation they could muster that would deter their slaves from setting out in the first place, so that physical punishment would serve as a last resort. The paterollers also used costumes and props to keep slaves from roaming at night: "frightening blacks by dressing in ghostly garb was an effective and important technique of control."[10] Planters usually did not want any real harm to come to transgressors, on whose labor they depended. As ex-slave Rev. Ishrael Massie explained, "Now sometimes ya had no trouble at dem meetin's [religious services] 'cause de marsters would say to dem ole paterollers, 'Ef ya ketch my nigger out, don't ya beat or bother 'im.' On de t'other han', ole mean masters would tell 'em to ketch dey slaves and beat 'em."[11] In the end, slaveholders had to weigh the possible loss of labor that might result from a beating against the seriousness of the slave's violation.

African-American oral tradition does reveal that some blacks developed countermeasures to defeat the purposes of their antagonists. By eavesdropping on their masters' conversations they learned the truth about the possibility of a free life in the North or in England. Then, with careful planning, many fugitives succeeded in escaping, avoiding the paterollers' pranks and whips altogether. They also sabotaged the efforts of the paterollers quite directly. In this, grapevines were more than mere channels of information: a favorite practice was to secure actual grapevines across frequently traveled roads to trip the horses as they galloped past. Mrs. Minnie Folks recalled how just such a plan came to be executed:

Ha! ha! ha! dar was one ole brudder who studies fer 'em one day an' tol' all de slaves how to git even wid 'em. He tol' 'em to tied grape vines an' other vines 'cross de road. Den when de paddyrollers come galantin' wid dere horses, runnin' so fas' you see, dem vines would tangle 'em up an' cause de horses to stumble an' fall. An' lots of times dey would break dere legs an' de horses too; one intervall one ole poor devil got tangled so an' de horses kept a carryin' him, 'til he fell off the horse an' nex' day a sucker was foun' om de road wher dem vines was win' aroun' his neck so many time jes had choke' him dey said, 'teetotally dead. Serve 'em right cause dem ole white folks treated us so mean.[12]

Mrs. Folks's anecdote sheds light on several aspects of African-American cultural tradition. The account itself demonstrates how slaves sometimes modeled their own behavior after that of the trickster heroes who dominated slave folktales. Tricksters, underdog dramatis personae also popular in many West African folktale traditions, are ostensibly powerless characters who use their wits and guile to sabotage physically and politically more powerful opponents.[13] Mrs. Folks is not only describing how trickster-style techniques were employed by slaves; her mirthful tone suggests that she is claiming a stake in these deeds herself by boasting about them. The same tone, as we shall see, is discernible in the renderings of many of the rumors and legends to be discussed in later chapters.

Forty Acres and a Mule

During the Civil War the idea that the Lincoln administration intended to seize the property of white slave owners and distribute it to the slaves was exploited by the Confederate powers to maintain morale and motivate southerners to spare nothing in its mission to defeat the Union.[14] Of course, the Confederates always expected to win the war between the states. They did not anticipate how this vision of land being allotted to former slaves might backfire if the unthinkable happened—if the North won the war. But indeed, by the time of Lee's surrender the belief that forty acres and a mule would be given to each former slave was firmly planted in the newly emancipated African-Americans' minds. In some southern locales, Union soldiers and the Freedmen's Bureau reinforced the notion by assigning newly freed slaves forty-acre parcels. However, no policy was ever established to systematically distribute land to each of the four million emancipated African-Americans.

The rumor did not die easily, though. As the historian Leon F. Litwack observes, "The feeling was sufficiently pervasive, in fact, to prompt thousands of freedmen in late 1865 to hold back on any commitment of their labor until the question of land had been firmly resolved."[15] The ex-slaves and their descendants came to consider the land that failed to materialize not as an unfounded rumor but as a failed promise: the government, in their view, was *supposed* to give the slaves land but reneged on the commitment. Indeed, over one hundred years later African-American filmmaker Spike Lee named his film production company "40 Acres and a Mule" as a testimony to the broken "promise."

The folk history shared by many African-Americans includes the perception that the U.S. government showed its true colors in refusing to redress the economic imbalances faced by ex-slaves following the Civil War. Uttering only official statements that there would be opportunity for all to share in the nation's wealth, Washington refused to implement a plan that might have genuinely empowered the freedmen.

Twentieth-Century Crises

From the Reconstruction era until now, many African-Americans have been inclined to believe that the government was insincere in its claimed support for racial equality. At several crisis junctures in this century, the dissemination of particular rumors and legends have had devastating effects on blacks—more devastating by far than the belief in forty acres and a mule ever had. These are the texts that have generated the most sustained scholarly interest. In consulting a research index for studies on rumor, in fact, one finds that works on race divide into two main clusters: one centered in the 1940s, the other in the mid-1960s and early 1970s. These clusters are not the result of a coincidence. In the 1940s, numerous academic attempts were made to explain costly outbreaks of racial violence and the ways rumors upset the nation's well-being during World War II.[16] The more recent studies, which explore the use of rumor during several epochs of U.S. history, were provoked by the race riots of the 1960s.[17]

World War

Most of the race rumors that arose in conjunction with this century's two world wars have also focused on white assumptions about blacks. In World War I and World War II, many of the rumors that circulated addressed the question of whether African-Americans were enemies or allies in the international conflict. At the beginning of both wars, it was said that blacks were going to extreme lengths to avoid having to fight—to the extent of faking imbecility and even contracting venereal disease. Other rumor cycles alleged that blacks were inclined to be more sympathetic to the enemy than to their "own" country. During the second conflict, stories spread in some white communities that African-American churches had established "swastika clubs" and "black dragon societies" to raise money for the Germans and the Japanese.[18]

In reckoning that the black patriotic impulse would be limited, whites were acknowledging the shortsightedness of their prior attitude toward racial equality. Old stereotypes that justified treating blacks as second-class citizens resurfaced in the texts alleging sexual misconduct and ignorance. Many of the better-known rumors focus on the ways in which stateside blacks were planning to take advantage of the draft-induced shortage of white males. Black men were supposedly approaching uniformed white soldiers and commenting, "Don't worry about your wife (daughter, sister, mother), we'll take care of her needs in your absence." Blacks were accused of stockpiling all manner of weapons, particularly ice picks, razors, and, of course, guns. It was alleged that Sears, Roebuck was "deluged with orders from Negroes for guns, pistols, shot, and the like."[19]

Joining black men in exploiting the nation during its time of need, allegedly, were black women, who were rumored to be staging their own rebellion against the status quo. Their inspiration was said to be Eleanor Roosevelt, the remarkable first lady who in fact had a well-earned reputation as a staunch advocate of racial equality. Stories arose that black domestics were making unreasonable demands on their white employers. A typical "Eleanor club" text claimed that after a white woman asked her cook to prepare dinner for her guests, "the cook turned the tables by demanding that her mistress be at her home by eight o'clock Sunday morning to fix breakfast for the cook's guests."[20] But black women were not merely antagonizing the white women for whom they worked; they were allegedly provoking all white women en masse. In addition to Eleanor clubs, African-American women were said to have formed "bump clubs," which encouraged members to set aside days to go to stores and intentionally bump into white women shoppers. This rumor may have been based on actual behavior; the folklorist Roger Abrahams reported that his black students claimed this was an actual practice described to them by family members.[21] However, it is quite plausible that these students were reporting in the style of a contemporary legend, in which narratives are authenticated by the remark, "I know it's true; a friend of a friend told it to me."[22]

The antiblack rumors that circulated during wartime reflect the ambivalence, insecurity, and uneasiness felt during a time of crisis. The dominant culture did not embrace the idea of training black men to shoot, but the idea that they share the risk of being shot at was perfectly acceptable. Blacks were empowered, in short, by America's need for them. A nation that had always tried to limit black access to weapons suddenly needed to train black soldiers. Few roles reinforce masculinity more than that of soldier. Whites knew, moreover, that they could not easily ask blacks to be soldiers while denying them the full rights of citizenship and increased access to the American dream.

In his important study of mid-twentieth-century rumors and race, the sociologist Howard W. Odum focuses largely on texts spread by whites alleging sexual misconduct and ignorance among blacks, featuring old stereotypes that justified treating blacks as second-class citizens. Only one six-page chapter titled "Rumors and Stories Among the Negroes" documents the beliefs that circulated within the World War II–era black population.[23] Notable among the rumors he reports are the folk ideas that white military policemen had shot a number of black soldiers; that southern-based white soldiers were mistreating the wives of Negro soldiers; and that in every battle a black soldier was to precede a white soldier.

These stories reflect the notion that the white military establishment was trying to maximize the chances that blacks were the Americans being shot at while minimizing the chances that blacks would be trained to do the shooting. In previous wars, blacks had been asked to take on particularly risky missions. Yet from the Revolutionary War through World War II, the weapons, pay scale, food, and training provided to black soldiers were nothing like those afforded to whites. The black soldiers who enlisted or were drafted during the Second World War may not have known the particulars of black involvement in earlier wars, but they did know that there was a tradition of ambivalence about arming black men. Given the disregard with which blacks were treated before World War II, the possibility that the military establishment wanted to place them between Axis bullets and white Allied bodies undoubtedly rang quite true to them.

Riot Rumors

Even more academic attention has been devoted to the rumor cycles that emerge in both black and white communities prior to, during, and immediately after outbreaks of racial violence. In addition to investigating the sources of particular rumors, numerous studies have focused on the causes of individual riots or episodes of extended racial turmoil. These accounts almost always include an extended consideration of the role of rumor in the incident in question.[24]

Most of this research is only partly germane to the present discussion. The majority of the documented rumors that accompanied pre-1960s race riots circulated largely among whites and reflect their fear and ignorance about blacks. Because whites were the aggressors in the pre-1960s race riots, Odum notes, "the main current of stories and rumors studied was that which swept through and influenced the white community and the resulting behavior towards Negroes" during several destructive melees.[25] The extant scholarship on rumors and race is in fact excellent; as a result, my own analysis will be cursory and somewhat selective, in that I will concentrate on those texts that gained credence among blacks particularly.

In their studies of the riot-rumors relationship, D. J. Jacobson, Terry A. Knopf, Elliot Rudwick, Tamotsu Shibutani, and others have identified various common denominators that link several twentieth-century civil disturbances. All agree that rumors and riots enjoy a nearly parasitic attachment. In chaotic circumstances, people are nearly desperate for news that explains what is happening. Shibutani notes, "Demand for news . . . is positively associated with the intensity of collective excitement, and both depend upon the felt importance of the event to the public."[26] Indeed, the rumors that emerge before, during, and after riots share so many characteristics that they constitute a powerful warning of impending trouble; yet authorities too often ignore the warning signs, with widespread death and destruction the result.

East St. Louis, 1917

Around the turn of the century, large numbers of southern blacks migrated to the industrial region of East St. Louis, Illinois, seduced northward by white recruiters who painted a utopian picture of ideal working conditions and harmonious race relations.[27] Quickly, however, the black laborers encountered an all too familiar level of racial hostility. Believing their jobs were threatened by the influx from the South, white workers were determined to diminish forcibly the burgeoning black population. Management practices only exacerbated the tensions as large numbers of newly arrived blacks were hired in an effort to weaken the labor unions. A newspaper advertisement for a union meeting scheduled for May 29, 1917, read: "Negro and cheap foreign labor [is being imported by the Aluminum Ore Company] to tear down the standard of living of our citizens. Imported gunmen, detectives and federal injunctions are being used to crush our people. Come hear the truth that the press will not publish."[28] The auditorium hired for the meeting could not accommodate the hundreds of white workers who showed up. Throughout the session, speaker after speaker denounced St. Louis's newest immigrants; "East St. Louis must remain a white man's town" was the common refrain.[29]

As the meeting was breaking up, several rumors spread through the crowd. They included the "news" that a Negro had just accidentally shot a white man in a robbery, a Negro had intentionally murdered a white man, a white woman had been insulted by a Negro, two white girls had just been shot by a Negro, and a white woman had just been shot by a Negro. Those assembled rushed forth into the streets, randomly attacking any African-American unfortunate enough to cross their paths. Some mobs headed for those businesses established and patronized by blacks. Most of these structures were completely demolished. Although the police allowed the whites to roam through the streets unchecked, they did arrest several blacks for carrying concealed weapons. The riot ended the next day, but only because the white aggressors were too tired to continue.

The next month saw sporadic outbreaks of violence. Virulent racism was not reserved exclusively to the white laborers. Rather, the newspapers, the police, and the mayor's office in effect excused the rioters themselves, finding blame instead in the behavior of the victims and the white management

officials who had lured the blacks to East St. Louis. A Topsy/
Eva rumor cycle emerged. Between the first outbreak of violence in May and the larger one that erupted in July, the
same rumor circulated extensively in both black and white
neighborhoods. In each version, one group maintained that
the other was planning a massacre for the July 4 holiday.

Both blacks and whites responded to this rumor by buying
firearms, not firecrackers. Of course, the whites tried to prevent the blacks from making such purchases: in the days following the outbreak of the rumor, "Detectives were stationed
at the bridge approaches to search and arrest Negroes attempting to transport guns while whites were allowed to pass without being stopped."[30] Blacks also acted on the rumor by leaving St. Louis. Most went to neighboring communities to wait
out the situation with friends or family. Throughout the month
of June random acts of violence were perpetrated against
blacks. On the evening of July 1, shots were fired from a passing car into several black homes. Shots were fired in return.
When a police car came to investigate, community members
mistakenly assumed it was the same vehicle that had carried
the earlier shooters. Blacks pumped the car full of bullets,
killing two white policemen. Word of this wanton black disregard for the white power structure swept the white community, and within hours a full-scale riot had broken out.

The next day white mobs patrolled downtown East St.
Louis, killing any blacks they could chase down. Once again,
fire became a powerful weapon as gangs descended on black
neighborhoods, set fire to the homes, and waited for blacks to
come out, shooting them as they ran for refuge. But "merely"
killing blacks proved insufficient for some of the rioters.

Victims were not permitted "to die easily," and when "flies settled
on their terrible wounds the dying blacks [were forbidden] to brush
them off." The mobs laughed at the terrible writhings of a Negro
whose skull had been partly torn away; even corpses were clubbed
and stoned. One man's face was a bloody mess, but when an ambulance arrived to take him to a hospital, rioters warned, "If you pick
up that skunk, we'll kill you too." The driver departed and the victim was thrown into the flames.[31]

Following the riot, appended versions of earlier rumors emerged on both sides as people tried to make sense of the event. Whites justified the violence by claiming that they had done what was necessary to prevent the "Negro murder plot" in which an organized assault force of 1,500 blacks was set to murder 25,000 whites starting on July 4 and take over the city. "By implication," Elliot Rudwick points out, "the whites who burned or shot Negroes on July 2 and sent the black armies fleeing across the Mississippi River [were] actually [claiming to have] performed a community service." Given the horror of the antiblack violence on that July 2, it would have been difficult for a post-riot rumor cycle to emerge in the black community that exaggerated the riot's damage.

Controversy did emerge over the victim count and the nature of the black retaliation during the riot. The atrocities performed on the black corpses led to conflicting estimates of the number of victims and the manner of their deaths. When blacks complained that numerous bodies had been thrown into a creek, their allegations were disregarded as "mere rumors." When several mutilated bodies were subsequently discovered in the creek, blacks were still accused of exaggerating the number of bodies disposed of in that fashion. Similar ambiguities arose owing to the extensive damage caused by fires. Coroners maintained that some physical evidence would remain for every body burned; African-Americans responded that some black bodies might have been consumed entirely by the flames. The exodus of so many blacks following the initial May fracas only added to the confusion. When blacks argued that a missing person was clearly a victim of the July 2 massacre, the official rejoinder was that such individuals had merely left town leaving no forwarding address.

Several aspects of the East St. Louis riot stayed alive in the imaginations of the next generations of African-Americans. Even those blacks who might not "know" the particulars of the events absorbed certain kinds of information from those who did. White racists, it was widely believed, would use fire, water, and ropes as instruments of torture to mutilate the bodies of blacks. Moreover, the inability of the law enforcement community to protect black citizens or punish the rioters proved that the North of the twentieth century could be as callous toward blacks as the South of the nineteenth century. Ostensibly "objective" investigators, it was felt, would always be inclined to give the benefit of the doubt to whites.

Chicago, 1919

Two years after the East St. Louis troubles, a major riot erupted in another Illinois city—Chicago—accompanied by rumors very similar to those that circulated in 1917. The racial climate in Chicago was as volatile as it had been in East St. Louis, and for much the same reasons: namely, a massive influx of southern black labor into the city and associated white anxiety. Before the actual outbreak of violence, Topsy/Eva rumor cycles circulated alleging that the other side was stockpiling arms with which to stage an attack on the July 4 holiday. And after the riot, which claimed twenty-three black and fifteen white lives, rumors spread that many more black bodies had been disposed of in a body of water.

In fact, the riot did not erupt until July 27, 1919, triggered by stories concerning the death of a seventeen-year-old black male. Eugene Williams was swimming at a beach where an unofficial color line separated white from black bathers. Although he entered the water from the black side, he soon found that he had crossed over the line. As white bathers began throwing stones in his direction and at the other blacks who had gathered at the water's edge, he panicked and drowned. Lifesaving measures were attempted by both black and white witnesses, but he was not revived.

Several rumors immediately swept through the crowd. One alleged that the boy's death had occurred when he was hit by a rock (though no bruises were found on his corpse). Another held that a police officer had refused to arrest the white man who had thrown the stone but had arrested a black witness. Blacks rushed the police, and for several days violence crippled Chicago.

Afterward, a Topsy/Eva rumor developed around "Bubbly Creek," with both sides claiming that bodies—black or white in line with the teller's race—were being tossed into Bubbly Creek by the other group. When no bodies were found in the creek, of course, rumors of a cover-up circulated. Rumors continued to emerge for several months after the incident. In a new twist, one rumor alleged that the violence had been part of a plot organized by Communist conspirators.

Belle Isle, Detroit, 1943

Rumors about the alleged disappearance of bodies into watery depths functioned as the immediate trigger of a riot in Belle Isle, Detroit, in 1943. Like East St. Louis and Chicago in the late 1910s, Detroit suffered a jolt to its racial equilibrium when a large group of southern blacks migrated into the urban center. On a hot June day, crowds of citizens, white and black alike, made their way to the beach at Belle Isle. A Topsy/Eva rumor cycle emerged, in which it was claimed that a woman and her infant had been accosted by members of the other race and thrown off the bridge. "The shared narratives," the folklorist Janet L. Langlois points out, "show that infanticide is a cultural code with overlapping meanings for blacks and whites in Detroit; one race's perception of the other's inhumanity [thereby] becomes tangibly expressed."[32] Less common but nonetheless inflammatory were rumors in which one side claimed that one of "their" women had been raped by men of the other race. In any event, hysteria was the result, during which new rumors spread in the white community that armed blacks from surrounding areas were heading for the city. The various stories circulated throughout the afternoon and evening, with violence marking that night and the next day.

Unlike the East St. Louis and Chicago riots, the Belle Isle riot was confined to one extended outbreak of rage. In a thirty-hour period, thirty-four people were killed. When the river was dragged, the investigators found no bodies—no white woman, no black woman, no white infant, no black infant.

Harlem

The events of 1935 and 1943 in Harlem are the notable exceptions to the pattern of white instigation in pre-1960s race riots. They were also characterized by property destruction rather than assaults on human beings. The first incident began after word circulated that white policemen had killed a sixteen-year-old black shoplifter in a Harlem department store. In fact, although an altercation had taken place between the young man, store managers, and the police, he had not been physically assaulted or murdered. Black witnesses to the heated verbal exchange were disturbed, however, when the police took the young man out through the store's basement and when, a short while later, an ambulance showed up. Throughout Harlem the word spread that a black teenager had been killed for shoplifting a cheap knife. When attempts were made to dispel the rumor by distributing a photo of the boy with a black policeman, another rumor surfaced alleging that the young face in the photo was not that of the real "victim."[33] No whites were killed in the ensuing day of violence, but numerous white-owned business establishments were destroyed.

Eight years later, again in Harlem, hostile words were exchanged between a black military policeman and a white police officer who had tried, over the MP's objections, to arrest a black woman on disorderly conduct charges. The white policeman discharged his revolver, wounding the black man in the shoulder. Word spread that a black soldier had been killed by a white policeman. Continuing a pattern established in the earlier Harlem riot, and which would continue with the black-instigated riots of the 1960s, the violence was directed at white-owned property, not white people.

The 1960s Riots

Most scholars distinguish between the outbreaks of racial violence before 1960 and those that occurred during that strife-ridden decade by saying that the earlier riots were launched by whites against black persons, whereas the latter—some of which might be better termed "skirmishes"—primarily involved blacks destroying white-owned property. But call them skirmishes or riots, the events of the 1960s, like those before them, were accompanied by distinct rumor cycles, of a sort we have encountered before and will meet up with again.

The sheer volume of episodes of racially oriented violence in the 1960s can be daunting. A survey conducted by Terry Knopf in conjunction with the Lemberg Center's Civil Disorder Clearinghouse, for example, counted over 1,200 "racial disorders" between January 1967 and October 1969 alone.[34] Obviously, it is beyond the scope of this study to review the circumstances of these outbreaks as was done for earlier twentieth-century incidents. However, Knopf's investigation of the role that rumor played in the troubles of the 1960s does lend itself to the present discussion. She identifies four major content themes in the 1960s rumor cycles: (1) predictions of violence, (2) police brutality, (3) white brutality, and (4) conspiracy by whites (as well as a fifth category, "other"). Rumors and legends about white conspiracies will be covered in the next two chapters of this book. As an example of a police brutality rumor, she notes an outbreak that occurred in Washington, D.C., after word circulated that a black man had been shot by a white policeman for jaywalking.[35] As an example of a white brutality rumor, she describes a story that sparked a 1967 Chicago outbreak in which it was alleged that white boys had pushed a black man in front of an elevated train. Within this category she also places those items involving accusations of sexual violence, such as rape and castration.[36]

Circumstantial Evidence

Several consistent features of the relationship between rumors and African-American behavior can be identified in the incidents described above. By looking at the similarities in the racial makeup of the communities involved in the unrest, the time of year in which the unrest occurred, the triggering events of the riots, and the rumors themselves, we can see why at certain historical moments rumors have played a role in creating crisis situations.

Maintaining a racial equilibrium satisfactory to both blacks and whites has always been problematic, whether in rural or urban environments. In the twentieth century, the eruption of race riots has generally occurred in locales where the black-white balance underwent a massive change. The white populations in East St. Louis, Chicago, and Detroit were hostile to the large-scale influx of black citizens into their cities. If the blacks did not anticipate this hostility, the discrimination they faced in residential, educational, and occupational opportunities served as a potent reminder of white duplicity: just as Reconstruction-era northern whites had broken an ostensible promise of land, so too were the northern whites who coaxed them away from the South with promises of equal opportunity in the industrial centers of the Midwest and Northeast unable or unwilling to make good their promises.

Although the Harlem riots and most of the 1960s disturbances took place in black enclaves, they, too, reflect a general dissatisfaction with the white-black balance of power. Blacks may have outnumbered whites in Harlem, but most of the property was owned by white entrepreneurs. In the inner-city areas that were the scenes of most of the 1960s riots, the same economic imbalance was still quite evident, and blacks greatly resented the dependence that this arrangement fostered.

As the above cases suggest, outbreaks of racial violence are more likely to occur during the summer months. It may be more than a mere coincidence that in at least two instances Topsy/Eva rumor cycles about planned racial violence were pegged for the Fourth of July—a day that, for different reasons, has strong significance for both blacks and whites.[37] In East St. Louis and Chicago, the first spates of violence took place in late spring; the next "big" holiday, an "off" day for workers, was July 4. If one were planning a full-scale racial assault, it would make sense to plan it for a day when people were not obligated to work. The fact that July 4 celebrates America's birthday—its independence—makes it even more potent symbolically. From the point of view of the whites, the southern blacks moving into their cities were making unfair claims on the American dream. For many blacks, the Fourth of July symbolized all that was hypocritical about that dream. As early as 1853, Frederick Douglass stated: "I am not included within the pale of this glorious anniversary . . . this fourth of July is yours, not mine."[38] When interviewing twentieth-century African-Americans about their holiday rituals, folklorist William H. Wiggins heard again and again the opinion that "we ain't got no business celebrating the 4th of July; we weren't freed, it wasn't our Independence."[39] For both whites and blacks, the possibility that the other group would select the Fourth of July to vent their wrath sounded entirely plausible.

Rumors about or genuine incidents involving aggressors of one race doing bodily harm to a symbolically significant individual of the other race preceded several of the violent outbursts in question. In other words, stories about average able-bodied white and black males getting into a fight in which one of them dies do not trigger riots. In the case of the Harlem riot of 1943, for instance, it is noteworthy that a black man *in a military uniform* was the alleged victim of the policeman's gun.[40] Blacks were becoming increasingly offended by a dominant culture that expected them to risk their lives in defense of a way of life to which they had only limited access. The altercation between the black soldier and white policeman brought down to a personal, identifiable level African-Americans' frustrations with this state of affairs. In general, there was little a Harlem resident could do to voice his or her disgust with the system; but the news that a black *soldier* had been killed by a white cop made the metaracial conflict comprehensible.

Similarly, when blacks heard that an innocent mother and child had been murdered (Belle Isle), or a youngster on the edge of manhood had been stoned to death (Chicago), or a black man-child had been killed by a white policeman in a store (Harlem 1935), they felt compelled to defend the assaults against precious members of the race. The rape and castration rumors of the 1960s are in this same mold.

Finally, several of the rumors involved particularly violent murders in which the bodies of the black victims were mutilated (East St. Louis) or entirely destroyed, either by burning (East St. Louis) or drowning (Belle Isle, Chicago 1919) or being pushed in front of a fast-moving train (Chicago 1967). These stories return us to the cannibalism texts and the concern with a fate in which one's whole person is consumed. In the face of major institutional, social, and economic discrimination, African-Americans are most likely to fight back when presented with news that one identifiable, symbolically significant black individual's body has been ravaged by white racist aggression.

Conclusion

Prior to the Civil War, enslaved African-Americans had access to few news venues other than rumors and contemporary legends. "Official" information about their collective and individual fates was certainly limited. Decisions about whether to run away or whether to perform an act that would likely result in being beaten or sold were based largely on a rumor mill that was often propelled by whites.

The sweeping changes wrought by Reconstruction improved blacks' chances of hearing for themselves the "news" that would shape their futures as free men and women. But however much their circumstances changed following the Civil War, blacks had good reason to be skeptical about their future share in the American dream. When the forty-acres-and-a-mule scenario failed to materialize, many African-Americans reckoned that post-Jubilee race relations would continue to be characterized by a familiar white supremacist dogma. Thus, many of the prewar rumor formulae remained applicable.

The crises of the twentieth century were also regressive in many respects. During the race riots and the world wars, whites resurrected old stereotypes and misnomers in order to justify the heightened antipathy evident in race relations. Blacks, too, found that traditional folkloric metaphors, ones in which the well-being of individual black bodies was shackled to the well-being of the race as a whole, still suited their predicament. Faced with unyielding second-class citizenship, the folk found that they could best make sense of their plight by reducing it to a personal level. With fire, water, and like weapons capable of complete bodily destruction, the powers that be seemed intent on eliminating blacks one by one from American streets, American cities, American factories—the entire American landscape.

Chapter Three

Conspiracy I

"They . . . the KKK . . . did it"

When confronted with evidence that Church's Fried Chicken was not owned by the Ku Klux Klan and was not contaminating the chicken so that male eaters would be sterilized, a bright young African-American female college junior responded, "Well, it's the kind of thing they would do if they could." No organization, legitimate or otherwise, has earned the mistrust of African-Americans more deservedly than the KKK. Throughout the late 1970s and into the early 1990s, the Ku Klux Klan has been blamed for much kinky and reprehensible antiblack violence in rumors and contemporary legends—including the Church's item; the story that the Klan produced a popular brand of clothing (Troop), profits from which they used to fund antiblack activities; the story that "Klan-owned" Tropical Fantasy soft drinks contain a sterilizing agent; and the rumor that the Atlanta child murders were attributable to KKK machinations. The last rumor differs from the other three in that while the Church's, Troop, and Tropical Fantasy items cannot be substantiated, a growing amount of evidence suggests possible Klan involvement in some of the deaths in Atlanta. In addition, the KKK is routinely associated with any unexplained civil rights violations. Even in Europe, where white supremacist groups have enjoyed some popularity of late, rumors have circulated in France and Great Britain linking the KKK to ownership of a popular brand of cigarettes.

Like almost all of my informants, the young woman cited above has never had any personal contact with the KKK. She knows no one who has seen a hooded Klansman. She claims to have learned very little about the group through her formal education. Her knowledge of the KKK and its goals and motives, rather, comes from the strong oral tradition of the African-American communities in which she has lived. Indeed, legends and anecdotes about the Klan have long been a staple of black folklore, perpetuating a profile of the KKK persona from generation to generation.[1] The particulars of this persona can be described as a set of powers. To many African-Americans, the Klan exists as the agency on which whites depend to mitigate or eliminate black access to those rights and privileges that white adults take for granted. As we shall see, the KKK asserted itself as a group capable of controlling nature, of controlling or eliminating black sexuality and reproduction, of controlling black political achievement, and of undermining any efforts by the white law enforcement community to defend African-American citizens. Even informants with no specific narrative about a KKK incident to share will almost always be able to talk generally about the group in terms of these traits.

The task of distinguishing genuine KKK activity from folk ideas about KKK activity is further complicated by the generic quality the labels *KKK, Ku Klux Klan*, and *the Klan* have assumed. In the minds of many of my African-American informants, any racially oriented crime can be attributed to Klansmen. This impulse is confirmed by Janet Caldwell, program associate for the Center for Democratic Renewal (formerly the National Anti-Klan Network), who writes, "As I study organized white supremacists and racism in this society even more closely, I find the question of defining a 'Klansman' or 'Klanswoman' to be quite different for Black folks than for Euro-Americans. Black people recognize the Klan mentality and Klan behavior quite readily. White people—particularly law enforcement—want some sort of formal proof of *membership* in a particular 'organization.' "[2] Ironically, this tendency to see the white sheets behind every antiblack assault has only empowered the still-active white supremacist group: the

KKK gets credit not only for its own crimes, but also for those carried out by *other* white supremacists not formally affiliated with the Klan. Consequently, the Klan's power is often stronger in the minds of many African-Americans than it is in actual fact.

Founded by a group of six bored and dissatisfied ex-Confederate soldiers in 1866 in Pulaski, Tennessee, the KKK with its outlandish garb and highly ritualized activities has remained a nemesis to African-Americans throughout its one-hundred-plus-year history. Although its very first activities resembled modern-day fraternity pranks more than malicious assaults, within several months the group's signature night rides and brutal violence, with blacks the central target, began to dominate the group's ill-conceived agenda.[3] Like the paterollers of the antebellum South, the KKK of the 1860s and 1870s employed an extensive repertoire of tricks and scare tactics in their attempts to keep Reconstruction-era free blacks "in their place." Many of these antipathy-laden escapades added new meaning to the "cruel and unusual punishment" idiom. Understanding why African-Americans have attributed corporate conspiracies as well as random unsolved racially motivated crimes to the KKK necessitates an understanding of just how perverse and destructive the KKK's verifiable crimes have been.

The Birth of the Klan

Both the era of Reconstruction—when "radical" Republicans based in the North worked to shift the white supremacist order and mindset of the Confederacy and create a more humble, egalitarian "new" South—and the first incarnation of the Ku Klux Klan span the years 1866–72. Although many of the techniques used by the postwar KKK were clearly inspired by the antebellum paterollers, changed economic, social, and political circumstances in the reunited nation had altered the balance of power in the South. Whereas prior to the war black lives were valuable commodities deserving of protection by the whites, after the war the economic incentives of property investment no longer applied. A political division thus emerged during Reconstruction that contributed to the African-American's tendency to view any racially bigoted policy as resulting from Klan activity. During their notorious night rides, Reconstruction-era Klansmen would call on local blacks who were affiliated with the hated Republican party—the party of Abraham Lincoln. Klansmen, of course, were anxious to restore the Democrats to power in the South, and it may well have seemed to the victimized African-Americans that all Klansmen were themselves Democrats and all Democrats were Klansmen.

The Klansmen who followed in the paterollers' wake felt no obligation to obey the edicts of any whites who objected to the mistreatment of African-Americans—who in any event were probably Republicans. Indeed, they enjoyed a virtual mandate to maim and kill their black victims—a mandate that, ironically, countered the paterollers' purpose of keeping blacks from finding their way North, for the cruel escapades of the postwar KKK were likely a profound stimulus to the widespread migration of blacks from the South. During Reconstruction, the African-Americans who were targeted were not those with wanderlust, but rather those who hoped to make good the promises of economic, political, and social equality extended by the northern Republicans in their effort to build a prosperous new South. Indeed, the abuses on black bodies that occurred between 1866 and 1872 challenged the severity of any that can be uncovered from the worst slavery regimes. Prompted to investigate, the House of Representatives issued a report on verifiable KKK activity that encompassed thirteen thick volumes.

During its formative years, the KKK enjoyed a rarely interrupted reign of terror so insidious and devised a dirty-tricks roster so gruesome that the reputation it earned carried it through the later leaner years, so that even today the Klan ethos is based on the legacy of those first six years. It is doubtful that the folk imagination could have invented more horrific atrocities than those actually perpetrated. The apparent unwillingness or inability of law enforcement agencies to curb the outrages only proved to African-Americans that they were on their own.

In the first two years following its inception in Tennessee, Klan violence spread largely unchecked throughout the South. When Grand Wizard Nathan B. Forrest granted an interview with the press, even the Congress became convinced of the extent of the group's power base: "The general had confirmed the existence of the Ku-Klux as a counterrevolutionary army, while up until now, it had been considered, if not a wild rumor or radical fantasy, then a harmless group of silly boys who played tricks on 'darkies.' "[4] These "tricks," which ranged from supposedly harmless practical jokes to outright atrocities, later became the foundation for numerous black legends. For example, mounted Klansmen would remove false heads attached to the top of their robes and hand them to terrified blacks to hold. Another prank involved the Klansmen hiding oilskin bags beneath their robes and then, pretending to have an insatiable thirst, asking frightened blacks to bring them prodigious quantities of water, which immediately disappeared—right into the bags by means of a concealed tube. Such ostensibly harmless pranks were meant to serve notice to blacks that these mysteriously clad horsemen had supernatural powers.

Most blacks were not duped by these claims. As one victim, Amzi Rainey, put it, "I went into this thing when they came to my house; they said they had risen from the dead; I wanted to see what kind of men they was. I went a purpose to see who they was; whether they were spirits, or whether they were human, but when I came to find out, they was men like me."[5] Although the Klansmen wanted to believe that their disguises and tricks would convince superstitious ex-slaves that they were supernatural beings, the blacks proved much less gullible than their pursuers assumed.[6] For many Reconstruction-era blacks, in fact, the sight of a mere ghost would have been preferable to that of the ominous, hooded, very much alive white men who knocked at their doors.

The anxieties and insecurities of the six founders of the KKK and the thousands of men who were recruited into the organization during Reconstruction are revealed in the ritualistic trappings they created. Their folkspeech, costumes, and activities suggest a powerful sexual ambivalence as well as a confusion about their attractions to and relationships with their black victims. In some ways, the participants seemed driven to assert their own sexual prowess by humiliating, castrating, or killing the sinister black male, whose purported "genital superiority" was so disturbing to white supremacists.[7] In other ways, however, KKK symbolism suggests that the participants felt driven to destroy black men not because they perceived them as competition for white women, but because they could not tolerate their own latent homosexual desires for the victims. In her study of racially motivated lynching and burning rituals in literature, the African-American literary critic and folklorist Trudier Harris noted:

In simultaneously perpetuating and attempting to destroy the myth of black male sexuality, the white men involved in the lynchings and burnings spent an inordinate amount of time examining the genitals of the black men whom they were about to kill. Even as they castrated black men, there was a suggestion of fondling, of envious caress. The many emotions involved at the moment perhaps led the white men to slash even more violently at what could not be theirs, but which, at some level, they very much desired (without the apish connotations, of course).[8]

For the most part, the Klan and like white supremacist groups made sure that there were few witnesses to these acts. Yet when victims' bodies were discovered the extent of the perversion was clear. Regarding a lynching that happened near her grandmother's home, the author Maya Angelou recalled: "We found out about a man who had been killed by white folks and thrown in the pond . . . the man's thing had been cut off and put in his pocket."[9] Occasionally, a black witness lived to describe an assault. When civil rights activist Fannie Lou Hamer was arrested in 1963, she was beaten in her jail cell. A fellow voter registration worker, Lawrence Guyot, was arrested and beaten as well. Comparing their treatment, Hamer said: "The beat him as bad as they beat me. The only difference was they taken paper and tried to burn his private off."[10]

These conflicting drives resulted in a complex web of sometimes contradictory but always destructive behavior. We should remember that, as ex-Confederate soldiers, Klansmen had just lost a long, hard-fought war. Even those inclined to reject symbolic analyses of sexual motivations are unlikely to question the link between losing a war and subsequent masculine insecurity. In the case of the Civil War, the situation was compounded by the sudden rise in the status of blacks. Still smarting from the assault on their masculinity inherent in defeat, many veterans of the Confederacy could not accept the idea of ex-slaves being on an equal footing with whites—of individuals they had always addressed as "boy" actually being men.

The reluctance of some white men to abandon the "boy" label has generally been linked to their desire to keep blacks in the subservient and dependent positions they held before the war. However, another interpretation may have some validity as well. At least since Plato's *Phaedrus*, a classical Greek dialogue in which male-male seduction is used to illustrate certain points, the younger of two male lovers—the object of the seduction—has been referred to as a boy. Perhaps the persistence of the "boy" label reflects not only a desire to maintain prewar oppressions, but also a subconscious effort to objectify black males as potential recipients of homosexual advances. As Harris notes, "Calling him a boy suggests . . . the strange lens through which the white man must view the black man sexually. 'Boy,' an effort at controlling language and thereby controlling the reality the language is designed to reflect, wipes out the symbolic, sexual implications of the black man as Man."[11]

If this were the only clue to possible homosexual underpinnings to KKK violence, it could be easily dismissed. But other aspects of the language and lore of white supremacy constructed by the Klan can be interpreted in like manner. With its elaborate initiation rites, secret languages, special codes, and private handshakes and gestures, the KKK established a masculine fraternal order complete with all the accoutrements of male-male bonding. The assorted costumes, regalia, and props adopted by various incarnations of the Klan and Klaverns are fairly well known; it is less well known, however, that some Klansmen padded their crotches to exaggerate

the size of their masculine endowments. Jackson Surratt, tes-
tifying before Congress in 1872, described his attackers thus:
"It looked like paper stuck up beside the head, and it run up
to a sharp point on the top, and they had their coats on and
[paper] under their breeches to make them look big—bulging
out."[12] Just as their explorer ancestors of the sixteenth century
had felt threatened by and envious of the size of African male
genitalia, so did Reconstruction-era Klansmen harbor mixed
feelings about the alleged difference in the sizes of white and
black sexual organs.[13]

Participation in KKK conspiracies allowed white men to
reclaim their own manhood while denying the same to blacks
or those who sympathized with black equality. As quickly as
radical Republicans gave ex-slaves access to the voting cham-
bers, seats in the state legislatures, the schoolrooms being
established by the Freedmen's Bureau, land ownership, and
their own families, the KKK mounted its crusade to impede
African-American claims to these previously whites-only domains. On an individual level, then, the goal of the Klan can
be seen as the boosting of their own sexual prowess by controlling or eliminating that of the black man. This goal was
matched on a political level as Klansmen attempted to maintain white dominance of the political arena by denying blacks
entrance to it.

While most people use the word *lynch* to refer to an illegal
hanging, the term actually incorporates a much broader range
of abuse. Creative Reconstruction-era Klansmen devised
many cruel fates for blacks, which contributed to their emerging reputation as demonically inspired monsters determined
to sexually humiliate those who threatened white supremacy.
Sexual metaphors abound in stories of KKK violence. In many
accounts, the desire to destroy or control the victims' sexuality
is quite apparent; in others it is less obvious.

Prior to the war, whites had been able to exert supremacy
over blacks by maintaining control over their slaves' sex lives.
When they wanted to increase the size of their slave population, they forced their slaves to procreate. When they wanted
sexual favors from black women, they could rape them with
no fear of reprisal. If they were dissatisfied with or disinclined

to support the babies born to the slave women, they could sell the offspring. After the war, they sought to reassert some of these prerogatives by raping black women, usually in the presence of their husbands or fathers. Not surprisingly, one of the most frequently cited justifications for KKK violence was contact between black men and white women; the slightest hint of such a relationship was sure to guarantee the arrival of robed crusaders in the middle of the night. Hangings were quite often preceded or followed by the castration of the victim. Many accounts speak of a black man whose attackers presented him with the chilling alternative of either being strung up or "just" castrated as punishment for having sex with a willing white female neighbor.[14]

Klan victims included whites sympathetic to blacks as well as blacks who might have violated the South's preferred power structure. Discovering that a white woman had hidden three African-American men in her home, for example, South Carolina Klansmen stripped her and poured hot tar in her vagina. (The choice of a black substance for that particular orifice seems more than coincidental.) The KKK also developed a fondness for forced couplings between blacks and the whites who had befriended them. A white southerner who allowed blacks to construct a school on his property was apprehended along with a married black couple in their sixties. The white man was forced to kiss the anus of the black man; when he proved unable to copulate with the black man's wife, his Klan attackers settled for his kissing her genitals.[15]

This last example illustrates that Klan violence was triggered by much more than allegations of black sexual misconduct alone. The scenarios described by the hundreds of black victims of the 1866–72 era negate the oft-cited rationale that the KKK was only trying to avenge assaults on innocent white women. Casting votes and holding political office were other symbols of white manhood that KKK members were loath to see bestowed upon ex-slaves. Amzi Rainey's testimony describes a standard encounter: "Then he asked me which way did I vote. I told him I voted the radical [Republican] ticket. 'Well,' he says, 'now you raise your hand and swear that you will never vote another radical ticket and I will not let them kill you.' And he made me stand and raise my hand before him and my God that I never would vote another radical ticket against my principle."[16]

With the demise of Reconstruction reforms, the dream of a new, more egalitarian South faded. Although the belated efforts of Congress did curtail KKK growth, the return to a social order similar to that in place before the war suggests that in some ways the KKK and the Democrats had "won." The African-American congressman Jefferson F. Long of Georgia addressed the House of Representatives on this issue before his all-too-brief term ended:

Why, Mr. Speaker, in my State since emancipation there have been over five hundred loyal men shot down by disloyal men there, and not one of those who took part in committing those outrages has ever been brought to justice. Do we, then really propose here today, when the country is not ready for it, when those disloyal people still hate this Government, when loyal men dare not carry the "stars and stripes" through our streets, for if they do they will be turned out of employment, to relieve from political disability the very men who have committed these Ku Klux outrages?[17]

The Democrats did, however, regain their grip on the South, and African-American citizens were forced to abandon most of the gains they had made during Reconstruction. Moreover, since the northern Republicans of the late 1870s, 1880s, and 1890s were less committed to southern black equality than their predecessors of the Reconstruction era, the status of Democrats as a formidable enemy was now much more pronounced. The implementation and codification of Jim Crow policies reinforced the emasculation of black men established by the Klan, while bold African-Americans who challenged the new status quo remained subject to correction by the robed vigilantes.

In 1901, Booker T. Washington wrote in his autobiography: "The 'Ku-Klux' period was, I think the darkest part of the Reconstruction days. . . . I have referred to this unpleasant part of the history of the South simply for the purpose of calling attention to the great change that has taken place since the days of the 'Ku Klux.' To-day there are no such organizations in the South, and the fact that such ever existed is almost forgotten by both races. There are few places in the South now where public sentiment would permit such organizations to exist."[18] As of the 1890s, however, Washington's observation was only technically correct. Although formal, functioning KKK groups were by then few and far between, southern blacks still ran a great risk of being apprehended for perceived violations of the "southern" way of life. White vigilantes, while not necessarily dues-paying Klan members, frequently invoked the Klan label and style in order to intimidate their victims. As the nineteenth century neared its end, new vigilante groups continued to emerge, such as the American Protection Association and the Whitecaps. The latter was clearly an imitation of the KKK, in that they adorned their countenances with white hoods and performed their dirty work at night.[19]

A contemporary of Washington's, the African-American journalist Ida B. Wells-Barnett, devoted her career to the risky cause of proving that Klan-style violence and values still threatened the well-being of southern African-Americans at the close of the nineteenth century. With painstaking care she compiled statistics on events that would have been within Booker T. Washington's memory: "During the year 1894, there were 132 persons executed in the United States by due form of law, while in the same year, 197 persons were put to death by mobs who gave the victims no opportunity to make a lawful defense. No comment need be made upon a condition of public sentiment responsible for such alarming results."[20]

Night Doctors

As blacks migrated from the southern rural roads to northern urban streets in the waning years of the nineteenth century, they brought with them their folklore. Just as their music, tales, and humor were reshaped to encompass the new challenges black folk faced, so were their narratives about white supremacist conspiracies adapted to fit their new life in the city. The comments of ex-slave Cornelius Garner in response to a question by a Works Progress Administration interviewer reflect this change: "De only Ku Klux I ever bumped into was a passel o' young Baltimore Doctors tryin' to Ketch me one night an' take me to de medicine college to 'periment on me. I seed dem a layin' fer me an' I run back into de house. Dey had a plaster all ready for to slap on my mouf. Yessuh."[21] Prevalent from the end of Reconstruction through the First World War, folk narratives about such encounters demonstrate that the powers established by the KKK were easily transferred to other possible sources of antiblack conspiracy. Gladys-Marie Fry, whose book *Night Riders in Black Folk History* remains the definitive source on so-called night doctors, defines them as follows: "The term 'night doctor' (derived from the fact that victims were sought only at night) applies both to students of medicine, who supposedly stole cadavers from which to learn about body processes, and [to] professional thieves, who sold stolen bodies—living and dead—to physicians for medical research. Night doctors were also known to black folk as 'student doctors' (referring specifically to apprentice physicians), 'Ku Klux doctors,' 'night witches,' and 'night riders.' "[22]

As antiblack conspirators, the Ku Klux Klan and the medical establishment may not seem very similar. From the perspective of black folk, however, these two groups can be seen to have shared several attributes. As Fry points out above, the night doctors, like Klansmen and the paterollers, were reputed to prowl after dark, thus limiting black nocturnal mobility. Moreover, both medical students and Klansmen are easily identified by their white garments; those charged with upholding the law allowed both groups to function with little fear of reprisal; and both groups demonstrated a marked indifference to the physical well-being of black bodies.

A final and significant piece of evidence on African-American attitudes toward these oppressors arises in oral testimony on the issue. Garner, like Minnie Folks in commenting on the tripping of paterollers' horses (see Chapter 2), closes his narrative by stressing his own street smarts in retreating from the possible threat posed by a "passel" of young doctors. His voice, in short, assumes a trickster tone. This poorly educated, recently transplanted ex-slave lets his audience know that he had enough mastery over his urban existence to outsmart a group of men inclined to do him bodily harm. The same is true of many of the accounts by former slaves of KKK encounters; for example: "One night dey come to our house after my husband to kill him, and my husband had a dream dey's coming to kill him. So he had a lot of colored men friends to be at our house with guns that night, and time dey seed dem Ku Klux coming over de hill dey started shooting just up in de air and shout, and dem Ku Klux never did bother our house no more."[23] This black woman, by emphasizing her husband's ability to cope with and deflect assailants in white, asserts their refusal to be victims. The historian Lawrence W. Levine, discussing the evolution of the black hero in folklore, notes: "Amidst the tales of Klan atrocity, intimidation, and murder, stories of courageous resistance came through again and again."[24] In African-American oral literary criticism about antiblack hostility this motif featuring the speaker's ability to cope with and indeed conquer the conspiracy when faced with it personally resurfaces through the use of a trickster tone.

Although it is likely that not all of the KKK narratives recited by African-Americans were based entirely in fact, the Klan and similar white segregationist groups clearly did pose a constant and genuine threat to the personal safety of rural blacks. The same cannot be said of night doctors. Despite exhaustive research, Fry uncovered no evidence of an early-twentieth-century demand for live bodies for medical study. However, she does note that the very first legends of such unscrupulous activity may well have been planted in the black folk imagination by southern whites anxious to prevent their labor force from leaving the region.[25] Like the antebellum-era ghost stories that warned slaves to avoid certain intersections and roads because they were frequented by spirits, the legends about malevolent doctors were likely intended to keep blacks from feeling control over their physical environment, especially at night. Yet the fact that so many of these accounts in the retelling close with a motif of conquest indicates that although blacks may have accepted the existence of night doctors, they converted the material to prove their mettle, boasting of their prowess in avoiding the alleged snares.

The Rebirth of the Klan

For white audiences, D. W. Griffith's 1915 epic film *The Birth of a Nation*, based on Thomas Dixon's successful 1905 novel *The Clansman*, recast Reconstruction-era Klansmen into noble white heroes and revived popular interest in the all-but-defunct group. As African-American leaders and organizations struggled to discredit the white supremacist vision depicted therein, they were forced to bear witness to the ominous enthusiasm with which the film was received, even by the White House. In describing the social and political reaction to the film, Wyn Craig Wade notes: "A 'Ku-Klux fever,' similar to that of Reconstruction, was revived in the North, and manufacturers responded with the production of Ku-Klux hats (patterned after the eighteen inch hoods in the film) and Ku-Klux kitchen aprons. New York society matrons held Ku-Klux balls. And on Halloween, students at the University of Chicago threw a party where two thousand young people cavorted in improvised Klan costumes."[26] The willingness of white America to embrace the film's distorted version of the post–Civil War era demonstrated to African-Americans just how fragile their status in the new century still was. And that fragility could be measured in very real terms by resurrected KKK groups, which began to pursue the bodies of blacks with renewed vigor.

The praiseworthy accomplishments of African-American soldiers in World War I further triggered the Klan fever inspired by the film. Just as blacks—many of whom had served gallantly in the Union army—felt justified in demanding equal rights during the hopeful era of Reconstruction, so did the black veterans who returned from Europe at the end of the "war to end all wars." They had defended democracy abroad; now they wanted the rights and privileges they deserved at home. Such an idea, needless to say, was as abhorrent to the white segregationists of the 1910s and 1920s as it had been to their predecessors of the 1860s and 1870s.

Once again, the trope connecting male sexual prowess with military acumen becomes applicable. The wearing of uniforms and carrying of weapons had been privileges that white American males wished to preserve for themselves. The fact that black men had adopted the garments and tools of war, and had done so with great success, pushed the white supremacists back into their hooded costumes. And as before, black demands for parity were interpreted as attempts to emasculate white men. The zero-sum notion persisted that if blacks were to be granted all of the rights of white males, white males would be forced to give up something of their own. While some of the ritualistic aspects of the Klan had changed since the 1870s, their preferred task of lynching and dismembering blacks remained the same. Wade notes that seventy-four blacks were lynched in 1919, and that many of them were wearing their military uniforms when apprehended.[27]

As always, the key message communicated by the white supremacists was a disregard for black bodies. When the African-American civil rights activist and labor organizer A. Philip Randolph called in 1922 for investigations into lynchings, he received a menacing package containing a black human hand. The box also contained a cryptic letter, which read in part:

There is no space in our race for you and your creed. What do you mean by giving us a nigger? Do you know that our organization is made up of all whites? We have sent you a sample of our good work, so watch your step or else you. . . . Now let me see your name in your nigger improvement association as a member, paid up too, in about one week from now. Don't worry about lynching in the South. If you were here you wouldn't talk about it. Now be careful how you publish this letter in your magazine [The Messenger] or we may have to send your hand to some one else. Don't think that we can't get you and your crowd. Although you are in New York City it is just as easy as if you were in Georgia. If you can't unite with your own race we will find out what's the matter with you all. Don't be selfish. Give your friends a tip.

K.K.K.[28]

Randolph makes a convincing case that his unwanted correspondents hoped to exploit African-American superstitions by sending him the severed appendage, though the KKK's consistent need to establish its dominance by controlling black bodies and body parts is equally evident.

The reborn Klansmen of the 1910s and 1920s thrived. Membership rolls bulged, and KKK chapters were established in the Midwest as well as in the familiar environs of the south. The problems that sporadically beset the thriving coalition were entirely internal. It was obvious to black organizations and officials monitoring the group's popularity that external law enforcement agencies gave little more than lip service to demands that they eliminate KKK violence.

This indifference on the part of the white establishment must be taken into account when considering the development of African-American folk belief about conspiracy. Whereas the growth of the Reconstruction-era Klan was checked within six years by a prolonged, extensive congressional investigation, the early-twentieth-century groups proliferated with no real threats from local, state, or federal law enforcement bodies. As we shall see in later chapters, the Justice Department and the FBI were particularly hostile to suggestions that they protect African-Americans from the Klan and Klan-style violence.

Fortunately for blacks and other targeted groups, the selfishness and arrogance of those who rose to power in the revived Klan periodically sabotaged larger group efforts. In the 1920s, for example, David Curtis Stephenson, grand dragon of the Indiana Klan, believing himself to be safe from criminal prosecution, made the fatal mistake of kidnapping and assaulting the beautiful young daughter of a prominent white family. The description of Stephenson's attack on Madge Oberholtzer suggests that an impulse to consume one's victims was still a cornerstone of Klan violence: "He just chewed that poor girl all to pieces!" "That sonofabitch acted like a goddamn *cannibal* with that girl!"[29] Of course, it took Stephenson's brazen attack on an upstanding *white* citizen to bring about his fall from grace.

Meanwhile, though, periodic reissues of *The Birth of a Nation* and the widespread success of *Gone with the Wind* in the late 1930s only reinforced the view that Klansmen were the heroic agents of the white majority. With few exceptions, the decades encompassing the Great Depression up to the birth of the civil rights movement in the 1950s were ones in which African-Americans, in both the North and the South, were forced to cope on their own with the threat of KKK violence.

With the beginning of the civil rights movement, televised coverage of conflicts between Klansmen and activists placed the issues in full view of the American public. The scenes of Klansmen harassing peaceful African-American men, women, and children increasingly contradicted the fictional ones depicted in *The Birth of a Nation* and *Gone with the Wind*. Nonetheless, the demands for equitable treatment by African-Americans and their allies once again propelled white segregationists into action. As civil rights activists accelerated their claims to schools, lunch counters, public transportation, and public office, the KKK carried out ever more inhumane corporal assaults on blacks and equal rights advocates. One group, after realizing that a white journalist and activist had infiltrated their klavern, threatened to "take him out in the woods, fasten him to a log with a staple around his testicles, set fire to the log, give him a knife and tell him to 'Cut or burn!' "[30]

Even a partial list of the crimes attributable to the KKK between the mid-1950s and the mid-1960s reflects a persistent preoccupation with much more than merely killing those who dared to question the validity of white supremacy. After using razor blades to castrate a black Alabamian, Klansmen bathed his wounds in turpentine and kerosene, then passed his testicles around in a paper cup.[31] James Chaney, Andrew Goodman, Michael Schwerner, Viola Liuzzo, and four little black girls in a Sunday School class were among the Klan's better-known victims. In addition to committing these and numerous other murders, the KKK also devoted itself to bombing and burning the homes, schools, and churches of African-Americans. Although a few of the more visible crimes, particularly those involving white victims, were eventually solved, the majority of anti–civil rights actions went unpunished. Martin Luther King, Jr., in remarking on the inability of federal investigators to resolve these crimes, captured the essence of African-American suspicions on the matter: "Rather than criticize the FBI, I have acted as a mediator, urging Negroes to keep faith with the FBI and to not lose hope. But you can't explain to a Negro why a plane can be bombed and its pieces scattered for miles and the crime can be solved, but they can't find out who bombed a church."[32]

KKK Lore, 1960–80

Assassinations

As we have seen, rumors and legends about Klan conspiracies emerge in relation to both genuine and perceived acts of anti-black hostility. Before examining the perceived animus implicit in rumors tying the KKK to modern American corporations, let us look at genuine KKK-motivated incidents of violence. Each of the assassinations in the 1960s generated rumors of Klan involvement, as did the spate of twenty-eight alleged homicides of young men and women in Atlanta, Georgia, during the late 1970s and early 1980s. While some of these crimes have been resolved to the satisfaction of law enforcement officials, enough mystery remains to feed folk speculation.

Within minutes after President John F. Kennedy (JFK) was shot on November 22, 1963, the rumors that a white supremacist group was responsible started to circulate in African-American communities across the country. The rumors did not stop after the arrest of Lee Harvey Oswald. They did not stop after the Warren Commission concluded that Oswald had not been part of a larger conspiracy. Today, nearly thirty years after President Kennedy's death, I still have no trouble finding African-Americans, some of whom were not yet born in 1963, who maintain that the KKK or a like-minded organization was involved in the plot to kill the president. The rumor theorists Ralph Rosnow and Gary Alan Fine remark, "John Kennedy's assassination produced a spate of rumors, many still alive in the hearts and minds of those disinclined to believe the findings of the Warren Commission. Leaving aside the justification of these rumors, it is not unreasonable to forecast that one hundred years from now stories will still be circulating about that fateful November day."[33] While the assassinations of Martin Luther King, Jr. (MLK) and Robert F. Kennedy (RFK) were more straightforward, because accomplished at closer range, the killers' professed motives were sufficiently weak that uncertainty remains about those ultimately responsible for these deaths.

All three of these leaders' deaths became shrouded in competing conspiracy rumors mere moments after the fatal bullets were discharged. Yet tracing such rumors is problematic because of the plethora of official and quasi-official accounts that crop up at the same time. To gain specific information about the post-assassination rumor mill, therefore, I queried informants who were at least teen-aged at the time of JFK's death. I asked them to try to recall what items were circulating between the news of the shots being fired, the first arrests, and the subsequent killing of Lee Harvey Oswald by Jack Ruby. I then asked how stories heard in the intervening years had influenced their own view of who was responsible.

Given the enormous ambiguity surrounding JFK's death, these interviews with both African-American and white informants revealed a surprising degree of consensus. Most informants recalled hearing or thinking in the first few hours or days that the KKK was behind the assassination, with three related circumstances pointing to this involvement. First, JFK was gunned down in the South (in Dallas, Texas), the Klan's home territory. Several older African-American informants claimed that they felt uneasy any time they heard the president was planning to travel to the South. Second, the quick and unsatisfactorily explained murder of Oswald by Ruby within days of the president's death suggested to many that one member of the conspiracy group was trying to eliminate another. Several informants even used Ruby's name as part of their proof: "Jack Ruby . . . doesn't that just sound like a southern cracker to you?"

JFK's visibility on the issue of civil rights was the third and perhaps central reason for believing the KKK to be the architect of the conspiracy. No president since Abraham Lincoln had gained such a reputation for being in favor of extending all the rights and privileges enjoyed by white America to the nation's African-American population. Whether or not that reputation was deserved is still a matter of debate. Many scholars maintain that Kennedy's reluctance to antagonize white southern voters and congressmen in fact slowed the process of social change to which he publicly professed allegiance. Employing a provocative illness metaphor, Martin Luther King, Jr., expounded on the early-1960s African-American view of JFK and his untimely death:

Suddenly the truth was revealed that hate was a contagion; that it grows and spreads as a disease; that no society is so healthy that it can automatically maintain its immunity. If a smallpox epidemic had been raging in the South, President Kennedy would have been urged to avoid the area. There was a plague afflicting the South but its perils were not perceived. Negroes tragically know political assassination well. In the life of Negro civil-rights leaders, the whine of the bullet from ambush, the roar of the bomb have all often broken the night's silence. *They have replaced lynchings as a political weapon* [emphasis added].[34]

King, too, focused on the locale of JFK's assassination in attempting to understand it. By linking the president's death with those of civil rights leaders and by connecting political assassinations with lynchings, MLK is evoking images of the Klan without ever identifying the group by name.

Competing conspiracy theories still surround JFK's death, and a broad range of culprits—including the Mafia and Cuban-based assassins, neither of which can be identified with white supremacist motives—have been implicated in his assassination. In all this, evidence of possible KKK involvement is scanty at best. Nonetheless, many African-Americans remain committed to the belief that the Klan was behind the attack. One male World War II veteran, after displaying an impressive familiarity with the full scope of conspiracy theories that have emerged, said in early 1990: "But, you know, I still think they [the KKK] might have done it. I still think that way. A lot of folks do." As long as JFK is perceived by the folk as having been in favor of racial equality and the KKK retains its reputation for bigotry, only the most compelling proof of another individual or group's guilt will remove this uncertainty.

The commitment of Martin Luther King, Jr., to racial equality is, of course, beyond dispute. As dramatic televised conflicts between the KKK and civil rights workers became commonplace during the late 1950s and early 1960s, the American public grew accustomed to seeing Klansmen denounce King—whom they openly referred to as "Martin Luther Coon"—and his comrades. It also grew accustomed to revelations of more destructive hostility as Klansmen claimed responsibility for burnings, bombings, and lynchings in their crusade to stop the movement. Thus, when a supposedly lone assassin gunned King down in April 1968, it was no surprise when the KKK was targeted as the possible instigator of the conspiracy. As one informant said, "After all, they had been trying to get him all along."

The history of antagonism between the KKK and King was a leading reason offered for the perpetuation of such rumors, though the fact that the shooting took place in the South was certainly a contributing factor. Clearly the folk perceive the South to be territory where the KKK can literally get away with murder, even of the most prominent individuals. The assassin's name, James Earl Ray, also generated suspicion, triggering images of the white hoods and robes that disguise many a red-necked southern white man. The greatest amount of speculation, however, arose on the occasion of Ray's trial. After pleading guilty and receiving the legally mandated ninety-nine-year sentence, Ray was marched off to prison without ever being required to explain why he had killed King. To many, such speedy "justice" pointed very clearly to a conspiracy cover-up.

Whereas the location of the shooting and the name of the principal suspect enhanced the KKK conspiracy rumors following the deaths of Martin Luther King, Jr., and President Kennedy, in the case of Robert Kennedy's assassination these factors probably mitigated the spread of such charges. To the folk, California does not qualify as KKK-controlled territory, and a name like Sirhan Sirhan hardly stimulates images of the Klan. While some informants recalled that rumors about the

KKK "doing it again" circulated briefly in the confusing immediate aftermath of the 1968 shooting, most of these were quickly laid to rest by the investigation—an investigation, moreover, that was much more conclusive than those that followed the deaths of JFK and MLK. Even though many informants perceived RFK as more committed to racial equality than his older brother, fewer had nagging doubts that the KKK might have been behind his death.

The Atlanta Child Murders

More than a decade after the assassinations of King and the Kennedy brothers, another series of puzzling murders began to unfold. This time the names of the victims were as anonymous as those of the previous decade were known, and indeed, the first few deaths caused little public concern or speculation. But like the assassinations of the 1960s' preeminent leaders, the deaths of twenty-eight young African-American people in Atlanta, Georgia, between 1979 and 1981 prompted numerous rumors in which organized white supremacists figured strongly.

In the preface to *The Evidence of Things Not Seen*, his book-length essay on the Atlanta child murders, the late African-American author James Baldwin explains his near obsession with these crimes in this way: "It has something to do, in my own case, with having once been a Black child in a White country."[35] Indeed, his interest in the case was so strong that it compelled him to return to the United States from his self-imposed exile in Paris. Seeking to understand the meaning of the seemingly senseless string of twenty-eight homicides that plagued Atlanta, Baldwin, like other African-Americans struggling to comprehend the crimes, probed beneath the surface of the Atlanta story as it was reported in the national media in order to determine if it revealed some disguised agenda. In needing to make sense of the seemingly senseless crimes, Baldwin was not alone; African-Americans much closer to Atlanta than Paris shared his preoccupation with this horrendous series of unexplained murders.

The fact that the city of Atlanta was the scene of this violence has a special significance. As Baldwin notes, many black southerners proudly identify themselves with the adage "I'm not from Georgia. I'm from Atlanta."[36] The city that Sherman burned during the Civil War, in which Booker T. Washington delivered his racially self-effacing compromise speech of 1895, and that witnessed several of the most bitter civil rights confrontations in the 1960s, had by 1979 emerged as a particularly comfortable environment for blacks. Whereas Memphis and Dallas were perceived as racist cities when JFK and MLK were assassinated in them in the 1960s, Atlanta's reputation had improved among African-Americans. Desegregation efforts had taken well in Atlanta, a large middle-class black community thrived there, and black leaders were visible in the city's highest offices. The home of several long-established black colleges, Atlanta was seen by many African-Americans to offer better educational and economic opportunities than any other southern or northern city. Rural Georgia may have been still beset by racial unrest and hostility, but Atlanta seemed to exemplify the potential for racial harmony in the "new" South.

This nearly idyllic situation changed dramatically in 1979, when young blacks began to disappear, only to be found dead on the city's south side. Over the next year and a half the number of victims climbed to twenty-eight, and meanwhile non-Atlantans flocked—some with, some without invitation—to the stricken city to offer their support. Psychics, the Guardian Angels, Frank Sinatra, Muhammad Ali, and Sammy Davis, Jr., all made the news when they extended their talents to Atlanta's beleaguered African-American community. With headlines such as "Terror on Atlanta's South Side" and "City of Fear," national news magazines ensured that readers could keep track of the steadily rising victim count and the law enforcement community's struggle to summon plausible suspects. Seeing the possibilities for outside exploitation, the families of the slain youths formed an organization to protect their own stake in the investigation.

Following a period of haphazard surveillance, officers of the law arrested Wayne Williams, a twenty-three-year-old African-American record promoter, and charged him with two counts of homicide. Alternately proclaiming his innocence and taunting the law enforcement community, Williams's hostility, arrogance, and alleged homosexuality further implicated him in the murder spree. His very public trial was marked by dissension between his attorneys and his family. After Williams was convicted of two of the murders on the basis of circumstantial evidence, the investigation of the remaining crimes was closed. In 1985, a highly controversial television docudrama refocused attention on the unanswered questions. Doubts about Williams's guilt were expressed by the victims' families and the community at large, but still the case remained closed and the records sealed. Finally, under pressure from the media and persistent family members, the "case" was reopened in June 1987. At the time of this writing, Williams remains in prison and no other arrests have been made.

The events in Atlanta constituted an obvious crisis for its African-American community. But the crisis was not limited to black Atlantans; its impact was felt by virtually all of those who had been "Black child[ren] in a White country." The "unofficial," unconfirmed "news" about the murders—that is, rumors and contemporary legends—caused the greatest dismay among African-Americans. For almost as soon as the extent of the crimes being committed against the young black population was realized, speculation about the probable assailants and their motives surfaced. What arose was a cycle of stories charging antiblack groups with conspiracy and, in many versions, the subsequent contamination of the bodies (a topic that will be discussed further in Chapter 5).

Tamotsu Shibutani, in his trenchant study of rumor formation, argues: "Rumors emerge in ambiguous situations. . . . If the demand for news in a public exceeds the supply made available through institutional channels, rumor construction is likely to occur. . . . The greater the unsatisfied demand for news, the more likely it is that rumors will develop."[37] Clearly, the situation in Atlanta was ripe for rumor formation. Neither possible motives for the murders nor plausible suspects were positively identified until the count exceeded twenty victims. Anxious to augment the inconclusive data being supplied by the investigators, the folk devised their own explanations for the appalling events.

Although some informants recalled rumors in which the crimes were attributed to one individual motivated by some sort of sexual perversion, the more popular rumors charged a conspiracy group, most frequently the KKK, with having committed the crimes. Many felt that the "individual sex perversion" explanation was not credible because the murders were not all executed in like fashion, race and setting being the only constants. Different techniques were used to kill the victims; the youngest victim was seven, while the oldest was in his twenties; and although most victims were male, two females were found dead during these months, their murders remaining unsolved. To most, the conspiracy seemed more plausible. African-Americans, after all, were all too familiar with organized groups whose expressed or implied agenda involved antiblack activity. The KKK was immediately implicated. Not only did the group have a long history of attacking relatively powerless blacks, but the perception that the KKK might have been behind the assassination of one or more national leaders in the previous decade added potency to the rumors. The idea was so compelling, in fact, that President Carter himself ordered the FBI to pursue this possibility of a white supremacist conspiracy in their investigation of the homicides. Yet even the FBI was not immune from these rumors; for as we shall see in the next chapter, it, too, was identified as a possible conspirator in the deaths in Atlanta.

Of all the rumors covered in this book, those linking the KKK with the Atlanta child murders have the most potential for accuracy. The folk may have this one right, at least in part. Nearly ten years after Wayne Williams was incarcerated, evidence began to surface that a judge had dismissed and law enforcement officials eventually destroyed a tape-recorded confession in which one white man told another that one of the killings was part of a Klan plot; in addition, part of an investigative file containing similar documentation was "misplaced." Since Wayne Williams entered prison, moreover, it has also been discovered that one of the prosecution witnesses—an individual, it turns out, with ties both to the KKK and to one of the murder victims—testified against him under a pseudonym. Williams and his attorneys have tried to use this information to win a retrial.[38] Indeed, the notion that the KKK might have been responsible for at least one of the twenty-eight homicides is quite plausible.[39] One must not overlook the Klan's resurgence in this century, following several decades in which it was presumed utterly impotent; to be sure, paranoia about the potential force of its hostility is not entirely unjustified.

The Ku Klux Klan and Corporate Rumors

In the introduction to his discussion of the ubiquitous Kentucky Fried Rat, Gary Alan Fine states, "Contemporary folklore themes are the attempts of people to negotiate their current reality, and to deal with the changes in their personal environment."[40] As if heeding this pronouncement, during the past few decades African-Americans have modified their folklore to accommodate the new challenges they face in a society still torn by racism. Just as at the turn of the century northward-migrating blacks evoked the dangers of their new urban environment in tales of malicious medical students, today social threats find expression in lore about malevolent corporations.

The KKK has figured prominently in at least four contemporary legend cycles in which modern corporations are the mechanism by which late-twentieth-century white supremacists pursue the bodies of blacks. The KKK, in other words, has traded its white sheets of yesteryear for the white shirts of corporate America. In one rumor, the KKK, who allegedly owns Church's Fried Chicken, has tainted the chicken recipe so that black male eaters are sterilized after consuming it. In a second, young African-American male consumers are unwittingly supporting the KKK by purchasing overpriced athletic wear manufactured by the "Klan-owned" Troop clothing company. Third, many believe that the KKK owns Marlboro cigarettes, a brand popular among black smokers, and is not only accruing financial benefits from but also deliberately causing cancer in African-American consumers. Finally, the Brooklyn Bottling Company, maker and distributor of a soft drink called Tropical Fantasy, which is said to contain a mysterious ingredient capable of sterilizing black men, is similarly alleged to be a front for the KKK.

In all the versions I collected of these four items, KKK manipulation of the corporate enterprise is the single most common and dominant motif. Informants never attributed the conspiracy, for example, to Lyndon LaRouche, the Moonies, skinheads, or any other likely source of modern intrigue. In this sense the rumors are very much like the conspiracy rumors and contemporary legends that have plagued many large American corporations, including Procter & Gamble, McDonald's, and Entenmann's. During the early 1980s, all three of these companies were implicated in rumors and contemporary legends linking the owners to religious cults. Of these, the stories that Procter & Gamble profits were supporting the efforts of the Reverend Sun Myung Moon, head of the Unification Church, proved to be the most tenacious. Believers stated that the Procter & Gamble logo, containing an image of a man in the moon surrounded by stars, confirmed the existence of a connection between the cult and the company. "Moonies," as members of the church were called, were also said to have taken over Entenmann's Bakery. As for McDonald's, it faced rumors claiming that its founder, Ray Kroc, was a member of the Church of Satan.

Fredrick Koenig describes corporate conspiracy rumors as "those in which the allegation connects a political, religious or ideological movement with a visible target: a successful commercial enterprise. The carriers of the rumor are members of a population who feel that the movement is undesirable and threatening."[41] Given the KKK's history of genuine malice, it comes as no surprise that the folk indeed do agree on its "undesirable and threatening" character. Moreover, the alleged goals of the KKK vis-à-vis these companies also bear a strong resemblance to those traditionally pursued by the KKK.

Church's

In her study of Klan-related lore, Fry notes that "the humor that is clearly present in black testimony concerning the paterollers is almost totally absent in discussions of the Klansmen. There was nothing funny about Klan terrorism, either in its supernatural manifestations or in its physical brutality."[42] In a conversation we had, she agreed that the group's potency in the mind of the African-American community no doubt exceeds its actual power. Indeed, my informants had no trouble believing the Klan was capable of devising a conspiracy of the magnitude asserted in the Church's rumor. When I asked one black female student if she didn't think the Food and Drug Administration (FDA) would have tried to stop the Klan from doctoring the chicken, she speculated that, on the contrary, the KKK would have had no problem gaining control of the FDA. Another female informant believed Klan infiltration was rampant in all phases of American life.

In many versions of the Church's-KKK rumor, informants "verify" the rumor by saying something like, "A friend of mine saw a story on it on '60 Minutes.' " Folklorists are very familiar with this type of authentication. Indeed, Jan Harold Brunvand adopted the term *foaf* to describe motifs in which informants authenticate their stories by citing a *f*riend *o*f *a f*riend who encountered a report in the paper or on television. In the Church's case, as in most others, the source named denies the accusation. "60 Minutes" never aired any such story.

On the surface at least, the Church's company has done nothing to "earn" this association with the Ku Klux Klan. The enterprise was started by George Church, a former chicken incubator salesman, in 1952 when he opened the chain's first store, actually a mere stand not far from a poor Spanish section of San Antonio, Texas. Soon another five stores appeared in Texas. In 1963, George Church, Jr., took over the business, building more stores in Texas as well as out of state. In April 1965, Church's Chicken Corporation went public, and it remained so until it was purchased by one of its chief competitors, Popeyes Famous Fried Chicken and Biscuits, in 1989.

These facts appear innocent enough. But several aspects of the company's overall corporate identity and philosophy could have contributed to the item's popularity. Koenig, for example, cites Larry Varney, a Church's public relations representative, who speculated that a news story in which the Ku Klux Klan was supported by white supremacist churches in their efforts to intimidate African-Americans may well have been misunderstood, with "churches" taken to mean the fast food company instead of religious institutions. Then too, in giving the company his own name, George Church in a sense paved the way for the public to associate it with houses of worship. As is well known, churches played a pivotal role in the civil rights movement. In many communities, houses of worship were the only public spaces in which African-Americans could meet. Moreover, many of the best-known leaders in the civil rights movement emerged from the ranks of the black clergy. In its attempts to prevent civil rights advances, the Klan was proven to be responsible for the bombing and burning of numerous black churches throughout the South. This flagrant disregard for the sanctity of churches no doubt left a lasting impression on the African-American mind. The notion that "Church's" could be responsible for such destructive behavior as the sterilizing scheme thus gained a perverse, ironic appeal.

None of my informants who expressed belief in the item knew that the company's corporate headquarters and place of origin is San Antonio. Most informants who were familiar with the company, whether believers of the rumor or not, associated the company simply with "the South"; a few claimed Alabama, a few Georgia, but no one thought that the company was located in the North. The company did, of course, concentrate on the South when it was starting up, so this association is not surprising. And association with the Klan is but a short leap, since the KKK is also perceived by most people to be based in the South. Over and over again, in fact, African-American informants professed more distrust for southern-based enterprises than northern. I have come to think of this as the "Dixie factor."

Just as the company's location and name may indirectly

support this rumor, so may their product. The Church's menu boasts a wide selection of foods much like those available at a soul food restaurant: okra, corn on the cob, biscuits and gravy, catfish, and southern fried chicken. If a white supremacist organization were going to use a fast food chain to infiltrate the African-American community, Church's would be made to order. Another observation made by many informants who believed the rumor concerned the location of individual stores. When I asked what substance would affect only *black* males, informants countered that that wasn't the issue; after all, Church's stores were always located in inner-city black areas where whites simply didn't go.

There is, in fact, some truth to this comment. According to a 1984 *Business Week* article, Church's was one of the last fast food companies to open mall and suburban outlets, preferring instead the inner-city sites mentioned by my informants.[43] In the greater Boston area, for example, as of 1987 stores were located in Dudley Square, right in the heart of Roxbury; in Central Square, the black part of Cambridge; on Dorchester Avenue, a thoroughfare that crisscrosses the white and black sections of Dorchester; and on Blue Hill Avenue, another thoroughfare that connects the largely black suburb of Mattapan with a black section of Boston. In racially conscious Boston, these are the kind of areas traditionally avoided by most whites.

One other dimension of Church's corporate persona lent credence to the rumor. Unlike most fast food franchises, Church's preferred not to advertise. In 1978, a year when Church's ad budget was one of the lowest in the industry, the chairman, George Church, Jr., claimed that other fast food chains rely too much on new products and slogans; these devices, he said, are "a trap executives can get into to save themselves instead of solving the real problems of their operations."[44] That attitude, naturally, kept the company's visibility low. Many white Bostonians were not only not familiar with the rumor, they had never heard of the company. In an age when most fast food companies bombard us nightly with their televised pitches, however, a company with little or no advertising becomes conspicuous, to those who know it, precisely because of its anonymity. Perhaps the folk assumption is that a company that doesn't boast about its product has something to hide.

In trying to cope with the rumor, the company maintained the same close-mouthed approach. As the chairman of the board, J. David Bamberger, put it in 1986, "Our policy in this rumor is to let our record in minority relations and hiring speak for itself. We don't wish to dignify such a malicious rumor." Bamberger was obviously quite proud of his company's efforts to effect integration. He claimed:

From its very humble beginning, one of our ideas for growth incorporated the idea of "making big people out of little people." . . . Today we have approximately 17,000 people in the company. Eighty-four percent of these are minority! This extends from our stores through the Board Room. Seventy-two percent of our store managers and fifty percent of our Board are minority people and this hasn't happened overnight because of a crisis, but rather over the years because of a philosophy.

Bamberger's response to my initial inquiry also contained a separate sheet identified as "references." It listed fourteen minority individuals and companies who would purportedly vouch for the company's integrity. The list was headed by Benjamin Hooks, then executive director of the National Association for the Advancement of Colored People (NAACP). Yet despite the company's good intentions and notable contacts, the rumor continued to have a negative impact. Bamberger candidly acknowledged, "There is no question but that it hurts our business and our employees."[45]

From the company's point of view, the rumor represents an unearned assault by a community it has endeavored to embrace. From the point of view of some within the African-American community, the rumor represents a plausible answer to nagging questions about why a franchise would actively seek to serve the needs of African-American consumers in particular.

A new wrinkle appeared in this corporate fabric in 1989 when Popeyes, headed by its notorious chief executive officer (CEO), Alvin Copeland, purchased the Church's company. In response to a letter I wrote inquiring if the rumor had any bearing on any aspect of the purchase, a public relations officer wrote:

As the result of your inquiry, we have researched the subject with great interest and can offer the following response to your questions. While it is true that the unfounded rumors had some impact on sales in the past, it was clearly isolated to a few specific markets and seems to have been ultimately resolved. Periodically it pops up again, and when it appears Church's has taken the following actions:
-attempt to isolate the origins of the rumor
-vigorously deny the rumor and attempt to contain it
-avoid any action that could fuel the rumor.
After evaluating the situation, it does not appear that there have been any long term or corporate-wide damaging effects.[46]

The tenor of this letter led me to conclude that the Popeyes corporation may have been unfamiliar with the rumor prior to hearing about it from me. Attempting to get a better understanding of what they knew and when they learned it, I wrote again. The pertinent sections of their response read:

Thank you for your recent letter. We recognize that your research into rumors and urban legends in the African-American community is related to research for your book. To answer your questions:
-The merger of Popeyes Famous Fried Chicken and Biscuits and Church's Chicken was a highly complicated business and financial transaction. The rumors were not a factor.
-The two restaurant chains remain distinct. Church's franchises continue to be identified as such, with no name or trademark changes. (The same is true of Popeyes.)
-Yes, as we understand, the rumors did adversely impact sales in about three isolated markets. They have been put to rest and have not been an issue for a number of years.[47]

Although my own fieldwork somewhat contradicts the third claim, it is too soon to tell whether the corporate changeover will allow Church's to lose the association with the KKK it gained in the African-American community. At the time of this writing, I still encounter people who refuse to patronize Church's because of what they have heard.

The takeover was not the end of the story, however, for before long the new parent company had another problem. In

REWARD

$25,000 Cash

To Whom It May Concern

This is about some unfair, misleading and totally false comments. Innocent people are being misled with lies that I am supporting David Duke. **This is absolutely not true.**

I want to set the record straight for the sake of fairness and truth. Most importantly, this is unfair to my 18,000 employees, black, white, of all races and walks of life. I feel it is my moral obligation to correct lies that are being spread and hope you communicate these facts to your family and friends.

In fact, I am and have been a long-time supporter of Senator J. Bennett Johnston including this campaign. He is a long time friend.

I do not usually make my political views public, but now I must because of these lies. I would not presume to tell anyone how to vote, but at least now you know where I stand.

I want to take the strongest possible legal action toward the source of these lies. I will pay a $25,000. cash reward for information which results in the successful criminal prosecution of the instigator of this lie.

If you or anyone else has any information or questions, I urge you to personally call my office at 736-4338. It is in the best interest of our community and our civic responsibility to rectify these lies immediately.

Sincerely,

Al Copeland

1. Flyer distributed in New Orleans by Popeyes in the fall of 1991.

the first week of September 1990, less than a year after it assumed control of Church's, phone calls began to come in from concerned consumers. They asked the operators if it was true that the company's CEO, Al Copeland, had donated $25,000 to the U.S. Senate campaign being waged by ex-KKK grand wizard David Duke of Louisiana. Kathryn More Wohl, the Popeyes public relations officer who investigated the Church's rumor, acknowledged that her first thought was to connect the item with the earlier rumor; that reaction, however, was not supported by any of her research into the new story.[48] To counter the rumor, Al Copeland held a press conference, and the corporation issued a flyer offering a reward for information leading to the arrest of the individuals responsible for spreading the rumor (Fig. 1). Copeland and Wohl saw the flyer as a mechanism by which they could spread the word of the CEO's innocence. They knew it was unlikely to result in anyone's arrest for rumor mongering.

Several aspects of the Popeyes corporate persona, the reputation of Al Copeland, and the political and cultural climate of Louisiana may have fused to generate the questions that ultimately led to the rumor. Again geography is significant, for both Duke and Copeland have strong ties with Louisiana. Much to the dismay of many Louisianans, the former grand wizard has used the state as his base of operations; his senatorial campaign and later his gubernatorial and presidential bids garnered national publicity as prominent Republicans hastily rejected the white supremacist planks of his platform. Yet those planks attracted a substantial following within the state, and for a while it seemed possible that an unapologetic racist might well be elected to represent Louisiana in the Senate. Of course, a significant number of Louisianans— those determined to alter their state's reputation for racism— shunned David Duke, and it is this group that particularly revels in the escapades of the fried chicken czar, Al Copeland, admiring his flamboyance and sometimes generous public spirit. A self-made multimillionaire, Copeland has a high profile in Louisiana, where his business generates both money and employment opportunities. Copeland's notoriety stems not from his political leanings, but from his business acumen and flashy personal style. According to a *Wall Street Journal* article, he participates in offshore power boat races, maintains a fleet of expensive cars for his personal use, and annually hires a regiment of Santa Clauses to distribute thousands of dollars' worth of Christmas gifts to Louisiana's poorest children.[49] A profile offered by an African-American female graduate student born and raised in Baton Rouge emphasized his power in New Orleans and its environs. Mentioning all of the examples noted in the *Wall Street Journal* sketch, she further claimed that he "owns the police force and uses his race boats to smuggle drugs." In the official record, he owes his wealth and personal success to the chicken company he named after the lead character in the 1971 hit movie *The French Connection*. In many respects, the corporate image of Popeyes is similar to Church's: once again we have a southern-based operation that specializes in foods symbolically potent to black consumers.

As Louisiana's African-American consumers see things, pa-

tronizing Popeyes is a point of ambivalence. The food is reasonably priced and reminiscent of the kind mother used to
make. Popeyes franchises are conveniently located and offer
prompt service. Many young black Louisianans get their first
real job at Popeyes. These are all reasons why African-Americans can feel good about patronizing the chain. Yet the same
factors have a down side. Sure, the chain employs many
blacks, but it is at the low-paying service-sector level that
African-Americans have been trying to leave behind. Thus,
while poorly paid blacks work hard serving fried chicken and
biscuits to other blacks, Copeland's name and white face appear in the local papers as he publicly spends Popeyes profits
on his speedboats and $125,000 cars. Then there is the matter
of the food itself. A handful of informants have repeated the
allegation that Copeland stole the fried chicken recipe from
a black maid who worked in his parents' home. In actuality,
Copeland comes from a very modest background. His family
did not employ domestics. The same legend has circulated
about Colonel Harlan Sanders, founder of Kentucky Fried
Chicken (KFC), and also about George Church. The presence
of this legend in the African-American community is not hard
to explain. Some blacks may need to rationalize their ability
to enjoy the "soul food" served at white-owned fast food
chains; the idea that the whites stole the recipes from trusted
black family retainers in essence gives their taste buds permission to covet the chicken.

Enter David Duke, who, as former grand wizard of the Ku
Klux Klan, established his name and reputation advocating a
white supremacist philosophy. In the summer of 1990, the
political atmosphere of Louisiana was charged, replete with
conflicting news of the sort that so easily breeds rumors. At
the same time that polls were reporting that Duke's chances
of winning the Senate race were improving, however, only a
small number of white Louisianans were publicly endorsing
him. To be sure, polls grant their respondents anonymity. Yet
that left African-Americans to speculate on which white Louisianans were veiled behind the secrecy of the polls. In the
minds of blacks, fried chicken czar Copeland's name and rep-

utation are also linked to his ability to personally profit from the tastes and labor of blacks. Not too surprisingly, therefore, Copeland came to represent the unknown Duke supporters, those ostensibly benevolent whites who secretly endorsed a white supremacist agenda. In a certain respect, in fact, the rumor linking Copeland and Duke empowered black Louisianans, for it led them to boycott Popeyes and thereby assert some mastery over their disturbing status as black citizens in a state that could produce and support the likes of a David Duke, former KKK grand wizard and U.S. Senate hopeful.

Troop

Unlike Church's and Popeyes, the now-bankrupt Troop Sport clothing company was fairly new when rumors linking it to the KKK emerged. Established in 1985 by Teddy and Harvey Held and William Kim, the company marketed a successful line of fashionable urban athletic wear. Popular among young African-Americans and Latinos, the high-priced clothing was in vogue for only a couple of years before rumors about the company surfaced in Oakland, California, in 1987. (See Figure 2 for the Troop emblem.) By 1988 several elaborations had been added, and the rumor had blossomed in some cities into a contemporary legend. In at least Boston, Philadelphia, Montgomery, and Memphis, word circulated that *Troop* was short for a slogan attributed to the KKK: *To Rule Over Oppressed People*. In some versions, this message was allegedly printed between the leather and the lining of the bomber jackets; in others, it was supposedly hidden somewhere in the shoes. In an attempt to disprove the rumor, Wesley Malloy, Troop's black marketing director, "went to Montgomery, Alabama to a store and cut open five pairs to prove that it wasn't like that."[50] But the story was not quelled. One of my informants, a West Indian male student from Mattapan, a largely black section of Boston, claimed: "A friend told me that a friend of his opened a Troop jacket with some scissors so that he could see the inner lining and printed inside was 'Thankyou niggers.'" A related motif developed in which it was

2. Troop emblem on the back of a running jacket.

claimed that the words "Thank you nigger for making us rich" were inscribed inside the tread of Troop's tennis shoes, though no examples of such shoes were offered as evidence. Just as informants frequently asserted the truth of the Church's rumor by stating that a friend had seen an exposé on "60 Minutes," believers in the Troop item authenticated their claims by noting that a report had been delivered on cable television or that rap singer LL Cool J, once a proud Troop enthusiast, had ripped off his jacket on the "Oprah Winfrey Show" and denounced the company. Other informants, however, contended that LL Cool J was in fact a "puppet" being used by the KKK to encourage young black consumers to buy the clothing.

The Held brothers, who are Jewish, and Kim, who is Korean, repeatedly disavowed any connection between the privately held company and the Klan. A regional sales manager backed them up, saying that if Held and Kim were "part of the Klan I'll eat my hat."[51] A black marketing director for the company further explained, "I've been to Korea and seen the whole operation for myself"—thus disallowing any hint of Klan involvement. Even representatives of the Klan itself responded rhetorically to journalists' inquiries about an association: "What would the Ku Klux Klan have to do with a bunch of gooks?" asked J. W. Farrands, imperial wizard of the Connecticut-based Invisible Empire of the Ku Klux Klan, referring in part to the fact that, like most sportswear, Troop's line was manufactured in Asia.[52] Several informants claimed that the KKK liked the idea of profiting off of young blacks' fashion vanity. Others stated that the white supremacist organization needed to make money after losing a civil case in Atlanta in which they were obliged to pay several million dollars to the mother of a black male victim.

Although the small athletic wear company, whose lifespan was less than five years, does not at first glance seem to share much with the over thirty-year-old Church's fast food enterprise, upon closer examination several common threads can be isolated. First, both the large fast food company and the small sportswear outfit targeted their marketing strategy almost exclusively at minority consumers. In both cases, my informants were quick to point out that the stores and products were highly visible in black communities but uncommon in white areas. At first, in fact, I found few white students who had even heard of the Troop company; one knew the products only because he had worked in a sporting goods store that stocked Troop merchandise. Troop's sales manager acknowledged that "ninety-five percent of our business was black or Hispanic."[53] African-American informants claimed that they had never seen whites wear the clothing. To a lesser degree, the same was true for Church's chicken: in some cities whites had not heard of the company, and black informants claimed that they rarely saw white people eating at Church's.

A second common aspect of the two companies is particularly provocative. While Church's became a public company, and Troop remained privately owned, both companies proudly chose the franchise route to take their wares to their largely minority public. Church's boasted of its long list of minority-owned and -managed franchises. And among the minority owners and managers of Troop's seventeen stores nationwide was former Detroit Tigers star Willie Horton. Intended or not, the suggestion of a white company implementing a "for blacks only" marketing strategy is apt to antagonize African-American consumers.

Third, the products of both companies generate a certain ambivalence among black consumers. The convenience factor associated with fast food, for example, is sometimes undermined by the knowledge that for less money one could prepare the same items in a more appetizing fashion at home. As Fine puts it, "Anxiety and guilt arise from the change from eating personally prepared food to eating what profit-making enterprises serve; these emotions have been projected onto the commercial establishment, and transformed into fear."[54] In a similar way, the peer pressure to be "with it" in the fashion arena causes many youths to covet expensive clothing when more modest goods would suffice; many young blacks would rather stay at home than go out wearing last year's sneakers.

Indeed, a disturbing turn of events occurred in the mid-1980s when crimes by black teenagers rose in number, triggered by the desire to have certain clothing items at any cost. When I first encountered the Troop rumor—which was also when I first heard of the company—one informant described the product to me as, "You remember hearing about those jackets that kids were shooting each other for last year? Well, those were three hundred dollars. Troop bomber jackets." By May 1990 the "sneaker wars" had escalated to the point where *Sports Illustrated* ran a cover story entitled "Your Sneakers or Your Life," chronicling the crimes generated in urban America by sneaker lust.[55] Of course, the corporations, not to mention the celebrity spokesmen they pay so handsomely to push their preferred footwear, absolve themselves of any guilt in this matter. Meanwhile, wearing certain fashionable prod-

ucts in certain urban areas can be dangerous, and even life-
threatening.

This allegiance to fashion is criticized by the folk. More
than one young black male informant expressed only disdain
for designer footwear and clothing. When I asked if they
would wear the clothing if it was given to them, they claimed
that they would not want people to think they had nothing
better to do with their hard-earned money than spend it on
fancy jackets and sneakers—thus displaying a sort of ethnic
snobbism in reverse. Even the company admitted that
Troop's most popular shoe, the seventy-five-dollar Cobra, had
"no real performance value."[56] From the perspective of the
now-defunct Troop company, an even more serious consequence of the rumor may be seen in the numerous informants
who decided to stop wearing the products, not because they
believed the rumors linking the company to the Klan, but
because they felt unsafe doing so.

A fourth common thread can be seen in some of the strategies the two companies used to cope with the rumor. Church's
was a bit slower and less aggressive in its response, but after
numerous complaints were logged they rallied minority support for their efforts (including, as we have seen, the then
NAACP president) and produced their record of minority hiring. Troop followed a similar course. In addition to the
NAACP and Operation Push, the company enlisted such
celebrities as athlete/franchisee Willie Horton and Gladys
Knight and the Pips into its $200,000 anti-Klan-rumor cam-
paign, which included displaying anti-Klan posters in its
stores.[57] In Chicago, Troop officials met with the executive
secretary of Alpha Phi Alpha fraternity, the oldest African-
American Greek-lettered organization, to ask them to try to
dispel the rumor through their chapters.

Despite these efforts, the final commonality between
Church's and Troop was the fact that both companies in the
end suffered severe financial losses. For the older and more
firmly established Church's, this outcome led to the sale of
the company to Popeyes. For Troop, it meant the company
was forced to declare bankruptcy. Both companies, however,
denied that the rumors were behind these changes. A

Church's spokesperson, for example, claimed that plummeting stock prices for the company reflected a downward spiral in the fast food industry generally in the late 1980s; and Popeyes denied that the rumor made Church's more vulnerable to their takeover. As for Troop, the owners of its parent company, Down Troop Sport, blamed the bankruptcy move on bad business decisions along with the public's fashion fickleness.

While Troop apparently targeted its products exclusively at African-American consumers, other athletic wear companies count African-Americans as a significant segment of their marketing plan. And some of these concerns have been linked with the KKK as well. Following the demise of Troop clothing in 1989, such rumors soon began to circulate with regard to Reebok as well as the popular but less well known British Knights athletic shoes. Although the Reebok variants of the KKK-Troop rumor were far outnumbered by items linking Reebok products to South Africa, a sizable number of informants did level this accusation. In the case of the imported British Knights, the rumor alleging Klan ownership was known both here and in the United Kingdom. Significantly, the popularity of the sneakers coincided with an increase in neo-Nazi and white supremacist activity in Great Britain. Perhaps inevitably, therefore, the rumor emerged that the products were named "knights" because the company was sympathetic to, and in some versions sponsored by a British chapter of, the Knights of the Ku Klux Klan.

The transference of the conspiracy motifs to other athletic wear enterprises supports the theory that the emergence and perpetuation of rumors linking a company with the KKK are not based on random factors. Rather, as the Church's and Troop cases reveal, certain key elements can be identified that allow one to predict what kinds of companies might be targeted with KKK involvement: namely, white-owned firms, large or small, with little advertising or advertising directed solely at black consumers, that establish nationwide franchises selling popular but nonessential commodities in primarily black neighborhoods. One way for the folk to show their concern about a desirable commodity with dubious practical value, particularly in a community whose financial resources are limited, is to subscribe to and circulate rumors that diminish the product's attraction. While it is unfortunate that apparently blameless companies and their employees have had to suffer because of these cycles, the fact that rumors function as a sort of self-imposed consumer harness within the African-American community is laudable. The thought of precious dollars being spent on luxury-style consumer items produced by white corporations violates the community's sense of the value of financial independence and self-determination and inspires action. Yet because fast food chains and clothing manufacturers lack the evil requisite for a formal boycott, particularly when the products are so appealing, an obvious and familiar enemy must be summoned. The Ku Klux Klan fits that bill admirably: African-Americans are willing to abandon any commodity tainted by the Klan, whether in fact or in fiction.

Cigarettes

More than one cigarette company has been linked in the popular imagination to the KKK. During the 1960s, for example, such a rumor circulated among African-Americans with regard to Kool, a menthol cigarette and, according to both tobacco industry market research and folk wisdom, the brand of choice among blacks who smoked. As one African-American female informant put it, "That's what people said. They said all of the brothers and sisters in the streets were smoking Kool. And that maybe the KKK had found a real good way to get them." Association with the Klan is suggested first off by the letter *K* in the name *Kool*. Moreover, by misspelling a word prominent in the folk speech of African-Americans to arrive at the product's name, the parent company, Brown and Williamson, unknowingly set itself up for folk speculation. In response to a 1990 query I sent to the Tobacco Institute, the major tobacco lobbying organization, Thomas Lauria, an assistant to its president, indicated that such rumors were not new to the industry:

You can be sure we share many of your concerns over these troubling, unsubstantiated rumors about white supremacist groups' alleged ownership of cigarette companies. One can assume these lies are most likely perpetuated by those groups or individuals who oppose tobacco interests and will say anything to disparage the industry. In fact, all but one of America's tobacco companies are owned by hundreds of thousands of individual stockholders, as well as institutional and corporate investors. "Tobacco" companies, per se, are now diversified, multi-product, multi-national giants who rank high in the Fortune 500. When taken together, the industries' multitude of stockholders represent a diverse cross-section of American society.[58]

Lauria's comments differ a bit from those of spokespersons for the other corporations we have been considering. The deleterious effects of fast food and expensive footwear, after all, are much more subtle than those of cigarettes. Whereas the chicken franchises and athletic wear firms were quick to distinguish themselves from the competition, tobacco companies worry less about threats from other cigarette manufacturers than about the growing strength of antitobacco interests. The very existence of the Tobacco Institute, a well-funded lobbying/public relations group, reflects their need for a certain solidarity.

The most prominent target of rumors alleging Klan links today is Marlboro cigarettes, a brand owned by the Philip Morris Corporation. Much to my surprise, the first ten or so versions of this item that I collected came from white informants in France and England. The French rumor specialist, Véronique Campion-Vincent, offered several versions; in addition, Janet Caldwell of the Center for Democratic Renewal, a well-respected white supremacist watchdog organization, learned while on a speaking tour of France that "there is a widespread rumor that Marlboro cigarettes are owned or manufactured or distributed by the 'KKK.' My host and interpreter warned me that at every location that question would come up and he was entirely right. In three separate towns, the audiences included this question among others. My host said he had encountered the rumor again and again—and that he had been shown the mystical letters—'KKK' in the logo of the cigarette pack."[59]

In the back of each of Jan Harold Brunvand's four books on contemporary legend, he includes his address and invites readers to send him versions of items they had heard. He forwarded several of these letters from readers in Britain that focused on Marlboro and the Klan. One writer reported a warning he had received after lighting up a Marlboro cigarette:

The logo design incorporated 3 representations of the letter K. . . . So far is plausible, the final "proof" was that if you tore the bottom of the packet open [in a particular way] . . . there would be revealed the head of a hooded klansman, the two spots, in black and gold, standing for eyeholes. To this was added the "fact" that Philip Morris, in person, was a noted Klan member and financier. The two spots are printers' proofs for colours used on packaging, a common enough practice, but further "proof" was supplied when it was pointed out that most printers use only a short line or two for such proofs. Although I personally never heard or saw the story carried in printed sources or on T.V. . . . Marlboro never the less stopped using the two spots on their boxes . . . With the withdrawal of the two spots, this story seems to have died a death, but even so, every now and then somebody will say to Marlboro smokers (there are a lot of us unfortunately) "you shouldn't smoke Marlboro, you know."[60]

Although the hooded Klansman in the package was not referred to by any of my American informants, several were familiar with the secret *K*'s on the package. What interested me more than the package clues, however, was the fact that the informants for this rumor were white, in several instances European, and not intended victims of Ku Klux Klan violence.

As I pursued the subject, of course, white and African-American informants did begin to surface. According to one white female who attended high school in Virginia in the early 1980s, the rumor was well known in her school. Other white male informants from New England claim to have known of the rumor for "many years." Yet a spokesperson for Philip Morris, interestingly, wrote in response to a query: "The rumor you recounted is distressing, we appreciate your bringing it to our attention. Your letter, in fact, is the first time we've heard this false accusation. We regret that any such unfounded rumors circulate and we hope our positive image will help to dispel them."[61]

In point of fact, the original Philip Morris was not a southern white tobacco magnate but rather a London tobacco merchant who rose to prominence in the tobacco industry in the 1850s.[62] The publicly owned American company was established at the beginning of the twentieth century; there is no evidence linking ownership of this corporation with the KKK.

We have seen how marketing strategies tended to perpetuate the Troop and Church's rumors; in the case of Marlboro, advertising may have helped to mitigate the rumors. For quite some time, the cigarette's trademark has been the Marlboro man: with his cowboy hat, his vest, and his horse, he is intended to represent the strong, silent, prototypical American pioneer—an image much more appealing to white male smokers than to African-Americans.

While I was working with African-American informants on this rumor in late 1989 and early 1990, the marketing plans of R. J. Reynolds, a Philip Morris competitor, for a new brand of cigarettes called "Uptown" began to appear in the media. These menthol cigarettes, it was reported, would be heavily advertised on billboards in black neighborhoods, in African-American newspapers, and in the major African-American magazines such as *Ebony, Jet,* and *Essence.* This agenda met with swift opposition from groups such as the American Cancer Society and the NAACP, who voiced outrage at a marketing strategy that targeted toxic substances at black Americans; in fairly short order, R. J. Reynolds abandoned its plans for the product. Before long, however, informants began to name R. J. Reynolds as the company with ties to the KKK. The same motif that had emerged in connection with Philip Morris—that is, that the company's founder was an original Klan member—was included in most versions of this text. John Singleton, the company spokesperson, explained: "I can assure you that there is no truth to the rumor that R. J. Reynolds Tobacco Company currently has, or ever has had, an affiliation with the Ku Klux Klan. On the contrary, Reynolds Tobacco has been supportive of Blacks and other minorities since Richard Joshua Reynolds, the company's founder, gave $500 in 1891 to the school that eventually became Winston-Salem University."[63] Singleton made no reference to the backlash over the proposed Uptown ad campaign.

The Uptown controversy refocused the attention of African-American leaders on the extensive and costly advertising directed at black consumers by both the tobacco and the alcohol industries. Because the toxicity of cigarettes and alcoholic beverages is well substantiated, concerned African-Americans have a quite legitimate reason for openly protesting these companies and their attempts to infiltrate black communities. And in fact, in many cities organized groups of African-Americans have started their own drives to paint over billboards in their enclaves that advertise such products. When they do so, the media identify them as protesters; if they attempted to do the same to a billboard advertising a more innocuous product, however, they would no doubt be dismissed as wanton vandals.

The historical relationship between persons of African descent and tobacco yields one of the more ironic elements of the purported connection between the KKK and the tobacco industry. A handful of crops—tobacco, a New World native, notable among them—were after all responsible for the dependency of early southern white Americans on a forced labor system and for the large-scale importation of Africans to the South. Since Emancipation African-Americans have continued to play a vital role in the production of tobacco. A fancy coffee table book, published in 1979, on the Philip Morris company's commitment to the art world and to an aesthetically pleasing workplace contains several artistically rendered black-and-white photos of African-Americans working in tobacco fields.[64] While many northerners are more apt to associate cotton with the labor of African-Americans, in my experience southerners of both races, particularly those from North Carolina and Virginia, will just as readily mention the sight of African-Americans handling those deadly leaves in the tobacco-growing regions of the South.

Given the documented dangers of tobacco use, the rising

cost of cigarettes, the fact that the crop has long been connected with the exploitation of black labor, and the tobacco
company's periodic forays into advertising targeted at African-
Americans, it is hardly surprising that rumors alleging a
KKK–tobacco company alliance often spring up. However,
the fact that no single population group is the intended audience of cigarette advertising has probably prevented such rumors from gaining widespread popularity.

Tropical Fantasy

In late 1990 and early 1991, crudely written flyers began circulating in black neighborhoods of metropolitan New York.
They contained a warning that black consumers should avoid
a popular fruit-flavored soft drink named Tropical Fantasy
(Fig. 3). The reason? Apparently the KKK owned the company, and the tasty beverages contained a secret ingredient
that sterilized black male drinkers.

Once again, no evidence can be found to support this allegation. The drink is the latest product of a small family-owned
enterprise named Brooklyn Bottling; when thirty-three-year-
old Eric Miller inherited the family business in 1990, he rein-
troduced an old line of fruit-flavored soft drinks with a new
name.[65] Twenty-ounce bottles selling in the half-dollar range
soon appeared on grocery store shelves in black neighborhoods. The drink was a big hit, but within a few months the
rumors hit the street. When sales of the soft drink plummeted,
the company's owners immediately tried to attack the rumor.
The Ku Klux Klan responded to reporters' inquiries by stating,
"The KKK is not in the bottling business."[66]

Why did this rumor develop about this particular company
at this particular time? Brooklyn Bottling resembles the other
companies beset by KKK allegations in only two significant
ways. First, it can be perceived as using a "for blacks only"
marketing strategy. The company sold Tropical Fantasy
chiefly in inner-city grocery stores, not in downtown areas,
and it avoided a large advertising campaign. Second, its product has a rather suggestive, enigmatic name. A large percentage of the black population in the targeted neighborhoods is

ATTENTION!!! ATTENTION!!! ATTENTION!!!

.50 CENT SODAS

<u>BLACKS AND MINORITY GROUPS</u>

DID YOU SEE   (T.V. SHOW)   20/20 ???

PLEASE BE ADVISE, "TOP POP" & "TROPICAL
FANTASY" *ALSO TREAT* .50 SODAS ARE BEING MANUFACTURED
BY THE KLU.. KLUX.. KLAN..

SODAS CONTAIN STIMULANTS TO STERILIZE THE BLACK MAN, AND WHO
KNOWS WHAT ELSE!!!!

THEY ARE ONLY PUT IN STORES IN HARLEM AND MINORITY AREAS
YOU WON'T FIND THEM DOWN TOWN....LOOK AROUND.....

YOU HAVE BEEN WARNED
PLEASE SAVE THE CHILDREN

3. Flyer distributed in New York City African-American communities from winter 1990 through the early summer of 1991.

from the "tropics"—the Caribbean islands—where luscious fruits and fruit drinks are plentiful. In designing and marketing such a drink, Brooklyn Bottling was treading on symbolically significant terrain, just like the southern white men who peddle fried chicken. Like many companies plagued by a rumor or contemporary legend, Brooklyn Bottling immediately assumed corporate foul play—and in this instance, the assumption may be partly correct (see Chapter 6).

Conclusion

Since its inception, the Ku Klux Klan has endorsed and followed through on an explicitly racist agenda. Replete with ritualistic emblems designed to intimidate, the KKK has carved out a seemingly permanent role as the enemy of African-Americans. My informant interviews revealed that African-Americans take a certain comfort from definable enemies. In the course of sharing their Klan rumors and legends with me, they often included comments about the difference between life in the North and life in the South. Almost always they voiced a preference for certain aspects of southern life: "They don't hide their racism there. You know who your enemies are. Not like up here." The continued existence of the KKK offers African-Americans an object to which they can affix antiblack sentiment and behavior.

To close this discussion of KKK lore and its tenacity, let us examine the performance context of just one of the texts cited above.[67] What follows is a description of one telling of the Church's rumor, provided by an African-American informant who recalled quite clearly his first hearing of it. In 1984 this student, who was then twenty-three, had a summer job at a branch of a large commercial bank in New England. Working with him was one other black employee, a "young lady" in the same age group as my informant. The two became friendly. One day they were discussing the pros and cons of various kinds of fast food, and the young lady warned my informant about the hazards of eating at Church's Chicken. She told him that Church's was owned by the Klan and that they were adding an ingredient to the recipe calculated "to make black men sterile and effectively wipe out the continuity of the black community." At first my informant stated that his friend had seen the "60 Minutes" exposé herself. When I pressed him, he conceded that perhaps a friend or relative of hers had seen the program. In any event, from that day in the summer of 1984, when he first heard the item, up to February 1986, when I collected it from him, my informant had not eaten at Church's. Although he claimed not to believe the rumor, when I asked him whether he would eat there again he said in a joking fashion that he didn't see why he should take any chances. He says that he believed the story for three reasons: he trusted the young lady; he trusted "60 Minutes"; and the story seemed to explain why there were so many Church's franchises in black neighborhoods.

The informant's credulity has further grounds, which stem, I believe, from the situation in which he found himself. For one thing, he and the young lady were members of the same folk group by virtue of their race, age, and occupation. Then too, the bank environment itself may have served as a catalyst for the telling of the rumor. As we saw, most of the other bank employees were white. Located in Boston, the bank reflected the community at large, in that although integration exists, it often proves to be quite superficial. According to my informant, the black and white employees worked together fairly harmoniously, but the two groups did not socialize outside of the bank. In addition, my informant felt that he underwent a proving period during which he was observed particularly closely by whites anxious to see if this young black male was smart and honest enough to work in the bank. Black employees in the bank as a whole commiserated about having to prove their mettle in a way not expected of the whites. Needless to say, blacks were poorly represented at the higher levels of the bank's management. Racial tension, in fact, was still quite pervasive in Massachusetts generally; the scars inflicted during the busing era had not yet healed, and periodic racial unrest was, in a way, to be expected. My informant and the young lady knew, for example, that there were many whites in Boston who did not want to see them working in a bank or attending the public schools.

Given the context in which she lived, it is easy to understand the young lady's purpose in spreading the Church's rumor. By sharing it with my informant, she was solidifying the bonds between them and, in a sense, bolstering their identity as potential victims of racist activity; in addition, a spotlight was trained on the potential aggressors, for one must never forget who the enemy is.

My informant accepted the rumor because it functioned as a metaphor for the struggle he was facing in his attempt to establish himself as a man in American society. The institutional racism he felt, however subtly, in the bank where he was working in his first "adult" job no doubt convinced him that forces were at work to deny him an easy transition into an adult male role. So when the young lady told him what she had heard about Church's, it made sense to him; his own experiences confirmed it.

The rumor flourished because it confirmed so many of the uncertainties of African-Americans' lives. As blacks, outnumbered and outranked by whites, my informant and his friend felt that much of their situation was expressible in "us versus them" terms. They ventured out into the white world to work and to attend school, not ever knowing if or when they would be confronted by racism. This rumor offered one certainty, one position that they could control. They might not know when a racist comment would come their way, but they did know that they could protect themselves by avoiding this restaurant and encouraging others to do likewise.

Like their parents and grandparents, contemporary African-Americans feel confident in naming the professed white supremacist organization as the enemy. The continued existence of the Ku Klux Klan, no matter how limited its actual power might become, together with the persistence of institutional and individual racism in this country, virtually guarantees that the Klan will remain a potent motif in African-American folklore.

Chapter Four

Conspiracy II

"They ... the powers that be ...
want to keep us down"

The Ku Klux Klan, given its long history of antiblack terrorism, is a natural target for rumors in which some assault on
the bodies of blacks is asserted. But other groups, groups generally perceived by the public as protecting American free-
doms, have been identified with antiblack activity as well.
In the late twentieth century, for example, informants have
pointed to the Central Intelligence Agency (CIA), the Federal
Bureau of Investigation, the Centers for Disease Control
(CDC), various branches of the armed services, the "administration," and the "government" generally as engaged in conspiracies detrimental to the physical well-being of African-
Americans. These rumors include among others: the belief
that the FBI, in cahoots with the CDC, committed the Atlanta
child murders that spanned the late 1970s–early 1980s (see
Chapters 3 and 5); the idea that the Reagan administration
wanted the AIDS virus to flourish in order to impede the
growth of third world populations; and the notion that the
"government" is directing illegal drugs into minority communities to keep the urban African-American population powerless. In one rumor cycle, Reebok, Inc., a major American corporation, is accused of using its profits to further another
government's economy—that of white minority–ruled South
Africa. In discussing all of these cycles, informants invariably

described the alleged conspirators as "the powers that be."

People who subscribe to these kinds of rumors are frequently labeled as unduly paranoid. The historian Richard Hofstadter maintains, "Certain audiences are susceptible to it [belief in a sustained conspiracy]—particularly those who have attained a low level of education, whose access to information is poor, and who are so completely shut out from access to the centers of power that they feel themselves completely deprived of self-defense and subjected to unlimited manipulation by those in power."[1] Hofstadter's assessment does not explain how contemporary legends alleging conspiracy gain popularity among African-Americans. This chapter will consider this question, as well as the texts and the people who share them, from several angles. First, possible historical antecedents will be reviewed. Then, the patterns of mistrust that have evolved will be examined: because relations between legitimate institutions and African-Americans have so frequently pitted oppressor against the oppressed, black folk history often seems to suggest that the government and corporate world are guilty until proved innocent. Finally, the contradictions between the stated goals of these agencies and their actual behavior will be explored; as we shall see, "guilt by association" is a strong contributing factor in the tenacity of conspiracy theories.

History

While at the end of the twentieth century it seems untenable that "official policy" might legitimate racist activity, it is important to remember that for most of the history of the United States, particularly in the colonial era, such a program was very much in place. The result was pervasive, *official* acceptance of a doctrine that considered the individual black body as a commodity available to whites to do with as they pleased.

From 1619 until 1807, the powers that be in this country allowed slavers to import unwilling Africans for sale as chattel. Internal slave trading as well as the illegal importation of Africans continued for the next six decades. In the framing of the Constitution, the question of congressional representation in the South was resolved by the infamous three-fifths compromise, under which five slave bodies were counted as equivalent to three nonslaves. The question of whether the Constitution's safeguards were intended to protect black men and women was decided for the antebellum era when the 1857 Supreme Court, under the leadership of Chief Justice Roger B. Taney, concluded that the founding fathers endorsed the position that black bodies were the property of whites. Taney argued, "No word can be found in the Constitution which gives Congress a greater power over slave property, or which entitles property of that kind to less protection than property of any other description."[2]

Throughout the slavery era abuses of African-American bodies were not merely the excesses of individual slaveholders; they were sanctioned by the laws of the day. A Virginia statute enacted in 1669 reflects the rationale used by the white southern power structure to justify exempting slave owners from punishment for murdering blacks:

1669. *An act about the casuall killings of slaves.* Whereas the only law in force for the punishment of refractory servants resisting their master, mistress or overseer, cannot be inflicted on negroes [because such punishment, for white indentured servants, merely extended their time commitment, whereas by 1664 blacks were slaves for life], Nor the obstinancy of many of them by other than violent meanes supprest. Be it enacted and declared by this grand assembly, if any slave resist his master . . . and by the extremity of correction should chance to die, that his death shall not be accompted Felony, but the master (or that person appointed by the master to punish him) be acquit from molestation, since it cannot be assumed that propensed malice (which alone makes murther Felony) should induce any man to destroy his own estate.[3]

In addition to legalizing the murder of blacks, slavery-era laws did not prohibit corporal punishment, rape, the separation of offspring from their parents, and numerous other assaults against African-Americans.

"Free" African-Americans fared little better. One particularly telling example is the way African-Americans willing to sacrifice their bodies for their country were treated. In every war from the French and Indian wars of the colonial era until

World War II, African-American lives were treated differently from those of their white counterparts. When "free" African-Americans were finally allowed to fight in the Civil War, they were told that their bodies were less valuable than those of white soldiers when the Department of War implemented a two-tier pay scale: one wage was established for white soldiers, and a lesser one for black.[4] The Confederate Army articulated its repulsion at having to face black men with weapons by brutalizing African-American prisoners of war and mutilating the corpses of black soldiers.

Official sanction of or indifference to assaults on African-American bodies did not end with the Civil War or the passage of the Fourteenth Amendment. As we have seen, official tolerance of antiblack hostility was commonplace long after the 1860s. In the last decades of the nineteenth century and the first decades of the twentieth, African-American leaders tried repeatedly to force local, state, and federal governments to enact and enforce serious antilynching legislation. Their efforts met with little success. Within police custody, African-Americans are more apt to suffer physical abuse than their white counterparts. Even today, African-Americans are disproportionately represented in police brutality statistics and on death rows.

In 1932, the supposition by governmental agencies that black bodies could be used in ways that white bodies could not took on a particularly gruesome twist when the Public Health Service (PHS; forerunner of the Centers for Disease Control) initiated a forty-year experiment on African-American men at the Tuskegee Institute in Alabama. Using the black hospital as their base, white doctors affiliated with the PHS invited hundreds of black men from the surrounding rural environs to undergo a free medical examination. After identifying 399 syphilitic men (who were told simply that they had "bad blood") as well as 201 syphilis-free men who would serve as a control group, the doctors enticed the men to participate in an observation study by offering them physicals, transportation to and from the clinics in an official car, hot meals on examination days, treatment for minor ailments, and a guaranteed burial stipend. As a result, the subjects enjoyed a certain status in their community, where such benefits were luxuries; indeed, many men not affiliated with the study, and even some women, begged to be included. For the syphilitic men, however, the experiment proved devastating, for no effective treatment was offered that might have alleviated the ravages of the disease; they were merely the subjects of medical observation. No comparable experiment was conducted on white males.[5]

In the 1970s, congressional investigations revealed that from at least the late 1950s until the late 1960s, the CIA developed and attempted to execute numerous assassination plans. For the African and African-American communities, the most notable of these was the 1960s blueprint to assassinate Patrice Lumumba of the Congo (now Zaire). More interesting than the existence of a plot by a U.S. government agency to murder a foreign leader was the weapon of choice: the diplomatic pouch containing the selected assassination tools included "an unusual assortment of items: rubber gloves, gauze masks, a hypodermic syringe, and lethal biological toxins. The enclosed instructions explained how to inject the poison into Lumumba's food or toothpaste to bring about his quick death."[6] Toxic toothpaste did not reach Lumumba's body, however. Before the CIA could carry out its plan, rival Congolese killers murdered the prime minister.

These incidences indicate that African-American mistrust of governmental agencies is not without merit. From the very policy that allowed Africans to be brought to the New World in the first place to the restrictions that prevent Haitians from donating blood (because of popular association between AIDS and Haitians), blacks have been subjected to a different set of rules than that applied to the majority. Official disrespect for the bodies of African-Americans has a long history in this country.

The FBI and the CIA as Antiblack Conspirators

The Federal Bureau of Investigation and the Central Intelligence Agency are often named in African-American legends and rumors as groups that perpetuate antiblack conspiracies. Indeed, specific conspiracies seem to be connected with one or the other group almost uniquely. For example, dozens of informants expressed familiarity with stories linking the FBI with the assassination of Martin Luther King, Jr., yet only a couple identified the CIA as the agency responsible. Conversely, many people linked the CIA with the spread of the AIDS virus in third world countries, while a mere handful pegged the FBI for that act. Based on my interviews, I suspect that some individuals confuse the domains of the two law enforcement agencies. Several people responded to queries about conspiracies by saying, "I heard that the CIA or the FBI did it." The "division of labor" between domestic and overseas law enforcement on occasion seemed far from clear; in the end, boundaries and jurisdiction were less relevant than the simple belief that either agency might have committed antiblack acts.

Conspiracy rumors concerning the assassinations of prominent 1960s leaders—John F. Kennedy, Malcolm X (in 1965), Martin Luther King, Jr., Robert F. Kennedy—are well known. Many informants born since that time can offer specific theories about these murders that they have heard at home and in peer grapevines. Given the stature of the victims, their violent deaths constituted true American crises. As the sociologist Tamotsu Shibutani puts it, "Any crisis, however mild, arouses popular excitement and leads to the formation of a *public* consisting of those who are in some way concerned with an event that has disturbed the routine of organized life."[7] The unending uncertainty over the identities of these alleged assassins contributed to the formation and perpetuation of these rumors. "If the demand for news in a public exceeds the supply made available through institutional channels, rumor construction is likely to occur."[8]

Although the public as a whole was affected by these assassinations, their individual and community impact varied. With only a few exceptions, the greater the informant's allegiance was to the assassination victim, the greater the degree of specificity she or he was able to offer. Because JFK was president and his was the first assassination of this unfortunate era, virtually all of the informants old enough to recall his death remembered clearly what they heard and when. In the case of Malcolm X's murder, the tightest narratives were articulated by Black Muslims. And African-American informants tended to offer more specifics about MLK's death than white informants. Another interesting difference in the reports concerns the time at which informants claimed to have heard and, perhaps, accepted subsequent rumors about these acts. African-American informants linking the KKK or official U.S. government agencies to the assassinations claimed that such items circulated almost immediately after the incidents. However, many white informants who connected the assassinations to an official agency said that they did not hear or come to believe these accusations until long after the murders were committed—specifically, until after Watergate and the mid-1970s congressional hearings on intelligence excesses.

An Era of Assassination

John F. Kennedy

Some of these patterns of difference can be seen in those items pairing the CIA and FBI with JFK's assassination. One thirty-six-year-old African-American female, for example, echoed the thoughts of many other black informants in attributing the murder to FBI director J. Edgar Hoover: "I heard this man didn't like the Kennedys and feared they would all be in the White House for the next twenty years. Since there wasn't any other way to get rid of the Kennedys, death was Hoover's only way to end their beginning of the takeover of the White House." Informants crediting the CIA with the act generally cited the agency's disapproval of Kennedy's foreign policy decisions as the motivating force; those who subscribed to this theory were largely white.

In the minds of the folk, JFK still retains folk hero status as a champion of African-Americans. Many African-American homes still feature photographs of Kennedy, frequently displayed next to ones of Martin Luther King, Jr. The following statement by an African-American man succinctly characterizes the view I recorded over and over again: "[JFK] died fighting for oppressed peoples." In fact, of course, President Kennedy's commitment to civil rights was moderated by his political ambitions, for he was unwilling to alienate southern white voters and the powerful Democratic congressmen they kept returning to office. Yet there is little doubt that JFK was disturbed by the FBI director's unabashed hostility to the civil rights movement; likewise, the young president's insistence that the FBI investigate alleged civil rights violations infuriated J. Edgar Hoover: "Hoover continued to equate the Negro question with subversion, and he found it especially irritating that the Kennedys expected him to defend racial agitators and oppose people who shared his own white, Christian vision of America."[9] Informants who subscribe to the theory that the FBI killed JFK tended to perceive the law enforcement agency as more powerful than the office of the president; the 1960 election of an ostensibly pro–civil rights president, in their view, was so threatening to the mainstream governmental power structure that one of its agencies sought to restore the status quo by killing the maverick chief executive.

The following opinion typifies my younger informants. Born seven years after Kennedy's assassination, this young woman reported: "One rumor that I heard about JFK is that one reason why he was assassinated was because of his involvement in the civil rights movement." She recalled hearing this from "one of my uncles and my father" when she "was little." She believed that her father and uncle find this explanation plausible, and for herself she maintained, "It has been covered up so much the truth will never come out." The fact that people close to her subscribed to this theory had strong rhetorical sway with her. The text is in fact a chapter in black folk history that has been passed on to her. A college junior at the time of our interview, she claimed to have only haphazardly covered the history of the 1960s in a classroom situation. Nor could she recall exactly whom her father and uncle accused of assassinating JFK; instead she employed the ubiquitous "powers that be" idiom to describe the conspirators. The only motif in her account that cannot be substantiated is the cause-and-effect relationship between JFK's civil rights policy and his death. Her family is correct in telling her that JFK had a reputation for being pro–civil rights; his public endorsement of that cause did put him at odds with other public officials. He was assassinated, and the reasons remain unclear to most Americans. For this family, the belief that he was killed for his civil rights policy fits their sense of American institutions better than any other of the many explanations for his death.

Oliver Stone's 1991 film *JFK* incorporates just about every rumor ever circulated about the 1963 assassination of the president—with one notable exception. In a brief scene supposedly taking place two years after the assassination, the white New Orleans district attorney Jim Garrison and his family are discussing new information about the murder at the dinner table. A uniformed black maid is serving the meal. With obvious surprise, Garrison says, for the first time, that the evidence indicates that Oswald did not act alone. The usually silent maid says that she knew that all along. Garrison never probes the maid's story. Rather, for the rest of the film Garrison methodically pursues every possible lead. He constructs a complicated conspiracy plot supposedly orchestrated by the Mafia, the CIA, the vice-president, the army, Cuban refugees, the Russians, and the leaders of several American businesses. At no time does he entertain the possibility that it was Kennedy's reputation as a supporter of black causes that led to his assassination. The conspiracy rumors that intrigued Garrison, and later Oliver Stone, were those that cast Kennedy's assassins as their own enemies, as individuals who wanted to kill the dreams of liberal, white young men who wished to change the power structure and curtail U.S. involvement in the Vietnam War. The conspiracy rumors that intrigued Garrison's maid and many other black Americans, in contrast, cast the assassins as *their* enemies—as white supremacists both inside and outside the government who wanted to kill the dreams of blacks who thought they finally had a president willing to include them in his vision for America.

Martin Luther King, Jr.

FBI involvement was asserted much more often in the case of Martin Luther King, Jr.'s death than of JFK's death. Although dozens of informants attributed MLK's assassination to the Ku Klux Klan, almost as many pointed to the FBI. Some informants even connected the two, with comments like "the FBI helped the KKK kill King." The standard reason given for such complicity was that the KKK needed the protection of the federal agency, and the FBI needed to make sure the crime was never traceable to the bureau. Some informants stated generally that one or the other was responsible: "I heard the FBI did it or the KKK—one of them groups." These individuals perceived no real difference between the nation's premier domestic law enforcement agency and the nation's premier terrorist group. With their conservative suits, haircuts, and cars and their penchant for secrecy, FBI men (who were almost exclusively white) did not seem all that different from Klansmen; after all, both groups consisted of handpicked like individuals who enthusiastically embraced a code that "protected" white citizens while ignoring or denigrating blacks. FBI director J. Edgar Hoover was identified by informants as responsible for MLK's death as frequently as the agency itself. I frequently heard comments like, "J. Edgar Hoover indirectly gave the order to assassinate King. King was getting powerful."

The prevalence and persistence of rumors linking the FBI to these assassinations reflect an explicitly negative folk profile of the domestic law enforcement agency. Genuine animosity on the part of the bureau and J. Edgar Hoover toward blacks is easily documented. Just as before the Civil War white public officials claimed that the guarantees of the Constitution were not intended to protect African-Americans, those who shaped the twentieth century's foremost law enforcement agency saw no need to include the rights of African-Americans within their jurisdiction. Even before Hoover's lengthy association began in 1919, the bureau had cultivated an antiblack attitude that reflected the general mood of the times. As one observer puts it,

For better or for worse, the history of the Federal Bureau of Investigation and the history of black America have been linked together almost from the Bureau's beginning in 1908. . . . The Bureau's decision[s] to avoid protecting civil rights and to spy on blacks were more in reaction to directives from the White House and the Justice Department than results of its own policy. In 1910, the second year of William Howard Taft's presidency and in response to a series of particularly brutal lynchings, the Department claimed "no authority . . . to protect citizens of African descent in the enjoyment of civil rights generally."[10]

Throughout Hoover's reign, the bureau monitored the activities of black leaders while excluding civil rights protections from their charge. In the 1920s and 1930s, for example, they pursued information that could be used to discredit black nationalist leader Marcus Garvey, yet consistently claimed that kidnapings and lynchings of blacks were not within its jurisdiction. In the 1940s, the bureau compiled dossiers on Benjamin J. Davis, Jr., a senior black member of the Communist party, and artist/activist Paul Robeson, even as police brutality in southern jails continued unabated. In the 1950s, the bureau virtually ignored the well-publicized case of fourteen-year-old African-American Emmett Till from Chicago, who was kidnapped and lynched after speaking disrespectfully to a white woman in a Mississippi store. Despite the testimony of a witness who identified the woman's husband and half-brother as Till's kidnappers, as well as physical evidence connecting the boy to these men, both were acquitted on all counts. In 1957, the bureau continued its surveillance activities, now focusing on Elijah Muhammad, founder of the Black Muslims, and Martin Luther King, Jr. In the years immediately prior to King's death, civil rights workers anticipated and received little protection from FBI offices. More than one informant claimed that even before the assassination, rumors circulated within their communities warning that the FBI would try to murder the leader. Even as late as 1990, charges of FBI racism have arisen; several separate cases involving complaints of black agents were scrutinized and eventually settled out of court.[11]

One of the best sources for understanding why blacks mistrust the FBI is David J. Garrow's extraordinarily detailed *The FBI and Martin Luther King, Jr.* Yet even Garrow, after reviewing volumes of records documenting Hoover's unrelenting animosity toward King, in an uncharacteristically contentious footnote condemns those who subscribe to rumors linking the bureau with the civil rights leader's death:

Suggestions that the FBI had anything to do with King's assassination are totally baseless, and are convincingly disproven by each and every study of the details of the event. People who continue to propound or believe such rumors are, in their own way, prisoners of the "paranoid style" of thought. . . . While some proponents of the FBI conspiracy notion may have acted largely out of self-interest, many others who have accepted the idea have reflected only gullibility and ignorance.[12]

Garrow includes in his book the letter the FBI sent to King in an attempt to drive the civil rights leader to commit suicide:

The American public, the church organizations that have been helping—Protestant, Catholic and Jews will know you for what you are—an evil, abnormal beast. So have others who have backed you. You are done. King, there is only one thing left for you to do. You know what it is. You have just 34 days in which to do. . . . You are done. There is but one way out for you. You better take it before your filthy, abnormal self is bared to the nation.[13]

In maintaining that those individuals who still harbor suspicions of an FBI–MLK assassination connection are "gullible and ignorant," Garrow reveals his own misunderstanding of the potency of rumor and the history of antiblack policies that African-Americans have experienced. Well after Hoover's death, FBI commitment to African-American civil rights was still weak, at best. From 1984 to 1986, the FBI engaged in an extensive campaign investigating alleged voting irregularities in the "blackbelt" of Alabama. Among the one thousand black voters interrogated was a ninety-six-year-old double amputee who had been voting only since the passage of the 1965 Voting Rights Act; forced to testify in court that she had received assistance in filling out an absentee ballot, she resolved never to vote again.[14]

While most informants were unfamiliar with the full range

of the antiblack agenda advanced by Hoover and the FBI, they perceived the bureau as hostile to African-American well-being. One black male informant reported, "I've heard that Martin Luther King was doing so much for the advancement of blacks and our nation as a whole that the whites could not bear to see a fully integrated society and they [the FBI] hired a man to kill him." In defending his acceptance of this text, the young man stated, "Yes, I do [believe it], and I know my family does because they know that this government is racist and no matter what they [the government] say, they don't want equality." Once again, the family's own version of political history proved more rhetorically persuasive than any the informant had encountered in a classroom; indeed, like the young woman who offered the JFK text above, this young man claimed never to have studied the 1960s in school.

Shibutani notes, "Observers sometimes designate as 'suggestible' anyone who accepts a report that the observers regard as ridiculous. . . . Suggestibility can only be measured in terms of what the subject takes for granted . . . acceptance of a given report may constitute suggestibility for persons from one cultural background but not for those from another."[15] Those individuals who suspect a connection between the FBI and the assassination of Martin Luther King, Jr., "take for granted" a history in which officially sanctioned antiblack actions are abundant; in other words, such a connection fits the black history to which they have been privy. I encountered informants from a variety of occupational and social backgrounds—businessmen, college students, professors, members of the armed forces—who defended the plausibility of this allegation, showing little evidence of being "prisoners of the 'paranoid style' of thought." For them, the notion that the FBI director who had tried to drive MLK to suicide might indeed have been powerful enough to have orchestrated his assassination, and in a way that defied detection, is entirely reasonable and in perfect keeping with the traditional antiblack hostility one finds in many branches of the government. As Shibutani puts it, "Far from being pathological, rumor is part and parcel of the efforts of men to come to terms with the exigencies of life."[16]

Malcolm X

The folk tendency to confuse the FBI and CIA appears prominently in the case of the 1965 assassination of Malcolm X.
Because this black nationalist leader's fame never matched
that of Martin Luther King, Jr., public interest in his death
was much smaller. As a result, there was much less consensus
regarding official involvement in the events that brought Malcolm X down. Very few white informants had heard or believed rumors linking his death to a conspiracy of any kind. As
for African-American informants, particularly Black Muslims,
they doubted the official explanation of his death—namely,
that Muslims orchestrated his death to punish him for leaving
the Black Muslims and establishing the rival Organization for
Afro-American Unity; rather, some party besides the Black
Muslims was generally imputed to be behind Malcolm X's
death, though no uniform explanation of who that party might
have been arose. One informant, an African-American prize
fighter born in 1962, revealed that his parents told him that
"the FBI or the CIA had something to do with it. They did it
because President Hoover [*sic*] ordered the assassination . . .
because he had it in for him, he didn't like Malcolm and what
he stood for." Claims that either "the FBI or the CIA" killed
Malcolm X were common among informants, more so than
those linking the assassination to one specific agency.

Unlike the assertions of motive for the assassination of JFK,
which varied considerably, the rationales expressed by informants claiming that Malcolm X was murdered by either the
FBI or the CIA are quite similar. While President Kennedy's
public life, of course, encompassed many issues in addition
to race, Malcolm X's claim to fame consisted almost solely in
his advocacy of an Islamic-based black nationalism; it was,
according to my informants, the militancy inherent in his philosophy that led the powers that be to kill him. Again, this
explanation for Malcolm X's death simply fit my informants'
sense of black history better than the official one implicating
a rival Black Muslim sect.

A Boston-born African-American male offered the following theory about the assassination of Malcolm X: "I heard it

was a CIA plot to kill him. They hired those Muslims who killed him so they wouldn't have to get their hands dirty. The people in the community always believed that Malcolm X was assassinated by the CIA." This young man said he had most recently heard the topic discussed in a barbershop where his uncle worked. All the patrons were black men, and they were reviewing the great leaders of the sixties. Although the men debated whether the actual assassins had been helped by the CIA or by the FBI or some other agency, no one doubted that the federal government was responsible for the murder. Once again only one motif distinguishes this barbershop explanation from the official one, that Malcolm X was assassinated by blacks. The CIA had plotted the assassinations of African leaders in the 1960s; the possibility that this seemingly omnipotent law enforcement agency might have engineered Malcolm X's death as well seemed a logical conclusion to the barbershop patrons.

Robert F. Kennedy

To paraphrase one African-American female informant with a Ph.D., by the time a murderer gunned down Robert F. Kennedy, most Americans were "desensitized" to the horror of assassinations. Many informants who had made specific comments about JFK and MLK had nothing to say about RFK. Others merely connected the younger Kennedy's death with his older brother's: if someone maintained that "the mob" had killed JFK, they also blamed organized crime for Robert's death. If J. Edgar Hoover was given responsibility for the president's death, then the director also "got rid of this Kennedy for the same reasons he got rid of JFK." The circumstances surrounding RFK's death were less ambiguous than those surrounding the other assassinations; moreover, Robert's death was much less of a crisis than the others. Consequently, fewer rumors sprang up, or else people merely piggybacked those they associated with JFK to explain his brother's death.

The Atlanta Child Killer

In attributing racist crimes to the FBI, people will make their judgment based in part on the relative stature and power of the alleged victim. Many whites and blacks alike doubt that even J. Edgar Hoover would have taken it upon himself to arrange for the killing of a U.S. president or a Nobel Peace Prize–winning civil rights leader. But the same people find it possible, and indeed likely, that the FBI might engineer the deaths of more anonymous Americans. This fact can be seen in the various Atlanta child killer rumors that point to the FBI (or, in some cases, the CIA, the army, or just "the government") as the perpetrator. Many of these versions contain an additional motif in which the agency in question was collecting the bodies so that medical experiments could be performed on them (see Chapter 5 for more on contamination motifs). Finally, some informants claimed that the FBI had not actually killed the victims, but they had covered up for the whites (usually the KKK) who had committed the murders.

In any event, the investigation of the string of murders that so plagued Atlanta clearly intensified the already charged feelings that existed between the FBI, which played a leading role in the case, and the African-American community. At the close of the Carter administration, the outgoing president called on the FBI to investigate the Atlanta crimes as well as other seemingly random attacks on African-Americans nationwide. Carter specifically asked the FBI to determine if the African-American victims had been the target of a conspiracy organized by white supremacists. In 1980 he told *Ebony* magazine, "The possibility exists that there is a conspiracy. . . . The FBI is concentrating on that with the utmost diligence and is making regular reports to me. It's hard for me to form an opinion without having actual evidence to base it on. . . . But, yes, the possibility exists that there is a conspiracy."[17] As the list of victims in Atlanta grew, the FBI's attention became focused primarily on finding the person or persons responsible for those deaths, with the task of uncovering an organized conspiracy being shunted aside.

Although the FBI's involvement began with Carter, the

first two years of the Reagan administration saw the most con-
centrated investigation into the Atlanta killings. The shift
from a Democratic to a Republican administration in 1980,
moreover, allowed the FBI to downplay possible racist motivations. In April 1981, FBI director William Webster announced that twenty-three of the murders had been "substan-
tially solved." One of the numerous agents assigned to the
case stated publicly that "some of those kids were killed by
their parents," the murders having been committed because
the children were a "nuisance." These statements infuriated
the local Atlanta investigators, who were by and large African-
Americans, in contrast to the predominantly white FBI con-
tingent. The two units also feuded over the strength of the
evidence that led to Wayne Williams's arrest on two counts
of murder. Fulton County's district attorney, Lewis Slaton, a
native white Atlantan, was very reluctant to arrest Williams
merely on circumstantial fiber evidence; his stalling infuriated the FBI, who felt the case was in the bag. This local-
versus-federal power struggle, needless to say, was played
out at great length in the local and national media.

When I sent a letter of inquiry, an FBI spokesman replied
briskly, seemingly oblivious to the possibility that the bureau's behavior might have been perceived as hostile by the
black community; of course, he denied the association:

It is hard to understand how anyone could believe that the FBI was
responsible for or in any way connected with the deaths of these
youngsters. Our concern was in bringing them to an end and appre-
hending the person responsible. I am unable to shed any light on
why such behavior would be attributed to the FBI or to speculate
concerning the origin of such a rumor. It goes without saying that
there is absolutely no basis for this rumor, and it is a disservice to
the fine men and women of this organization who have dedicated
themselves to safeguarding the American people.[18]

The first informant to tell me that the FBI was responsible for
the deaths, an African-American female in her early twenties,
recalled having heard it from Dick Gregory in a college lecture in the mid-1980s. Several subsequent informants heard
the story from a friend who they thought might also have got-

ten it from the social activist/comedian. Although most of my informants said that they heard the rumor "on the street" or "in church," Gregory may have been a strong force in its dissemination—though where he got the story from remains unclear.[19] Jan Douglass of the Center for Democratic Renewal attributes the popularity of the rumor to him.[20] Yet whether Gregory was the rumor's primary source is less important than the fact that his rendition of it rang true for many members of his audiences, providing plausible answers to the unresolved questions of the case. Orally and in print, these individuals then shared these answers with the larger community, sometimes modifying, sometimes amplifying the core material to create a cycle of rumors and contemporary legends. If Gregory or any other charismatic speaker had posited a theory about the killings that did not fit the audience's understanding of black history, it could never have gained such widespread credibility.

The FBI's posture throughout this case was perceived as antagonistic by many in the United States. In its criticism of the local law enforcement community, public accusations of the victims' own families, and push for the arrest of a black suspect on little evidence, the bureau was conforming to the antiblack pattern so firmly established during the Hoover dynasty. These factors contributed to the FBI's emergence as a suspect in the minds of some African-Americans. The number of homicides in Atlanta was great and the clues were scarce; who better than the savvy, well-trained FBI agents would have had the skills necessary to commit the crimes and then cover their tracks? Herein, too, lay an explanation for why the supposedly all-knowing federal agency was unable to solve the murders in an unassailable fashion.

Approximately half of the informants who connected a law enforcement agency to the killings offered no motivation other than a racist desire to eliminate as many African-American males as possible. The other half claimed a more sinister motive, saying that the bodies were taken to the Centers for Disease Control for interferon experiments. At issue here, however, is the fact that informants considered these crimes the result of a conspiracy between at least two agencies of the federal government, the domestic law enforcement agency and the nation's public health agency.

Of course, the CIA had no direct or indirect role in the investigation conducted in Atlanta; therefore, fewer informants implicated this agency than implicated the FBI. Nonetheless, it is possible to understand why the CIA was mentioned. The CIA, after all, had, like the FBI, also been implicated in rumors alleging racist activity, particularly in the third world, where the agency was known to have plotted assassinations as well as coups and other violent acts, ostensibly in the name of U.S. national interests. When asked about rumors connecting the agency with the Atlanta killings, the CIA spokesperson, like his FBI counterpart, denied any involvement: "I can state categorically that the CIA had nothing whatsoever to do with the case of young black citizens who were murdered in Atlanta during the period 1979–82. We have no idea how rumors might have started linking the CIA with those crimes."[21]

Rumors and contemporary legends capture modern anxieties by commenting on the effects of urbanization, mass society, technology, and strained ethnic relations. Clearly, the events in Atlanta constituted a crisis, one large enough to evoke mass public sentiment. The "public"—in this case, black Americans both within Atlanta and all over the country—was starved for satisfactory news: the relationship between them and the conveyors of official news (the whites) was so laden with mistrust and apprehension that the "official story" contradicted the worldview of many African-Americans. As one by one young Atlanta-based African-Americans disappeared or were found dead, the "public" was reminded just how tenuous its claim to law enforcement protection had always been. The local police did not recognize the seriousness of the crimes until several bodies had been found; meanwhile, the media exploited the grief of the victims' families. Because they were committed in Atlanta, the southern city reputed to have conquered its racist legacy and opened the doors of opportunity to all, the crimes were even more likely to promote speculation about a covert political agenda. When law enforcers, whose television counterparts always manage to solve crimes in under sixty minutes, failed to identify a suspect quickly, doubts mounted. Why were the parents of the victims being blamed? Too many coincidences seemed to incriminate the federal law enforcement agency itself. Perhaps, disturbed by the progress being made by Atlanta's black middle class, they had opted to curtail future achievement by eliminating the youngsters who would one day stake their own claim. Or maybe the agency was providing a way for those who actually committed the antiblack crimes to go unpunished. Just as representatives of the government had sanctioned racist assaults on black bodies in the past, so, it seemed, was this government anxious to impinge on the physical well-being of African-Americans. And as we saw in Chapter 3, KKK involvement in some of the murders may yet prove to be true, which may in turn indicate an official cover-up.[22]

The rumors and contemporary legends that emerged with regard to the Atlanta child murders addressed the ambiguities that continued to perplex the folk. They also provided a network that restored, in part, a sense of ethnic empowerment for African-Americans. The rumor theorist Terry Ann Knopf argues, "Like hostile beliefs, rumors create a 'common culture' within which leadership, mobilization, and concerted action can occur spontaneously. Crystallizing, confirming, intensifying hostile beliefs while linking them to actual events, rumors often provide the 'proof' necessary for mass mobilization."[23] In collecting these rumors and legends between 1986 and 1990, nearly ten years after the crimes were committed, I discovered that the ability to name the perceived oppressors/conspirators still gave people a sense of power over them. The process of identifying or naming contributes to an atmosphere of communal problem-solving. Unable to prove that the all-powerful FBI was guilty or that Wayne Williams was innocent, the folk could at least posit an alternative explanation that fit their worldview. And, in part, they just may have been right.

Politics and Sneakers

Two aspects of African-American culture in the late 1980s and early 1990s intersected to generate a slightly different kind of conspiracy rumor from those discussed above. First, high-priced athletic footwear increased in popularity among the young. Although by no means an exclusively African-American phenomenon, this fashion craze caused considerable concern among blacks. Wearing the "right" sneaker became essential for many young people, whose parents' limited budgets, however, often allocated funds only for the least expensive sneaker. Second, a "new" officially sanctioned oppressor was discovered as anti-apartheid activists focused public attention on South African politics. When popular recording artists refused to "play Sun City," instead producing a record album and a music video, the inequities of South African politics were catapulted into the domain of young adults.[24] The political consciousness of white American youths was also elevated by celebrity condemnations of apartheid. But once again, young African-Americans, because they felt they shared a common heritage with oppressed black South Africans, embraced this cause on a more personal level.

As the price of the athletic footwear and celebrity attention to South African politics increased, a rumor merging these seemingly disparate phenomena began to circulate. In its most popular versions, the rumor maintains that Reebok, manufacturers of one of the best-selling lines of athletic footwear, is owned by South Africans or manufactured in that country. Subscribers to the rumor claim that the white power structure of South Africa is surreptitiously profiting off young African-Americans' lust to have the right shoe; that is, it is essentially engaged in an anti–African-American conspiracy.

In a 1990 interview, the Reebok International vice-president for corporate communications, Kenneth R. Lightcap, dated the rumor at a "couple of years" old.[25] My informants also said that they had first heard the rumors circa 1987–88. By 1989, I was able to collect it from the East Coast to the West, primarily from young African-Americans, but also from whites. Most of these informants were well entrenched in the youth culture that embraces anti-apartheid efforts and follows the latest fashion trends. The rumor is also well known to African-American parents of preadolescents and adolescents who have ambivalent and sometimes downright hostile attitudes about the expenses incurred by their fashion-conscious children.

Like most corporate leaders besieged by a rumor, Reebok representatives are perplexed by this charge of wrong-doing. At first they speculated that the company name might have triggered the rumor. Steven Encarnacoa, a former marketing director for Reebok, asserted that the company's founders, Joe and Bill Foster, turned to the dictionary for a name for the bootmaking company they started in the late 1950s; they "picked the name Reebok . . . a light, nimble gazelle. . . . Coincidentally that species is found almost exclusively in South Africa."[26] Lightcap, in speculating on the source of the rumor, mentioned the association with the South African gazelle, the similarity between the words *reebok* and *springbok*—an annual South African rugby match—and the fact that the corporate symbol for the Reebok brand is the British flag. These coincidences generated a guilt by association, according to Lightcap, who concluded: "There's enough comfort to the rumor to feel good about passing it on."[27] To date, I have not encountered any informants familiar with the reebok animal or the springbok match. However, some informants, particularly those with a British Caribbean background, do associate the British flag with racism and colonial oppression. Corporations frequently attribute negative rumors to disgruntled ex-employees or the competition. Although Reebok officials did not expressly accuse their competitors of starting the rumor, they do think that they have taken advantage of the rumor's popularity.

The Foster brothers were making their boots in England, but since 1984 the Reebok company has been American, located on Boston's south shore. The breakdown of ownership of Reebok is as follows: 32 percent is owned by Pentland Industries, 28 percent by individual shareholders, 22 percent by various institutions, and 18 percent by the Paul Fireman (CEO of Reebok) family. The company went public in 1985. Approximately half its products are manufactured in Korea; the remaining half are made in other Asian countries, including China and Taiwan. According to Lightcap, Reebok has no suppliers or subsidiaries on the continent of Africa. The

version of the rumor that most concerns the company alleges
that it distributes its shoes in South Africa. As company officials acknowledge, the products in fact were sold in South
Africa until 1985. Pointing out that other U.S. shoe companies
still peddle their footwear in South Africa, Reebok representatives claim that "C. Joseph LaBonte (1986), then Reebok's
president, led the company out of South Africa and was consequently sued by the [South African] distributor."[28]

To the company, its status as the first major U.S. shoe company to withdraw its products from the South African market
makes the allegation even more disturbing. Proud of its record
on human rights and its support of the African-American community, Reebok has gone to great lengths to dispel the rumor.
Kenneth Lightcap spends a great deal of time on the road,
pleading Reebok's case to African-American college groups
as well as community and political groups. Signs disavow-
ing the South Africa connection are very much in evidence
in Reebok outlets. A handsome flyer entitled "Reebok: On
Record with Human Rights" contains disclaimers from both
African-American athletes and well-known anti-apartheid
groups. For example, next to a picture of Olympic decathlon
gold medalist Rafer Johnson is the following statement: "Reebok to its credit cut off its business ties to South Africa before
many corporations opted to leave. In addition, what has made
my relationship with Reebok compelling is its corporate embrace of human rights." The flyer also reprints a letter to Reebok employees:

> To: Reebok Employees
> From: Randal Robinson, TransAfrica
> June 23, 1989
> Those of us who have been in the struggle to end apartheid have
> used various strategies to reach that goal. One of our most effective
> approaches is to highlight and reproach American corporations
> which are doing business in South Africa. We have been very suc-
> cessful in getting hundreds of corporations to withdraw from bol-
> stering an economy based on oppression. In addition, we have been
> keeping the glare of public scrutiny on those still operating in South
> Africa. It is incumbent, therefore, that we in the anti-apartheid com-

munity salute those corporations that are actively involved in peace-
fully transforming South Africa into a democratic state. Yours (REE-
BOK) is one such corporation. Your chairman and president, Paul
Fireman and Joe LaBonte respectively, have demonstrated above
and beyond all expectations their commitment to human rights and
a free South Africa.

Though your company has been daunted by a rumor that it is
doing business in South Africa, Reebok is now the only company I
am certain is not doing business in South Africa. Furthermore, it is
one of the few corporations, if not the only one, that has embraced
human rights as a corporate value.

Thus I would like to salute Reebok and all of its employees for
their dedication to human rights, a free South Africa and a responsible corporate America.[29]

As a further demonstration of the company's commitment to
the rights of oppressed South Africans, Reebok and its dy-
namic CEO, Paul Fireman, played a very prominent role in
Nelson Mandela's eight-day visit to the United States in June
1990.

One reason Reebok may have been targeted in the rumor
is its position at the top of the athletic shoe industry. Few
American companies can boast as much success as Reebok
has enjoyed since 1985. In that year they stated, "We are the
largest company when you consider what we own—producer
of athletic footwear and apparel, given the fact that we have
somewhere between 28 and 30 percent of the athletic footwear
and apparel market, the fact that we not only own the Reebok
brand, we own Avia, which has a little over 4 percent of the
market; so we are the largest athletic footwear manufacturer
in the world."[30]

The following synopsis of one telling of the rumor high-
lights many of the issues implicit in its circulation. In 1988,
an early informant to share the rumor with me was the African-
American stepmother of a teenage male. After spending "over
fifty dollars" for a pair of Reeboks for the boy, three weeks
later she found them in the garbage. When she confronted
him, he claimed that his schoolmates had chided him for
"wearing South Africa on his feet." As an individual personally committed to anti-apartheid efforts, she did not insist that

he wear the shoes, though she did rescue them from the trash. Knowing of my interest in such matters, however, she asked me to investigate the accusation. When I told her that my research indicated that Reebok was not owned by South Africans, nor were their products made by South Africans or even sold in South Africa, she asked her stepson to start wearing the shoes again. Nevertheless, he continued to be verbally accosted by peers who were not satisfied with his explanation that his mother's college professor's research debunked the rumor. Concerned for his personal well-being, his stepmother soon bought him another brand of sneakers.

This informant's rendering of the rumor, like many others I collected, includes a reference to the price of the product. Both parents and adolescents bemoaned the spiraling costs of athletic footwear. This telling detail became particularly pronounced in versions collected after the late-1989 introduction of Pump basketball shoes—a $170 pair of sneakers complete with inflatable soles. For example, when asked generally about a conspiracy and an athletic wear company, one informant stated, "Reebok makes those $170 shoes in South Africa." For this individual, the cost factor was part of the definition of the product. In other versions, informants closed their telling of the rumor by commenting on the product's price tag: "and they [South Africa] are making a lot of money off of them shoes."

This last informant, like many over the age of thirty, heard the item from a high school or college student. Clearly these texts are best known to this age group. Although this woman did not wear Reeboks herself, other informants over thirty did; and, upon hearing the item from younger people, they too abandoned the shoes. One African-American mother of three commented, "They are just sitting there in my closet now, hardly worn at all." When I asked this woman why she hadn't thrown the sneakers away if she thought wearing them was politically incorrect, she repeated that they were just like new.

The stepson in the item above was verbally accosted for wearing the shoes. Unfortunately, some young people have been physically accosted as well. Many informants claimed to have witnessed such altercations in public places, with one or more individuals berating another for wearing the shoes. Thus, people who do not subscribe to the rumor often abandon the product anyway; they do not want to be physically assaulted because of their choice in fashion footwear.

Considered together, these individual motifs in the Reebok rumor add up to a narrative that reflects a great deal about contemporary African-American culture. The consistent attention to cost suggests that the community may be in the process of reshaping some of its consumer values. With the price of a pair of name-brand sneakers hovering above one hundred dollars, some African-Americans are rebelling against the companies that carry on the fashion wars. Rather than boycotting expensive shoes because the money could be better spent elsewhere, people subscribe to the rumor to validate the consumer decision. Granted, the above informant eventually gave in to her son's wishes and purchased another pair of pricey shoes. And many of those who condemned Reebok were wearing other expensive brand-name shoes at the time of the interview. Nonetheless, the fact that the Reebok and the Troop items began to circulate at about the same time would seem to indicate that a critical self-consciousness is growing within the community regarding the allegiance to trendy footwear.

According to the stepmother above and numerous other informants, the threat of physical force promoted adherence to the unofficial boycott as well. In the 1980s, urban fashion and urban violence became linked as some individuals without the funds to purchase the latest gear simply stripped the clothes, jewelry, or shoes off a well-dressed victim. To avoid assault, therefore, many people identified places where they would or would not wear desirable clothes. A young woman might be reluctant to wear her designer coat to school or to a movie, for example, but would feel safe wearing it to church, a suburban mall, or a family reunion (see Fig. 4). Gold jewelry, particularly neck chains, was often hidden while outdoors, then displayed once the wearer felt safe in an enclosed envi-

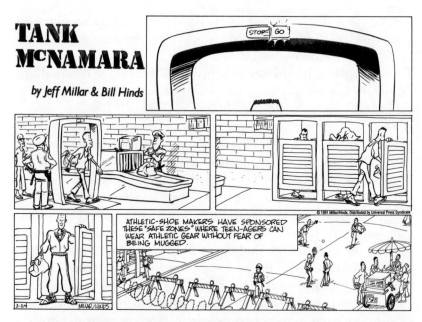

4. Cartoonists Jeff Millar and Bill Hinds capture the anxiety faced by young African-Americans who seek safe places to wear popular clothing. (Tank McNamara © 1991 Millar/Hinds. Reprinted with permission of Universal Press Syndicate. All rights reserved.)

ronment. When these rules were violated, a person might pay the highest price of all:

For 15-year-old Michael Eugene Thomas, it definitely was the shoes. A ninth-grader at Meade Senior High School in Anne Arundel County, Md., Thomas was found strangled on May 2, 1989. Charged with first degree murder was James David Martin, 17, a basketball buddy who allegedly took Thomas's two-week-old Air Jordan basketball shoes and left Thomas's barefoot body in the woods near the school. Thomas loved Michael Jordan and the shoes Jordan endorses, and he cleaned his own pair each evening. He kept the cardboard shoe box with Jordan's silhouette on it in a place of honor in his room. Inside the box was the sales ticket for the shoes. It showed he paid $115.50, the price of a product touched by deity. "We told him not to wear the shoes to school," said Michael's grandmother, Birdie Thomas. "We said somebody might like to take them and he said, 'Granny, before I let anyone take those shoes, they'll have to kill me.' "[31]

Although my research uncovered no deaths as a result of wearing the politically incorrect Reeboks, the threat of any kind of a physical assault might well steer many people to leave the shoes in their closet.

During the late 1980s and early 1990s when I was collecting this rumor, African-Americans demonstrated an increased sensitivity to the issues of the anti-apartheid struggle. Throughout the eighties, activists urged institutions of higher learning and corporations to stop doing business in South Africa. Films like *Cry Freedom* (1987), *A Dry White Season* (1989), and *A World Apart* (1988) depicted the day-to-day life of apartheid victims. When a much more commercial film, *Lethal Weapon 2* (1989), was released, many reviewers commented on the identity of the villains—white South Africans. With the demise of the cold war, Americans needed to find their evil elsewhere. South Africa fit the bill nicely.

Unfortunately, most African-Americans could do little to voice their allegiance to black South Africans. African-American businesses tend to be too small to have ever invested in South Africa, and boycotting travel to South Africa was generally precluded because few individuals have the means to consider such a trip in the first place. Although college-aged students could participate in campus calls for divestment, younger students, to my knowledge, had no such opportunity to wage their protest. Nevertheless, individuals could articulate their solidarity by relinquishing one desirable wardrobe item. A woman whose once-treasured Reeboks were now collecting dust in her closet described how much trouble she was having finding another pair of shoes as comfortable; other informants also mentioned how pleasurable their shoes had once been. Yet they were willing to make this sacrifice to support the cause of black South Africans. Refusing to wear Reeboks was something tangible that they as individuals could do.

Talking about their refusal was part of this process. Many of my informants lapsed into a trickster tone as they described how they were avoiding the all-powerful shoe company. An eighteen-year-old African-American male who claimed that "Reebok supports apartheid" continued, "A female black friend told me. At first Reebok was my favorite shoe; after she told me, I stopped wearing the shoes, and I told others and they stopped." When a young man takes a stand based on negative information given him by a young woman, he is bringing himself closer to her. When parents refuse to wear a product because their teenagers have expressed concerns over the manufacturer's political agenda, they are strengthening the bond between themselves and their offspring. Refusing Reeboks becomes a family matter, and several individual acts of defiance add up to a communal show of support for the cause. Sharing the rumor and joining the boycott enables individuals to perceive themselves as powerful.

Conclusion

What do these contemporary legends about political assassinations, child killings, and sneakers reveal about the relationship between the power structure and African-Americans? When the contents of the folk texts are juxtaposed to the historical circumstances of the incidents in question, it becomes apparent that only a narrow stream of "information" distinguishes the folk explanation from the official one. The powers that be are not, after all, unblemished innocents; federal and local law enforcement agencies have a long record of racially problematic policies, and capitalist enterprises of all sorts have employed an impressive range of marketing strategies to make their high-priced products attractive to African-American consumers. The 1960s assassinations, a long string of unaccountable homicides, and the rapid rise of an athletic wear company are all the kinds of events that trigger folk speculation. In seeking to fill in the gaps between what is known about these events and what remains a mystery, the folk will rely on their sense of black history to construct motifs consistent with past experience but applicable to the issues at hand.

Chapter Five

Contamination

"They want to do more than just kill us"

In the preceding two chapters we have focused on groups identified in African-American folklore as antiblack conspirators. Let us now look at texts in which the conspiracy in question is intended specifically to contaminate blacks in a physical way, either directly or indirectly. The majority of people who spoke with me about the Church's rumor, for example, allege much more than a simple KKK plot to capitalize monetarily on a product preferred by African-Americans. The first informant who shared the item told me, "They're doing something to the chicken so that when black men eat it, they become sterile," and this comment accusing the KKK of imposing a sinister form of ethnic birth control pervades my fieldwork. The same motif dominates the Tropical Fantasy cycle. Many informants who claim that the FBI was responsible for the Atlanta child murders elaborate by reporting that the bodies were taken to the Centers for Disease Control in Atlanta for biological experiments. A college-aged African-American female said, "I remember hearing that the killings in Atlanta were related to the genocide of the black race. The FBI was responsible and using the bodies for interferon during research." (Interferon is an antiviral glycoprotein produced by human cells exposed to a virus; according to certain research reports of the late 1970s and early 1980s, the scientific community was well on its way to testing it so that it could be marketed as a genuine "miracle drug.")

In some folk items, contamination is a much more prominent motif than conspiracy. Growing public awareness of the
threat implicit in the acquired immune deficiency syndrome
(AIDS) epidemic caused various contemporary legends to
arise connecting this fatal, sexually transmitted disease with
an ethnically based contamination plot. Some informants, for
instance, claimed that AIDS was developed from experiments
having to do with disease, chemical, or germ warfare. These
experiments were supposedly conducted in Haiti or West Africa, populations that the experimenters (usually identified as
some group affiliated with "the government") perceived to be
expendable. As one informant reported, "The United States
government was developing germ warfare when it got out of
control. AIDS was the project, and they tried it out in Africa
first to see if it would work. It did." Others claim even more
heinous motives, saying that the disease was developed for
the express purpose of limiting the growth of third world populations. A New England–born thirty-nine-year-old African-
American female offered this succinct version: "AIDS originated in Africa by the [U.S.] government in that it was a
conspiracy to kill off a lot of black people."

This chapter will explore the evolution of contamination
motifs in these and other late-twentieth-century examples of
black folk discourse. *Contamination* will be used to refer to
any item in which the physical well-being of individual black
bodies is being manipulated for racist reasons. The modes of
contamination implicit in the Church's, Atlanta child killer,
and AIDS items differ in their immediate effect, but ultimately serve the same end: to curtail the growth of the black
population. Although black consumers of Church's chicken
and Tropical Fantasy suffer no visible effect, their ability to
procreate is blocked by some mysterious ingredient in the
food. Black AIDS patients have been afflicted by a deliberately introduced fatal virus; their deaths are imminent. And
the victims of the Atlanta child killer are not merely killed,
which reduces the size of the African-American population;
as part of two-pronged conspiracy, their bodies are also violated in an attempt to perfect a miracle drug. Because the
historical information about several of these items was in-

cluded in the previous two chapters, the focus here will be on the symbolic ramifications of contamination.

Dangerous Chicken

Approximately half of my informants claimed that the Klan's goal in its ownership of Church's was to put something (spices, drugs) into the chicken (either into the batter or flour coating, or, by injections, directly into the chicken) that would cause sterility in black male eaters. Similar aims and tactics were true of the Tropical Fantasy conspiracy. This motif contains the specificity and narrative closure that folklorists often find in contemporary legend texts. However, the other texts I collected lacked any such closure. Most informants used the present tense and described the contamination as an ongoing, relatively unfocused conspiracy. Typical of the comments I collected was, "I heard that the Klan owns Church's chicken and has been lacing the batter with a spermicide." Several people suggested that the KKK's goal was to "make blacks infertile." Thus both men and women have something to fear. One black female informant claimed that eating the chicken "makes something go wrong with pregnant black women so that their children come out retarded."

Typically, food contamination rumors and contemporary legends are associated either with instances of accidental, incidental contamination (the Kentucky Fried Rat, the mouse in the Coke bottle) or with premeditated food substitution, ostensibly for the purpose of increasing the company's profit ("wormburgers," the use of dog food on fast food pizzas). In the latter case, the company is not trying to hurt its customers, but rather to decrease costs through the use of socially distasteful but essentially safe ingredients. In the Church's rumor, by contrast, greed is not stated as a strong motive for the Klan. Although a few informants contributed versions that lacked any contamination motif, maintaining merely that the KKK owned the company, not a single informant speculated on how much money the Klan could make by selling fast food fried chicken to African-Americans. The white supremacist organization's goal, simply put, was to implement domestic genocide.

To those outside the rumor's public, the mechanism of contamination makes the accusation seem highly implausible. I encountered very few white informants who were familiar with the rumor. Upon hearing a summary, most responded by asking, "How is this mysterious substance supposed to distinguish between white male eaters and black male eaters?" When this question is posed to blacks, a common explanation is that most Church's franchises are located in black neighborhoods. Similarly, those who believe the Tropical Fantasy rumors note that the beverage is sold in inner-city ma-and-pa grocery stores, not at downtown soda counters. Hence, the KKK runs very little risk of sterilizing white male consumers. Other informants suggest that a substance has been discovered that impedes the production of sperm in black males but is harmless when consumed by whites.

When the Church's rumor surfaced in San Diego in 1984, Congressman Jim Bates arranged to have the Food and Drug Administration test the chicken using gas chromatography and mass spectrometry. After finding no evidence of foreign materials, an assistant of Bates together with two West Coast Church's officials held a press conference to share their findings with the public.[1] Tropical Fantasy was tested in 1991. A female informant told me that the Klan had probably "fixed things up with the FDA" so that the test on Church's would come out negative. Although I performed no scientific investigation of the chicken myself, I queried University of Massachusetts biologists and chemists about the possibility of such tampering. They maintained that there is no known tasteless, odorless substance that could be disguised in the chicken that would result in sterilization with no discernible side effects. I asked a black male student who overheard one of these conversations if he still believed the rumor. He said he did not. I asked him if he would patronize the nearby Church's. He said he would not.

To better understand the appeal of the contamination motif in the Church's and Tropical Fantasy rumors, it is useful to look at a very similar rumor. In speculating on just how the alleged sterilization agent in the chicken could function, none of my informants made any specific reference to the "ethnic weapon." This is the label that the U.S. intelligence community applied to rumors alleging that government scientists had developed a substance that could kill blacks but leave whites unharmed. These rumors, which appeared in leftist publications in the mid-1980s, caused great concern for the United States Information Agency (USIA). However, officials charged with exploring the reports drew no connections between them and other items of folk belief concerning people of color; rather, they claimed that the Soviet Union had designed and disseminated the rumors. In a publication familiarizing members of Congress with the scope of communist propaganda activity, the agency introduced the segment on the ethnic weapon thus:

Since at least 1980, the Soviet press has been circulating claims that the United States is conducting research on or has developed a so-called "ethnic weapon," which would kill only non-whites. The Soviet media typically also charges that the South Africans—or less frequently the Israelis—are supposedly collaborating with the United States in this research. The Soviet goal in this campaign seems clear: to make it appear as if the United States and its alleged collaborators are pursuing racist, genocidal policies.

The Soviet charge is absurd on the face of it. Even if the U.S. government wanted to produce such a weapon, it would make no sense to do so, given the multi-ethnic composition of the American population and the armed forces. The only plausible group that would want to produce such a weapon would be unregenerate white supremacists—a portrait of the U.S. government that Soviet disinformation specialists apparently want their audiences to believe.[2]

These comments are followed by various statements by scientific authorities explaining why such a substance could not be developed, as well as forty-five references in left-wing and communist publications to the U.S. government's role in the development of such a weapon.

Because none of my over two hundred Church's and Tropical Fantasy informants mentioned the "ethnic weapon" by name, I can only conclude that this rumor was not embraced by the African-American population. Whether communist-inspired journalists actually planted the rumor or simply reported one that was gaining popularity is less relevant, in my view, than the fact that the item did not capture the African-American imagination. Why did a rumor alleging the KKK's malevolent involvement in a fast food company find more acceptance than one claiming the government was manufacturing a weapon for racial genocide?

In the various left-wing print references cited in the USIA pamphlet, the so-called ethnic weapon is either a perfected substance or one still under development. Except in one item linking it to the AIDS virus, there are no hints that the weapon has been deployed. Nor are there any real indications of how, when, or why it would be used. The threat is in its mere existence—in the possibility that the U.S. government might want to have such a weapon, in the fact that it could not be used in a clandestine manner, and in the fact that the potential victims have no control over its implementation. In the Church's and Tropical Fantasy texts, by contrast, a form of random deployment is at work. Any African-American who chances to eat at Church's or sip a Tropical Fantasy soft drink is a potential victim. Yet in these cases, people can avoid victimization by refusing to purchase the product. The Church's and Tropical Fantasy rumors, in short, give people some control over their fate, whereas the ethnic weapon texts do not.

The other primary difference between the Church's rumor—as well as the other contamination rumors—and the ethnic weapon item resides in the mode of contamination. With the ethnic weapon, there is no clue as to how the victims will be infected with the deadly substance or what modus operandi will govern the weapon's use. In the other items, however, the contamination is more specifically rendered: poisoned food or soft drinks, postmortem intrusions, and sexual intercourse are concrete threats. In short, rumors that contain specific physical consequences are more likely to seize the interest of a public than ambiguous, unspecific ones.

With motifs pinpointing a particular company, a known antiblack conspiratorial group, a familiar prepared food, and a detrimental outcome, the Church's rumor contains all of the nuances the ethnic weapon rumor lacks. Because a person can do something about the threat contained in the Church's item simply by not patronizing the restaurant, it is ultimately a much less ominous rumor. No informants who professed belief in the Church's story believed themselves to have been sterilized permanently because they consumed the chicken before they heard the item. No one said anything like, "It's too late for me now." Instead they merely observed, "So I haven't eaten any since."

Like other folk groups, African-Americans assign food and its preparation symbolic importance; food choice is part of the ordering process by which humans endow the environment with meaning and feeling.[3] At first glance, a fast food chain that provides decent, familiar foods at a friendly price is offering a fair service and product. But by removing the preparation of an ethnic food from the home kitchens most strongly identified with it, the Church's corporation unwittingly intruded on sacred territory.

Ethnic foods, as a rule, are prepared and consumed by the very people who have created the dishes or by descendants who have had the recipes handed down to them. On special occasions or in special settings, these foods are shared with outsiders eager to participate in "equal opportunity eating." Church's created a new, public context for the sharing of what had thus far been considered communal foods—and foods, moreover, that carried with them strong symbolic associations. Nor are these associations necessarily positive. American popular culture has long perpetuated a stereotype in which blacks are portrayed as inordinately fond of foods that can be eaten without utensils, such as fried chicken and watermelon. Given this background, it is not surprising that blacks wish to approach these foods, particularly when offered outside the home, cautiously. The anthropologist Mary Douglas has pointed out that people with a minority status in their society are often suspicious of cooked foods as well as protective of the body's orifices: "If we treat ritual protection of bodily orifices as a symbol of social preoccupations about exits and entrances," she writes, "the purity of cooked food becomes important. I suggest that food is not likely to be pol-

luting at all unless the external boundaries of the social system are under pressure."[4]

The popularity of the Church's rumor indicates that the
black community perceives itself as vulnerable to the hostile
desires of the majority population, which, it seems, will stop
at nothing to inhibit the growth of the minority population—including the use of polluted food to weaken individual sexual capacity. In this case, indeed, the threat to fertility
comes from a source that employs the name of the very religious structure presumed by the black community to offer the
most safety: the church.

The key to understanding the item's popularity, however,
resides in the power it bestowed upon its public to seize control over a perceived threat to all African-American people.
In the spring of 1990, an African-American female Californian
discussed it as if it were ancient history. She recalled first
hearing it "a long time ago," and concluded her commentary
by stating, with obvious satisfaction, "A lot of these Church's
have closed up now." Like many other informants who used
similar closing motifs, she believed that a battle had been
"won."

Atlanta Bodies

Whereas most of those who knew the Church's item mentioned both the conspiracy and the contamination motifs,
there was less consensus in testimony about the Atlanta child
killer. While over half of the informants offered only a conspiracy text, some 20 percent of the total followed up the conspiracy allegation with the claim that the conspirators (the
CIA/FBI, either alone or in cahoots with the KKK) were kid-
naping the children, killing them, and then using their bodies
for medical research. Even more specific were those who
identified the Centers for Disease Control in Atlanta as the
setting for the research and interferon as the substance being
investigated. Two informants even went on to say that the
desired substance was removed from the victims' genitals
with a syringe.

The incorporation of these motifs into the Atlanta lore was

no doubt stimulated by concurrent developments. In the late 1970s and early 1980s, just when the Georgia city was coping with its tragedy, the medical and business communities were making the news with stories about interferon, a substance believed to promise a breakthrough in cancer research. Coincidentally, Atlanta is also the home of the CDC, the nation's agency for public health research. Just as other Atlanta-based institutions lent their particular expertise and resources to the murder investigation, the CDC eventually did so as well. Employing a paradigm oriented to the confinement of disease epidemics, the CDC suggested ways in which the murder "epidemic" might be kept from spreading. Unfortunately, outbreaks of murder and outbreaks of disease cannot be controlled by the same measures, and the agency's contribution proved quite ineffective in the end. Published in 1984, their report concludes:

Although child homicides have not been uncommon in Atlanta, the cluster of unsolved child homicides in 1979 to 1981 was an outbreak that did not seem attributable to lack of effective police work. Expansion of the case definition failed to show further related cases. Defining those factors associated with risk may help parents and public health and public safety authorities take appropriate measures to reduce such risks should such a problem recur.[5]

The CDC maintains that it was at no time involved with interferon research; however, given its prominence as an internationally respected problem-solving institution, its location in the same city as the murders, its inability to contribute anything genuinely useful in the solution of these homicides, and a troubled record with the African-American community, it is not surprising that some interpreted its role in such an ominous fashion.

Like the FBI, the CDC, through its affiliation with the U.S. Public Health Service (PHS), has a history of weak relations with the African-American population.[6] It was under the auspices of the PHS that a destructive experiment was conducted from the early 1930s until the early 1970s on a group of adult black males in rural Alabama. Telling four hundred sufferers of syphilis that they were treating them for "bad blood," doctors merely examined them regularly in order to observe and document the debilitating effects of the untreated disease.[7] The discovery of penicillin in the late 1940s, however, meant that doctors had a sound treatment for this malady that had plagued humankind for centuries. By withholding penicillin from those African-American patients who had been participating in the study, the doctors in control of what is commonly called the Tuskegee experiment violated an Alabama health statute which required that the drug be given to anyone known to be suffering from the disease. Although the study was not a secret one, it did not become public knowledge until the early 1970s. The doctors involved, as well as a large specialized audience who read progress reports in medical journals, saw no reason to hide or be ashamed of the investigation. Allan M. Brandt, a medical historian, states, "During the forty years that the Tuskegee Study continued, it was widely reported in medical journals without raising any significant objections on the part of the profession. Indeed, only reports of the study in the general press in 1972 finally brought it to an end."[8] The public disclosure of the experiment resulted in an outpouring of rage from the media and African-American groups. Senator Edward Kennedy took up the cause of survivors and the heirs of deceased participants, who were eventually awarded an out-of-court settlement by the government. Although spokespersons for the CDC did acknowledge moral and ethical errors in withholding treatment from the subjects in the 1940s when Public Health Service doctors could have offered medical relief, they were reluctant to denounce the experiment. "We are trying to apply 1972 medical treatment standards to 1932," was the comment of one CDC representative.[9]

This example of flagrant disregard for African-American physical well-being confirmed for many what they already suspected. Together with the fact that the experiment was conducted from Atlanta, two additional aspects bear on the development of the later child killer legend. First is the fact that the disease being observed was syphilis—which is sexually transmitted—and the subjects were all male. The later disappearances and homicides also, in all but two cases, involved only males. Thus, both cases can be seen as attempts by complicitous whites to rid America of as many black males as possible. The second noteworthy dimension of the Tuskegee experiment lies in the doctors' rationale for requesting additional funding after the effectiveness of penicillin on syphilis was documented: now that the disease was treatable, they argued, no other opportunities would arise to ascertain its long-term effects. In other words, white doctors were using black human guinea pigs to understand better how to treat white patients. The claim that CDC doctors needed (black) corpses for interferon tests likewise suggests a willingness on the part of the public health authorities to sacrifice black male lives in order to save white ones.

Around 1980, no other potential "miracle drug" was getting as much media attention as interferon, a naturally produced substance that was found to combat a wide range of common diseases. In the medical pages and the business pages, article after article projected the riches that individuals who invested heavily in the emerging biotechnology industry would accumulate. Touted as a cure for cancer and viral illnesses, the drug had a huge potential market. Yet its practical status was still not assured, for more research was required—research that could plausibly involve human experimentation. The setting, in short, was ripe for legend formation.[10] Who could help but note the irony that, at the same time human bodies were being destroyed with such violence, a potentially lucrative substance produced by the human body was being celebrated as a cure-all. Although the CDC played no direct role in interferon experimentation, folk speculation arose linking the well-known research facility with the inexplicable homicides occurring in its own backyard.

While many informants claimed to have heard the rumor from a friend or relative, several attributed the CDC-interferon link to comedian and social commentator Dick Gregory or author James Baldwin. In his book *The Evidence of Things Not Seen*, in fact, Baldwin identifies Gregory as *his* source, though his version of Gregory's story differs from most of those I collected from informants who heard Gregory lecture. Baldwin, with acknowledged ambiguity, states: "[Gregory] suggested . . . that the key to the Terror was in the nature of a scientific experiment. I am being deliberately vague, but the nature of the experiment was based on the possibility that the tip of the Black male sexual organ contained a substance that might be used to cure cancer." After claiming that Gregory's suggestion did not convince many Atlantans, Baldwin reflects: "I tend to doubt Dick's suggestion because—apart from the fact that I want to doubt it—it seems such an untidy way of carrying on a scientific experiment. But, then, one is forced to realize that a scientific experiment *must* be untidy: that is why it is called an experiment."[11] In the end, however, the original source for the rumor is less important than the fact that it was sufficiently plausible to enough people to guarantee it a healthy tenure on the rumor circuit.

The interferon explanation satisfies the obvious question of why a government conspiracy would undertake the homicides in the first place. If the FBI or CIA indeed risked exposure by becoming involved in such a plot, they must have had a "noble" goal. The idea that the bodies were required for a medical experiment appeals to the belief that whites consider the destruction of blacks as warranted when the majority population ultimately benefits from it. As one African-American male raised in New Jersey claimed, "I heard it was the CIA or the government who was killing the children for experimenting with their bodies, blood, etc. It's been said that only black children's biology was the source of human flesh needed for these experiments."

This perception that a politically and economically powerful population feels entitled to strengthen itself by destroying the bodies of citizens from weaker populations can be examined in another contamination cycle that, similarly, is laden with racist overtones. The "baby" or "body parts" rumors that spread in the international press during the late 1980s alleged that wealthy U.S., European, and/or Israeli citizens have been pretending to adopt Latin American orphans for humanitarian reasons, while in fact they intended to kill them to use their internal organs and appendages for transplant operations for themselves or their children. This cycle does not suggest a focused conspiracy; rather, it details a danger to all peoples of color in the Western Hemisphere. As such, according to the French folklorist Véronique Campion-Vincent, it "deserves to be examined by folklorists and sociologists, who will have more to say than politicians, propagandists, even political scientists about the meaning of belief in such a story."[12] Yet the U.S. government summarily denounced the rumor as a clear example of communist-authored disinformation; accordingly, the USIA limited its investigation to the realm of contemporary politics. After tracing the story's origins to media revelations about unscrupulous adoption rings operating in Honduras, one report concluded:

It is sometimes difficult to distinguish which of the appearances of the allegations is due to unintentional misinformation and which is due to deliberate disinformation. But, one thing is certain. The original misinformation would not have spread so far and wide if it had not been for the way it was cynically used and embellished with deliberate distortions in a disinformation campaign by several communist countries, with the Soviet Union and Cuba taking the lead.[13]

Yet even without the aid of communist propaganda machines, very similar legends have circulated in oral tradition. If the baby parts story was manufactured by the communists to fuel anti-Western sentiments, its authors understood a great deal about folklore.

This theme connecting the dominant population's need for physical components of the minority population is common in folk discourse. Thus the Atlanta and the body parts legends, with their strong racial and urban aspects, resemble the well-known "castrated boy" legend, in which a child is abducted and castrated or killed in a public setting. In the oldest variants of this legend, the victim is a non-Jewish boy whose blood is needed by Jews for Passover.[14] Indeed, prior to the twentieth century the "difference" between the abductors and the victim was most often religion. In this century race began to appear as frequently as religion, at least in versions collected in the United States, with numerous versions reported of the Topsy/Eva contemporary legend cycle in which a black (or white) preadolescent male is castrated by one or two white (black) males in a public restroom.[15] In 1988, without giving any racial clues, I asked a classroom of students if any of them could recall having heard such a story. One white student and one black student proffered a classic Topsy/Eva pair: the white student's narrative involved a young white adolescent being castrated by two black men in a department store in Phoenix (where she lived during her teens), while the African-American's version placed the story in Alabama, with the young victim a black and the assailants white "rednecks."

In these and in many racially oriented legends, the assailants are often said to be motivated by plain meanness or sexual perversion. In the Atlanta, body parts, and anti-Semitic variants, by contrast, the aggressors' need for a certain physical substance forces them to castrate or kill their enemy. The age range and gender of most of the Atlanta victims no doubt summoned up this staple of legend, and, as it has been for thousands of years, it was reshaped to fit the circumstances. Campion-Vincent notes that such seemingly disparate stories share a cluster of related motifs:

the unveiling of a conspiracy, or discovery of a hidden order as meaningful evil, is substituted for meaningless chance or hazard;

a hostile outgroup, scapegoat for the group's tensions, is denounced; often, too, the group's own elite are presented as part of the conspiracy;

absolute evil is contrasted with utter innocence; the victims are the weakest of the group, but also the incarnation of its future: its young children;

the victims are drained of their blood, symbol and essence of life; often they will be cannibalized by outsiders who need *our* [referring to the victims of the conspiracy] vital force.[16]

When they appear in fictional form in a folktale, these motifs supply a potent charge. When they emerge in real-life situations—when the disappearances of real little African-American boys are not satisfactorily explained or when domestic adoption constraints take individuals to poorer countries to find children—it means that affected individuals, frustrated by gaps in the "official" story, are finding their own explanations for inexplicable events.

Once again the anthropologist Mary Douglas's work on pollution sheds light on the popularity of these motifs. She has argued that symbols of group conflict are frequently revealed in forms that emphasize the human body. Body parts become synecdoches for the body, and the body becomes a synecdoche for the group. Thus, attacks on single black individuals are perceived as affronts to the entire African-American community. To protect their "body parts," African-Americans believe that they must guard themselves both as individuals and as a people from white animosity. "When rituals express anxiety about the body's orifices," Douglas writes, "the sociological counterpart of this anxiety is a care to protect the political and cultural unity of a minority group."[17] By circulating these rumors among themselves, African-Americans are seeking to gain some measure of control over threats to their presence and status in a hostile environment.

The Atlanta murder spree activated familiar uncertainties for many black Americans. The tenaciously troubled relationship between blacks and whites caused many blacks to perceive the murders as attacks on them as a people, not just as random attacks on individuals. Occurring nearly thirty years after the onset of the modern civil rights movement, these apparently racist assaults and the substandard investigation into their cause functioned as clear reminders that racial equality has not been realized. In responding to the crisis, African-Americans used folklore to effect solidarity and group cohesion and as a way to combat perceived attempts to destroy the group.

AIDS

At the same time that African-American attention was focused on the events in Atlanta, the first hints of another crisis were beginning to appear in the news as the Centers for Disease Control revealed evidence of a public health problem of devastating impact. And just as the legacy of racism hampered the murder investigation, so has it clouded scientific efforts to understand AIDS and to contain its spread.

Given the opportunity, most folklorists would have predicted that the AIDS epidemic would generate much rumor mongering. From the beginning, the pieces of information that trickled out about the disease cried out for communal interpretation: a previously unknown fatal malady that threatens some groups more than others—gays, intravenous drug users, blood transfusion recipients, Haitians; a disorder transferred by sexual contact or the exchange of blood and bodily fluids; an illness that erupted during a presidential administration at best unsympathetic to the initial populations most threatened by the epidemic; an epidemic that the media chronicled reluctantly at first—no, the best and most imaginative minds among us could not have invented a better folklore-generating disease than AIDS.

One of the first AIDS jokes to gain prominence went:

Q: What is the hardest part about telling your parents that you have AIDS?
A: Convincing them that you are Haitian.

Indeed, in the early days of AIDS research, scientists called the at-risk groups the "four H's": homosexuals, hemophiliacs, heroin addicts, and Haitians. Before long that list grew to include groups that could not be identified with an "H." With the possible exception of hemophiliacs, there is no doubt that these initial groups share a marginal status in our society. As early as 1981, gay activists were pointing out that the government had "dropped millions of dollars into research to determine the cause of Legionnaire's disease, which affected relatively few people. No such outpouring of funds has yet been forthcoming to research the hows and whys of KS [Kaposi's sarcoma—a harbinger of the AIDS virus], a rapidly fatal form of cancer that has claimed far more victims in a very short period of time than did Legionnaire's disease."[18]

More so than most of the other texts discussed in this book, AIDS origins stories are known to a public beyond African-Americans. Unlike the Atlanta child killer or Church's chicken, namely, AIDS is indiscriminate in picking its victims—the list of which, moreover, has grown to include more and more groups beyond the "four H's." Shibutani points out, "Spectacular events with possible consequences for millions result in a sudden increase in demand for news that cannot be satisfied even by the most efficient press service."[19] AIDS certainly falls in this category, and indeed, the rumors are abundant. For instance, I encountered many informants, gay and heterosexual alike, who believed that the disease was an experiment in biological warfare intended to diminish the world's homosexual population. Narratives about "AIDS Mary" also were reported, in which a somewhat naive, young heterosexual man allows himself to be seduced by an irresistible woman; the next morning he finds that she has disappeared, the only trace of her being a lipstick message on a bathroom mirror: "Welcome to the world of AIDS."[20]

Discerning the folkloric elements of these theories is problematic for several reasons. For one thing, the media has played a significant role in reporting and perpetuating AIDS material, making it difficult to distinguish between AIDS lore and AIDS fact. To the layperson, the complexities of the disease and the research into it can be confusing. For example, several informants claimed that the alleged biological warfare experiment began when scientists injected the experimental substance into African green monkeys. At first glance, such a statement might appear outlandish. Yet although respected AIDS researchers do discredit such theories, they in fact believe that African green monkeys may become key in understanding the disease's origins.[21] Many theories about the disease, moreover, are spread in both oral and print discourse, making it nearly impossible to determine if an item is the product of communal folk imagination or of evidence gathered by responsible authorities. Finally, to investigate AIDS from any angle at all is to investigate a mystery that is still unfolding. Because what is unknown about AIDS exceeds what is known, we cannot know what is in fact correct. In other words, some of the theories about AIDS origins that circulate orally may turn out to contain pieces of the truth.

Despite these obstacles, I think it is important, in the context of a chapter devoted to African-American beliefs about

contamination, to include a section on AIDS beliefs. In collecting this material, I was always particularly careful to ask
the informant about his or her source and whether or not this
was an item in folk circulation. Given the growing sophistica-
tion of the media and technology generally, variables that will
surely influence the future shape and direction of folk transmission, I hope that this study will offer some insights into
how folklorists can face these challenges.

After the "four H's," the next populations linked with the
AIDS virus were Africans and African-Americans. With titles
such as "Special Help Needed to Halt Black AIDS Cases,"
"AIDS More Prevalent Among Black Military Recruits,"
"Black Health Professionals Urge AIDS Precautions," and
"Black Man's Teeth a Deadly Weapon, Jury Rules," newspaper, magazine, and television reports have depicted AIDS as
a particular threat to the African-American community since
1982. Although the media have proved adept at reporting
the ostensibly disproportionately high number of diagnoses
among blacks, the reasons why one ethnic group might be
more vulnerable than another are less clear. It is therefore not
surprising that such people have responded with their own
theories about the disease's origins.

I began collecting stories about AIDS as a possible conspiracy against a particular community in the summer of 1987; my
informants include white and black college students, blue-
collar workers, professional people, prison inmates, members
of the armed services—in short, a broad cross-section of the
population. As a result, I have several hundred examples of
AIDS origins beliefs, and many make specific reference to a
conspiracy or contamination plot directed against people of
color.

Several motifs recur frequently. (1) Some branch of the U.S.
government is usually the author of the conspiracy (informants have identified the CIA, the army, the Reagan administration, the Pentagon, the Centers for Disease Control, the far
right, and "the superpowers"), though a couple of informants
in 1987 referred to the "Chicago" version popularized by the
national media, in which Jewish doctors were the culprits. (2)
The contamination targets of the conspiracy are labeled as

Africans or descendants of Africans, either directly or by implication—for example, Haitians, Africans, blacks, black babies, the lower classes, and the outcasts of society. Many informants identify more than one group, claiming, for instance,
that the conspiracy was intended to limit both the gay and the
black populations. (3) The conspiracy is described usually as
either an experiment or as the intentional use of biological/
chemical/germ warfare; hence, the goal is either to learn more
about an experimental weapon or actually to use a known
weapon against a targeted group. (4) The spread of the disease
through groups other than those intended by the conspirators
(such as white heterosexuals) is cited as a big mistake made
by those in charge when the disease became too powerful for
them. (5) Authenticating motifs frequently provide closure in
one of two versions that are not mutually exclusive. An informant might say, "That's why the disease is rampant" within
one of the identified groups or why it is so widespread in a
specified locale—Africa, Haiti, inner cities, San Francisco.
Or the informant will make the familiar comment, "I know it's
true, I read it in the paper/saw it on television"—identified in
folklore shorthand as *r.i.p.* (read it in paper). And indeed, the
media, particularly left-wing publications but also black-
owned, gay-owned, and even straight, conventional forms of
the print and television media, have discussed various versions of this conspiracy motif, whether as fact, possibility, or
hearsay. The idea of the army's inflicting AIDS on undesirables, for example, gained prominence in an Ann Landers col-
umn in 1986. Many informants who identify a specific media
source will also claim to have heard the item "in the street."

Informants almost always begin their reports with a motif
identifying the conspirators—usually "the government" or
"government scientists," though the other parties implicated
could be considered symbolic equivalents for the government. Statements singling out the far right, the Reagan administration, the CDC, and like groups all clearly refer to groups
perceived to have the power to conduct such a mission. The
CIA was the agency most often named. As one informant put
it, "[AIDS was] a chemical experiment sponsored by the CIA
that went awry." Yet I would say that the conspirator's precise

identity is far less important to informants than the contamination plot itself. Informants, after all, have no particular stake
in claiming that the CIA conducted the experiment, as opposed to some other government agency. The frequency of
the CIA attribution appears to stem from the popular association of that agency with covert foreign affairs, making it the
logical group to instigate such an action.

Not surprisingly, the CIA itself views the situation from a
different angle. In response to my inquiry about this association, a CIA spokesman wrote:

We believe that rumors linking the CIA with the development or
the spreading of the AIDS virus, especially in Africa, may be the
result of what we would call "disinformation" efforts of hostile intelligence services to damage the United States. The CIA has had
absolutely nothing to do with either the development nor the
spreading of AIDS or any other virus. The CIA is not carrying out
experiments in this regard and you may document this by corresponding with either the House or Senate Select Committees on
Intelligence which monitor Agency operations. The CIA has under-
taken to try to understand the effects of the AIDS virus around the
world, since it is clear that the spreading of such a disease could
constitute a threat to US national security.[22]

Once again we seem to have a "blame the Russians" explanation for the dissemination of material perceived as disruptive.
In official documents informing American policymakers of
the alleged scope of Soviet disinformation campaigns, in fact,
various versions of the rumor are offered. A 1988 report, for
example, states, "The largest Soviet disinformation campaign
of recent years has made the totally false claim that the AIDS
virus was created in a U.S. military facility at Fort Detrick,
Maryland." None of my informants named the Maryland or
any other military installation by name, though several did
claim the virus was developed in a government, CIA, or CDC
"laboratory." The above report continues, "The main 'source'
for the Soviet allegations, Dr. Jacob Segal, argues that AIDS
must been created at Fort Detrick because it appeared first in
New York which Segal describes as the 'nearest big city' to
Fort Detrick. In fact, New York is 250 miles from Fort Detrick.
Baltimore, Washington and Philadelphia are all closer."[23] Ac-

cording to this convoluted reasoning, because Dr. Segal has a flawed knowledge of northeastern geography, his hypothesis about AIDS dissemination is necessarily inaccurate.

The reports to Congress as well as the letter responding to my inquiry are as provocative for what they do not say as for what they do say. It is troubling to note that in denying the U.S. government–AIDS connection, U.S. Information Agency officials begin by stating, "Science has not yet reached the stage where it would be possible to create artificially a virus as complex as AIDS."[24] By making "science" the subject of the sentence, the report authors seem to be directing attention away from the role Americans have, according to Soviet propagandists, allegedly played in the conspiracy; after all, "science" cannot create a virus, but scientists could. This statement would be more reassuring if it were followed by a disclaimer along the lines of, "and American scientists would not engage in such a research project." But it is not. The authors also make no reference to any other forces that might have fueled the spread of the rumor/disinformation. Implicit in their commentary is the assumption that if the Soviet Union had not perpetuated this information, it would not be circulating among Americans.

Discussion of the conspiracy targets revealed only one real pattern. If an informant had a connection to a particular group of people of color, he or she was more likely to name that group as the intended victims. For example, many Haitians responded to my query with accusations similar to one from a male Haitian postal service employee who claimed that the CIA planted AIDS on that island to curtail "Haitians immigrating into the United States illegally." Like many Haitian informants, this one identified the United States' dislike of former president-for-life Jean-Claude "Papa Doc" Duvalier as instrumental in the decision to spread the disease. Similarly, Africans, as well as people who had recently traveled to Africa, identified that continent as the target of the conspiracy. An African-American female college professor recently returned from Zaire claimed to have heard that the virus was "tried out" both in that nation and in Uganda. Informants with no particular allegiance to Africa or Haiti usually combined the two locales in their commentary. A Jamaican-born female college student, for example, reported that "the AIDS virus was started in Africa and Haiti by the government." Other informants used general labels such as "non-whites," "Africans," "minority people," and "blacks" to refer to the targeted groups. These patterns are not absolute. While not all Haitian informants claimed that the contamination was conducted in their homeland, some did. That is, informants are more likely to focus on a locale they identify with, but that does not mean that all members of a given group personalize the threat.

The contamination motif commonly emerges in one of two ways: the AIDS virus is characterized as either (a) the aftermath of a biological warfare experiment that was tried out on Africans or Haitians or (b) an intentional use of biological warfare *intended to* diminish the African or Haitian population. The former explanation was more common among those I interviewed. While the second option attributes a much more sinister motive to the perpetrators, the first assumes more than just a marginal hostility. After all, few people would disagree that an "experiment" in biological or germ warfare is apt to have negative consequences; in using human guinea pigs, the experimenters are clearly risking the well-being of people they presume to be "disposable." An unemployed white male reported, "The AIDS virus was created in a CIA laboratory. The CIA brought it to Africa to test on blacks, thinking they could watch it, but it got out of control. This is why doctors cannot come up with a vaccine that will work on it. It has to be man-made." Here again we find, as in the Atlanta child killer legend and the castrated boy legend, the rationale that the powerful group needs the oppressed group's bodies for their own enrichment. If people do not know how the tools of germ or biological warfare are tested, they may well assume that the power in question would look for an impotent (pun intended) population on which to refine its weapon. Utility, not evil, motivates the powerful ones.

Diabolical malice is abundant in the second option—the notion that the AIDS virus was intended for the purposes of African genocide. These versions clearly reflect a belief that "they" are out to get us. One young woman who identifies herself as a black American/Seminole Indian stated, "The story was told to me by an aunt. Apparently the CIA was testing to find a disease which would resist any cures known to man. They did this testing somewhere in Africa [South]. The purpose of finding this incurable disease was to bring America back to the old days of the moral majority. Therefore this disease was to be transmitted sexually among the outcasts of society, namely people of color and gay men."

No doubt much of the momentum for the contamination beliefs is provided by a group of highly credentialed authorities who maintain that AIDS is just the latest form of genocide practiced by the U.S. government. Tracing this impulse backward through "Cointelpro" (the code name for an FBI campaign conducted in the 1960s and 1970s to undermine the credibility of "radical" black leaders), the Tuskegee experiment, and slavery, they make the case that whites have always been anxious to rid the world of blacks. Advocates of this theory include medical doctors, college professors, writers, and ministers. A partial list includes James Small, a black studies professor at City College of New York; Robert Strecker, M.D., Ph.D.; and Louis Farrakhan, leader of the Nation of Islam.[25] They also cite cryptic references contained in the World Health Organization bulletin and the Congressional Record. In an articulate and nonequivocating manner, they contribute their theories at any forum that invites them.

For every expert willing to argue that AIDS is the result of a grotesque genocide conspiracy, several others can be cited who debunk these theories and the evidence on which they are based. Both white and African-American experts have little respect for the proponents of conspiracy theory. Chief of infectious diseases at Howard University Hospital, Wayne Greaves, M.D., laments, "I'm too busy worrying about caring for sick patients and educating people about AIDS to get caught up in this kind of inane rhetoric."[26] Once again, the bottom line for most of these experts is not that the United States would never conduct such research, but rather that the scientific community is not sufficiently advanced to create a virus as complex as AIDS.

The facts that the scientific community has discovered

about AIDS often evoke a familiar cluster of stereotypes about blacks. Sexual contact and the sharing of hypodermic needles are two of the most common ways of contracting the disease. The virus destroys the body's immune system, whereupon the victim becomes vulnerable to a wide range of debilitating and fatal infections. The incubation period for the disease is long: an infected individual might show no signs of the disease for as long as ten years after being exposed to it. To avoid contracting the disease, we are told to eliminate the exchange of potentially hazardous blood and body fluid and to practice safe sex.

Persistent beliefs about black sexual licentiousness have permeated Western culture ever since English explorers found their way to the west coast of Africa in the 1550s. Even four hundred years later, following a much acclaimed sexual revolution that supposedly gave permission to nonblacks to enjoy sex as well, many in the dominant culture still assume that people of color overindulge their sexual desires. Since AIDS is in part a venereal disease and a disproportionate number of blacks are succumbing to it, these beliefs continue to be reinforced. Many informants raised the possibility that the whites who might have designed AIDS as an antiblack weapon did so because they were either envious of or felt threatened by black sexual freedom. These jealous scientists made sure their genocidal weapon could be sexually transmitted, for that would guarantee that the disease would spread quickly through the diaspora.

And if unsafe sex didn't bring the disease to blacks, those hypodermic needles that inject illegal drugs into their bloodstreams would do it. Several informants specified "low-class," "underclass," or "inner-city" blacks as the main targets of the conspiracy. Implicit in these comments is the rationale that the conspirators were willing to exclude from annihilation those blacks who adhered to the life-styles endorsed by white society.

Finally, one of the most insidious aspects of the disease is its long incubation period. If one were going to design a disease for genocidal purposes, it would certainly be convenient if it were capable of residing dormant in the body for a while.

Ultimately it will kill its host, but in the meantime he or she will be unknowingly spreading it, with the conspirators likely escaping detection.

Social critics who recognize familiar cultural issues in AIDS discussions acknowledge the strong force coincidence is apt to exert. In her treatment of these AIDS origins beliefs, the essayist Susan Sontag prefaces her comments by drawing attention to the psychological impact the Africa association can have:

Illustrating the classic script for plague, AIDS is thought to have started in the "dark continent," then spread to Haiti, then to the United States and then to Europe, then . . . It is understood as a tropical disease: another infestation from the so-called Third World, which is after all where most people in the world live, as well as the scourge of the *tristes tropiques*. Africans who detect racist stereotypes in much of the speculation about the geographical origin of AIDS are not wrong. (Nor are they wrong in thinking that depictions of Africa as the cradle of AIDS must feed anti-African prejudices in Europe and Asia.) The subliminal connection made to notions about a primitive past and the many hypotheses from animals (a disease of the green monkeys? African swine fever?) cannot help but activate a familiar set of stereotypes about animality, sexual license, and blacks.[27]

Commenting on popular perceptions of the disease, the writer Cindy Patton notes:

AIDS is a class illness: people who share certain common characteristics are vulnerable to particular types of diseases (in this case sexual practice, poverty, immigrant status, and race are other qualities that define disease classes). Put another way, types of people get the diseases they deserve. As AIDS turned up in other populations with no clear parallels to the "gay lifestyle," contagion theories gained popularity. (You can almost see it: Haitians! Intravenous drug users! What next? Say don't those fags vacation in Haiti and consort with lowlife drug elements?—and poof! a theory is born.)[28]

Virtually all of my informants suggested that the epidemic proportions the disease has assumed were in fact a mistake. The conspirators never intended for the population at large to be at risk from the disease. In Dr. Frankenstein fashion, they created a monster that they could not tame; now the best they can do is try to prevent the conspiracy from being revealed and hope that scientists will discover a cure. As one woman maintained, "I have heard that U.S. scientists created AIDS in a laboratory (possibly as a weapon to use against an enemy in the event of war), and they needed to test the virus, so they go to Africa, as they (Africans) are expendable, introduce the disease, and then are unable to control its spread to Europeans and Americans." This motif lends some sense of personal control to those who perpetuate it. The implication is clear that some unseen force has gotten even with those conspirators who generated the dreaded disease, for it now victimizes individuals outside the targeted groups. As a consequence, the government is saddled with a huge financial burden because it must underwrite research for remedies and cures to alleviate the potential impact on whites.

AIDS origins stories as they are disseminated among blacks reveal several facets of the contemporary African-American worldview. Those individuals who find these stories credible consider the "powers" that run America—be they the president and Congress, the intelligence community, the medical establishment, or the right wing—to be consistently ambivalent and perhaps even hostile to African-American well-being. If some "good" for those in power can be gained, the conspirators will gladly sacrifice persons of color—foreign ones in particular, but members of the urban underclass as well. Whereas in the interferon motif of the Atlanta rumors the powerful are depicted as willing to kill a few dozen African-American individuals to perfect a drug that may save countless lives, the germ-warfare-gone-amiss motif in the AIDS lore suggests that no *black* human price is too high to pay in the search for viable instruments of destruction. The fact that some informants maintained that the intended targets of the conspiracy include others aside from Africans or their New World descendants suggests that a certain solidarity might be emerging among groups traditionally at odds with the system. The number of white informants who professed belief in genocide/germ warfare theories, moreover, suggests a feeling that blacks just might be correct in their suspicions about the ill-conceived motives of the government.

With their appealing "divine justice" motif, AIDS origins beliefs allow those who share them to have a laugh at the expense of the makers of the weapon. The ultimate power is not bestowed on the conspirators who planned to eliminate blacks; rather, it is claimed by the disease itself, which became stronger and more destructive than its makers ever anticipated. Now the conspirators are at risk from their own creation, and the folk can console themselves by noting that some force in the world might always step in to prevent the oppressors from succeeding in their evil plans.

Conclusion

The contamination motifs that link Church's chicken, Tropical Fantasy, the Atlanta child killer, and the AIDS epidemic in African-American folk belief are metaphorically the same. The bodies of the individuals purportedly defiled by the chicken, the soft drink, the interferon experiment, or the disease stand as symbols of perceived animosity against the race. Moreover, issues relevant to black sexuality are implicitly or explicitly raised in all of the contamination cycles. Church's and Tropical Fantasy are said to sterilize. The powers that be wanted black genitals in order to extract a potentially useful drug. To curtail the growth of black peoples, scientists developed and disseminated a disease that could be sexually transmitted. Those who subscribe to these rumors reason that the dominant group is preoccupied with the minority group's sexual capacity. This is the one attribute people of color possess that whites cannot steal from them for their own use. But they try. They will extract a substance from a youngster on the brink of sexual maturity in order to devise a miracle cure. They will unleash an epidemic in order to refine a biological weapon. The popularity of these texts, and their connection to the centuries-old castrated boy legends, suggest that allegations of individual sexual impropriety intended to destroy the minority group are apt to erupt whenever the relationship between two groups is charged with mistrust.

Members of the less powerful group will find evidence of conspiratorial activity in the behavior and attitude of the more powerful group. Mysterious deaths and unexplained epidemics within the minority group's population will be attributed to the conspirators' desire to curtail the group's size and limit its access to power. In order to diminish the impact of the potential threat, the less powerful group will create motifs to satisfy the circumstances at hand: if the two groups do not share the same attitudes about sex, this disparity will find its way into the discourse; if young men are disappearing in the same place where medical miracles are being probed, a connection will be drawn; if a previously unknown disease ravages the minority population more than the dominant one, the disparity will be noted; if the dominant culture is pushing something that holds symbolic significance for the minority group, the idea may emerge that that thing has been designed to contaminate.

These motifs will be rendered in items of discourse that can be easily shared by the members of the minority group. Rumors, legends, and other unstructured forms of speech will circulate within the group, providing an outlet for frustrations as well as a means for fostering in-group solidarity. While the content of these motifs suggests that those who find them credible are insecure, the process of rendering such motifs in folkloric discourse, which is then shared with other group members, can function positively, by providing mechanisms through which to monitor the intentions of the dominant group.

Chapter Six

Consumer/Corporate
Conflict

"They won't get me to buy it"

Troublesome Commodities

In April 1991, Eric Miller, head of Brooklyn Bottling, was
fighting to retain his company's hold on the inner-city soft
drink market. Sales of Tropical Fantasy, a popular beverage
introduced less than a year earlier, were plummeting. Inner-
city customers, largely black, who had been the primary consumers of the product were now passing up the forty-nine-
cent twenty-ounce bottles in favor of smaller containers of
national brands such as Pepsi and Coca-Cola. The reason
for the switch? A conspiracy motif—Ku Klux Klan ownership—had become wedded to a contamination motif—"the
mystery ingredient sterilizes." The rumor spread orally, and
soon other familiar contemporary legend motifs became evident. The fact that the television news magazine "20/20" had
exposed the sinister soft drink was offered as authentication,
as was the product's believed absence in areas where whites
might drink it. Xeroxlore quickly surfaced and further perpetuated the rumor.[1]

Like most companies that are the victims of contemporary
legends, Brooklyn Bottling maintains that the rumors were
started by vindictive former employees or unscrupulous competitors. Although most social scientists who study corporate

165

rumors maintain that business rivals do not start or perpetuate such rumors, the bottlers of Tropical Fantasy have in fact amassed an impressive amount of evidence which suggests that if their competitors did not launch the story, they might well have actively perpetuated it.

In this chapter, I will examine the consumer/corporate conflict as it pertains to African-American culture. After briefly reviewing the companies that have been the target of rumors or contemporary legends among blacks particularly, I will identify a cluster of attributes that these companies share, and that some African-American consumers consider to be particularly ominous for their community (Table 1). From this examination we can develop a hypothesis about the corporate products and policies that will most likely stimulate black customer ambivalence of the type manifested in contemporary legends, a folk idiom used by blacks to justify their reluctance to patronize certain companies. The fact that Brooklyn Bottling shares only some of the characteristics exhibited by those companies will be used to support the company's conclusion that its competition may have started or at least actively exploited the Tropical Fantasy rumor.

From the corporate point of view, any rumor that casts a shadow on its products or reputation is an evil. As Fredrick Koenig, a social psychologist who studies the impact of rumors on American corporations, puts it, "Next to an act of terrorism, what corporations fear most is that they may be targeted with an outlandish tall tale."[2] Journalists, African-American elected officials, watchdog groups that monitor white supremacist trends, and folklorists have scrutinized the targeted companies and reached the conclusion that they are innocent of the allegations in question. Nevertheless, these companies do maintain practices and policies that can jeopardize black consumers.

Chicken

Fast food restaurants and contemporary legends have had a long and, from the companies' perspective, distressing relationship. Any entrepreneur considering a franchise operation

TABLE 1. *Mercantile Rumors in the Black Community*

Company	Alleged Conspirators	Goals
Beverages:		
Adolph Coors Company	Ku Klux Klan	sterilization/use of profits to oppress blacks
Tropical Fantasy	Ku Klux Klan	sterilization
Fast Food		
Church's Fried Chicken*	Ku Klux Klan	sterilization
Kentucky Fried Chicken	Ku Klux Klan	sterilization
Popeyes Famous Fried Chicken & Biscuits	Ku Klux Klan/ present owners	promotion of David Duke
Tobacco:		
Kool	Brown & Williamson/ Ku Klux Klan	sterilization
Marlboro	Philip Morris*/Ku Klux Klan	sterilization
	R. J. Reynolds/Ku Klux Klan	sterilization
Any menthol	Present owners (various)	increase in cancer rate in black men
Athletic Wear:		
Adidas	South African Co. or Gov't.	use of profits to oppress blacks
British Knights	Ku Klux Klan/South African Gov't.	use of profits to oppress blacks
Converse	South African Co. or Gov't.	use of profits to oppress blacks
Nike	South African Co. or Gov't.	use of profits to oppress blacks
Puma	South African Co. or Gov't.	use of profits to oppress blacks
Reebok*	Ku Klux Klan/South African Gov't.	use of profits to oppress blacks
Troop*	Ku Klux Klan	use of profits to oppress blacks

* Represents best-known items

featuring fried chicken would do well to study the folklore, for such poultry-pushing enterprises—among them Kentucky Fried Chicken (KFC), Church's Fried Chicken, and Popeyes Famous Fried Chicken and Biscuits—seem inordinately destined to confront contemporary legends. That linking KFC with a deep-fried rat is one of the most tenacious stories in American folklore scholarship.[3] Known to all, this contemporary legend narrates the unintentional contamination of a customer who purchases a fried rat served up as a piece of chicken.

When I first collected rumors linking Church's and the KKK in 1985–86 (see Chapter 3), nearly all of my informants identified Church's as the culpable corporation.[4] Likewise, when I asked students in an African-American folklore class about rumors linking the KKK to a contamination plot, all but one of those who knew the item named Church's. In subsequent years, however, the same rumor alleging the ongoing contamination of fast food chicken by a company secretly controlled by the KKK has diffused; now, the two other major fried chicken concerns are also apt to be singled out by those African-Americans familiar with the rumor. When I queried 110 students in an African-American studies class in 1990, half of those who knew the item identified Church's as the guilty company; the other half linked the rumor to either KFC or Popeyes.

Although ultimately Popeyes, after it assumed control of Church's, was able to mitigate the impact and dissemination of the rumor connecting CEO Al Copeland to ex-KKK Grand Wizard David Duke, the parent company has not been immune from association with other items. Several informants, for example, claimed that Copeland stole his recipe from a black female domestic servant who once worked for his family. Other informants told a similar story about KFC founder Colonel Sanders's formula for finger-lickin' good chicken and about the Church's recipe. I call this the "Imitation of Life" cycle, after the 1930s melodrama in which a white businesswoman builds a fortune from her black maid's pancake batter recipe.

Beverages

Like the fast food chicken companies, the Adolph Coors Company has been the object of several folk allegations. More so than other company leaders under consideration here, members of the Coors family have often taken controversial public stands on charged issues. It is therefore not surprising that rumors have emerged about the company and its product.[5] In the black community, the most popular one alleges that Coors family members belong to the KKK, with profits from the brewery being used to perpetuate the Klan's antiblack agenda. Although many of the professed opinions of the Coors family are decidedly conservative, I uncovered no evidence linking members of the Coors family with the KKK.

Tropical Fantasy's battle with Klan rumors began at the end of 1990. By early 1991 young blacks were handing out flyers stating the allegation and substantiating it with the false claim that an exposé had appeared on the TV newsmagazine "20/20." Graffiti artists have used their talents to perpetuate the rumor as well. The *Wall Street Journal* describes this scene: "A burned-out building covered with graffiti includes the slogan: 'Oppressors are not our protectors.' Just under that spray painted warning a chalk-scrawled postscript adds: Tropical Fantasy."[6] According to *Newsweek*, "Angry customers have threatened distributors with baseball bats and pelted delivery trucks with bottles; some stores even refused shipment."[7]

While the most potent folklore genres of the postindustrial age—rumor, graffiti, Xeroxlore—were being put to work to spread the notion that Tropical Fantasy was a KKK-inspired anaphrodisiac, the company fought back with all the standard damage-control tools. They had their products tested by the FDA and made the results public; they hired a truck to drive around black neighborhoods with a billboard denying the KKK allegation; they hired a black public relations team to propose strategies by which they could reclaim their customer base. Individuals respected in the African-American community were enlisted for the campaign. The mayor of New York, African-American David Dinkins, guzzled the soda on television; community clergymen denounced the rumor.[8] Finally, although the story maintained a tenacious hold, some of the strategies—which in the end included giving away free samples[9]—paid off, and after three months of poor sales orders for the soda began to pick up.

Before long, similar fruit-flavored soft drinks marketed in other East Coast cities were being named in rumors. Sales for such drinks as A-Treat and Top Pop diminished. The Pennsylvania-based bottlers of Top Pop did not launch an aggressive counteroffensive; rather, the company's president, Jeffrey D. Hettinger, issued a one-page denial and responded to subsequent inquiries by saying only, "At this point in time, I think the least said, the better."[10] In this he followed the lead of many companies named in contemporary legends, who choose not to confront the charges directly lest the publicity backfire and fuel the story's dissemination.[11]

These small but smart soft drink bottlers have more than just a suspicion that their larger competitors started or at least fueled the transmission of this particular rumor. Before the allegation emerged, the success of Tropical Fantasy, which black consumers seemed to prefer over the big-name colas, was irksome to the drivers who delivered Pepsi and Coke to inner-city grocery stores. Small beverage companies are accustomed to sometimes nasty fights over the limited refrigerated shelf space available in corner groceries. As the editor of a beverage trade magazine put it, "It's hard to think there's space in coolers for anybody aside from Coke and Pepsi."[12] Investigators eventually traced the flyers back to someone who allegedly received them from an employee of Pepsi.[13] If the rumor was being fueled by the competition, moreover, the culprits were most likely the union truck drivers for the northeast Pepsi and Coca-Cola bottlers, not the companies themselves. Given the notorious territoriality of unions in the greater New York area, the drivers might well have welcomed any opportunity to eliminate the competition's attraction to the black community. One store manager acknowledged that "a Pepsi salesman warned him: Don't buy it—I'll give you no credit."[14]

Tobacco

For at least thirty years, the KKK has figured prominently in black-oriented rumors about the tobacco industry. Several informants who smoked in the sixties, for example, recalled a rumor alleging that Kool cigarettes, a menthol brand preferred by many African-American smokers, was owned by the KKK—with the substitution of a *k* for the *c* in *cool* serving as confirmation.[15] In the early 1990s, similarly, several black smokers told me that Marlboro was Klan-owned, one "proof" being the presence of three hidden *K*'s on the package.[16] Many informants claimed that Philip Morris and R. J. Reynolds, the men for whom the larger American tobacco corporations are named, were original members of the KKK. In other versions of the rumor, rather than linking specific tobacco manufacturers with the Klan, informants claimed that those companies marketing menthol cigarettes have been increasing the amount of menthol in the formula to accelerate the formation of lung cancer in black smokers or to cause smokers' lungs to bleed. It is, after all, common knowledge that blacks prefer menthol cigarettes over regular ones.[17] Nonsmokers who knew the items were generally quite vague about the threat; most could only recall hearing from a smoker that the KKK owned one of the tobacco companies.

Athletic Wear

The chicken, beverage, and cigarette rumors all contain conspiracy and contamination motifs: the Ku Klux Klan owns the corporations in question; the ingestion of the tainted chicken and the contaminated drinks causes sterility; smoking the wrong cigarettes will increase one's chances of contracting cancer. Because athletic wear is not orally consumed, it makes sense that rumors about such companies lack overt contamination elements. These stories do, however, highlight conspiratorial practices—as we have seen in Chapter 3, on alleged links between the KKK and Troop athletic wear, and Chapter 4, on Reebok and South Africa. Nike, British Knights,

Puma, and Converse have also been connected to antiblack conspiracies.

Common Threads

What do cigarettes, chicken, and sneakers have in common? Why have several companies that manufacture these goods been the target of rumors that some blacks find so seductive? What kinds of companies might anticipate similar attacks in the future? The answers to these questions lie in the way these companies, their leaders, and their products are seen by the folk who disseminate the rumors. In particular, the reputation of businessmen associated with the product, product price, corporate marketing strategies, the utility of the product, and risks implicit in the use of the product can be threaded together to disclose an atmosphere in which conspiracy and contamination rumors might be generated.

Products or places having strong symbolic potency for African-Americans may inspire folk speculation that is then manifested as rumor or contemporary legend. Similarly, names and spellings of products can stimulate strong associations, often negative, that find their way into rumors. Consider, for example, the very name *Church's* and the fact that a white-owned company so named is selling chicken to black people.[18] Because houses of worship have been the traditional religious, political, social, and cultural oases for African-Americans, any company named Church's will be monitored closely. Similarly, British Knights sneakers and Kool cigarettes both trigger a Klan association, the first because Ku Klux Klansmen refer to themselves as Knights, the second simply because of the misspelling of *Cool*. The controversy over Tropical Fantasy soft drinks, tellingly, emerged in communities populated largely by Caribbean-born blacks, who clearly were not drawn in by any sense of nostalgia associated with the name. Gary Alan Fine has pointed out that the folk may associate Adolf Hitler with the Adolph Coors Company, thanks to their similar first names.[19] When Reebok company executives were trying to pinpoint how the association with South Africa had come about, they recalled that a reebok was a South African gazelle. As for Troop athletic wear, in addition to being an unfortunate acronym—*To Rule Over Oppressed People* —the name is a noun describing a unit of military personnel as well as a verb denoting aggressive military marching. Modern-day white supremacist regimes, of course, are known for their militaristic aggression and survivalist tactics.

Companies with their headquarters or production bases in the South are also apt to draw the attention of black consumers. This could be called the "Dixie factor." Although in the minds of many African-Americans the South still represents an overtly racist history and philosophy, these blacks will generally voice a preference for some aspects of southern life. One informant summed up this attitude by saying, "In the South, they [whites] don't try to play like they are your friends like they do up here [Boston]. You know where you stand with them down there." It is no accident that virtually all of the fast food chicken corporations and major tobacco companies have strong corporate ties to the South. Many informants compared their own or a family member's southern fried chicken recipe to that served by Church's or KFC. Another common observation was of the tobacco stench in certain North Carolina communities and of the presence of black men and women in the tobacco fields and processing plants.

Athletic wear, too, has strong symbolic significance for African-Americans. After all, the sports and entertainment industries were probably the first real loci of high-status opportunities for blacks. As a result, sports figures and even whole teams are the heroes of many young African-Americans. These same youths frequently state that their greatest chance for financial success is in professional athletics. In their preparation for this possibility, which begins at a very early age, wearing the correct sneaker is quite important.

Subliminal Messages

Superficial factors alone do not necessarily destine a company or product to be named in a rumor. In addition to sharing these coincidental threads, most of the companies and products described here also possess less obvious common denominators that contribute to the black public's wariness. In their comments on the rumors about athletic wear, cigarettes, and fast food chicken, informants repeatedly emphasized three elements: product price, potential risks, and negligible utility. The following formula is a useful way of looking at the relationship among these three factors.

$$\text{Price} + \text{Risk} > \text{Utility} = \text{Rumor}$$

In discussing cigarettes, for example, informants would complain about the rising cost of a pack of cigarettes and the health hazards of smoking, liabilities that far outweigh any positive utility associated with smoking. Most smokers claimed that the desire to look mature or cool to a peer group caused them to begin smoking in the first place. But by the time I interviewed them, addiction seemed to be their only reason for continuing; no one claimed that any real good came from the habit. It is much easier to identify the positive aspects of eating at fast food restaurants, such as low cost relative to other types of restaurants and ease of preparation. Even so, a certain ambivalence about these convenience factors was evident in informants' comments as well. After reciting a rumor about Church's or Popeyes, for example, informants were apt to comment on the cost of eating out versus the cost of purchasing and preparing fried chicken at home, the calories and fat content of the fast food chicken, and the basic wisdom of patronizing such establishments. One African-American woman wove into her telling of the Church's/KKK rumor the observation, "You know, with Church's, their food is so greasy, there has got to be a *lot* of cholesterol in it."

In their recitations about Reebok or Troop, informants paid a great deal of attention to the rising cost of the product; indeed, I noted a marked increase in the Reebok/South Africa stories after the $175 Pump basketball shoe entered the marketplace. One informant responded to a query about the Reebok rumor by mentioning both the cost and the risk factors: "I'm not sure if it's an actual conspiracy. However, there is no doubt in my mind that athletic footwear companies actively seek the African-American market. They may inadvertently encourage illegal activity and foolish spending." Here, "illegal activity" can range from stealing the money to buy the coveted shoes to snatching the shoes off the very feet of an unsuspecting wearer. In other words, the risks associated with athletic wear were often identified as matters of personal safety. Violence is in fact a deplorable by-product of the youth culture's infatuation with trendy fashion. Informants recited numerous instances in which individuals wearing designer products were physically assaulted and even killed for their clothing by their peers. Given the high financial cost of Reebok and Troop products and the potential for physical intimidation, the genuine usefulness of such items, particularly for individuals who are not athletes, was deemed low by informants. One woman concluded her version of the Reebok rumor by criticizing companies that "encourage poor blacks [to] spend their money on useless items, thereby keeping them poor."

In each of these examples, a perception had developed in the rumor-telling public that the costs and risks associated with a particular product outweigh its usefulness to the consumer. The likelihood that beliefs about a skewed price/risk/utility ratio will generate rumors increases for companies that employ specific kinds of marketing strategies. Both too much and not enough advertising are suspect in the minds of the folk—a theme that I call the "for blacks only" motif.

While selling their products in the black community, Troop, Church's, and Tropical Fantasy did negligible advertising. Informants were disturbed by the incongruity of a large company that brings its products into the black community unaccompanied by the standard advertising campaigns of modern-day America. In asserting the plausibility of the Church's rumor, informants referred to the chain's high visibility in black communities only. Troop's dependence on minority consumers was even more apparent; that clothing line was blatantly marketed to appeal to black and Latino youths, with no real effort made to hype the products to white customers. Indeed, many of my young white informants had never even heard of the Troop company. The infamous flyer that spread word of Tropical Fantasy's alleged white supremacist ties contained the following rationale: "THEY ARE ONLY

PUT IN STORES IN HARLEM AND MINORITY AREAS. YOU WON'T FIND THEM DOWN TOWN . . . LOOK AROUND. . . . "[20]

If Church's, Troop, and Tropical Fantasy aroused black consumer suspicion with their advertising silence, Reebok and Philip Morris did the same by bombarding black consumers with carefully crafted appeals to purchase their products. These two highly competitive companies, of course, simply wish to attract as many consumers as possible, regardless of color. Yet both companies have also developed marketing strategies targeted specifically at a black audience. Like most major athletic wear corporations, too, Reebok hires celebrity spokespersons, many of whom are professional black athletes, and sponsors many of the kinds of athletic events attended by young blacks. The corporate competition for the African-American market is in fact so strong that some observers have blamed not only Reebok but all the large athletic wear companies for fueling violence in the black community, a violence inspired in part by lust for their high-priced products.[21] Philip Morris will not break down its advertising budget, but one need only peruse the pages of *Ebony, Essence,* and *Jet* magazines to find numerous ads displaying attractive, sophisticated-looking African-Americans holding that company's cigarettes. Philip Morris also supports many visible black enterprises, sponsoring such well-known artistic companies as the Alvin Ailey Dance Troupe and underwriting leadership grants in inner-city areas; in this way the company is making sure that its name is associated with goodwill toward the African-American community.

Companies in two of the industries discussed here—athletic wear and tobacco—have been the objects of intense scrutiny by African-American leaders. In August 1990, the Reverend Jesse Jackson urged black consumers to boycott all products manufactured by the Nike corporation, and he offered several reasons.[22] The company, he claimed, while marketing its very expensive athletic wear to appeal to black consumers, had shown little corporate responsibility in its dealings with blacks. Although African-American consumers purchase 30 percent of all Nike shoes, blacks had no Nike executive positions, no subcontracting arrangements, and no

seats on the company's board of directors; moreover, the footwear giant did not advertise with black-owned media outlets.
With the possible exception of such celebrity spokesmen as
film director Spike Lee and basketball superstar Michael Jordan, both of whom received large sums in exchange for product endorsements, Nike simply was not sharing its profits with
blacks.

The most prominent and outspoken African-American critic of cigarette companies has been President George Bush's
secretary of health and human services, Dr. Louis Sullivan.
Appointed in 1989, Sullivan led the successful attack on R. J.
Reynolds's plans to market its new Uptown menthol cigarette
specifically to black consumers.[23]

While the fast food chicken industry has not been singled
out in like manner, the 1980s and 1990s have seen increased
attention devoted to the nutritional habits of minority communities. In particular, Secretary Sullivan and other public
health authorities have lamented the high rate of heart disease
among African-Americans, a condition that is linked to fried
foods and foods with high sodium contents—staples in the
diets of many African-Americans. Few individuals outside the
fast food industry itself would defend the menus of any fried
chicken franchise as harmless for black Americans concerned
about their cardiac well-being.

The grounds on which these prominent African-American
authority figures have challenged these companies and their
products may seem more legitimate, or at least more tenable,
than those rooted in the rumors and contemporary legends
we have been discussing. But let us not forget the timing
and impact of the folk discourse. Although these items are by
nature difficult to date, certain coincidences are pertinent.
My fieldwork suggests, for example, that the tobacco rumors
began to surface in the mid-1960s, not long after Surgeon General Luther Terry's now-infamous report on the health hazards of smoking. The Church's/KKK rumors gained popularity
in the early to mid 1980s, at about the time widespread concern with cholesterol and fatty foods emerged. The athletic
wear rumors also gained credence in the mid-1980s, shortly
after the first shooting deaths linked to designer sneakers and

jackets. In short, the perpetuation of these rumors suggests
that the folk take quick action as soon as negative evidence
begins to implicate a company or industry. Well before Sullivan, Jackson, and other authorities began to urge blacks to be
wary about certain products, members of the community itself
had initiated a process of separation from the once-coveted
items. In fact, these rumors might be construed as early warning signs signaling the emergence of ambivalence over potentially hazardous products and allowing the folk to justify their
disloyalty to commodities that shortly before had enjoyed
considerable favor.

While most consumer products can probably be considered
"nonessential," some pose a genuine threat to our well-being.
If the companies that produce them have made them extraordinarily attractive, they become particularly hard to surrender. When members of a folk group begin to sense that certain
goods are not good for them, they will share their suspicions
with like-minded members of the group. African-Americans,
like all consumers, have few viable weapons with which to
deflect the increasingly sophisticated appeals of Madison Avenue. Corporations invest enormous amounts of money and
energy into convincing the public to purchase nonessential
items—such as fast food, athletic wear, and cigarettes. Eventually, however, consumers will fight back with the few resources available to them. None is more potent than the folk
idioms of late-twentieth-century life.

Gary Alan Fine has argued that when a certain type of product stimulates anxious rumors among consumers, related
products are likely to generate similar stories.[24] With multiple
modes of discourse, black consumers will fight against the
ubiquitous billboards, glossy advertisements, coupons, and
television commercials. For some black consumers, the ex-
hortations of African-American authority figures about the
negative aspects of a product will be enough to convince them
not to buy it. For others, the belief that the Ku Klux Klan is
benefiting from the money spent will be a stronger incentive
to boycott a product than the less volatile invectives of a black
man in a three-piece suit. I have found, moreover, that blacks
wanting to make intelligent consumer choices will generally

try to absorb all the information about a company they can. More often than not, they will weave the "truth" they uncover into their recitation of a specific rumor.

The price/risk/utility formula works least well with the rumors about Tropical Fantasy. At forty-nine cents for twenty ounces, the product is far more affordable than any of its competitors. While soft drinks may be nonessential products, they do not pose the health risks that tobacco and fried foods do (though the sugar content might be considered a risk to persons with a weight problem). So how can we explain the impact of this rumor? Let us recall that the Tropical Fantasy item may well have been perpetuated by "outside agitators," whereas the chicken, athletic wear, and tobacco allegations were sufficiently powerful that they needed no external catalyst. Although the product's provocative name and a marketing strategy targeted at black consumers may have been enough to provoke a folk response, Brooklyn Bottling is perhaps justified in its suspicion that corporate competitors or delivery drivers for those competitors actively fueled the rumor's dissemination.

The price/risk/utility formula, I believe, can help to illuminate industry policies and practices that are prone to generate black consumer ambivalence. The Tropical Fantasy case study indicates that unscrupulous businessmen may be learning how to manipulate folklore for their own purposes. Clearly, the folk imagination does not randomly identify products to avoid. A logical and practical process is at work, with the power of folk belief behind it.

Chapter Seven

Crack

*"See, they want us to take
all of those drugs"*

As I was conducting fieldwork for this book, I encountered informants who, while relating a text on the deleterious side effects of fast food chicken or the government's complicity in the spread of AIDS, made oblique references to the problem of illegal drugs in urban America. At first, such comments seemed tangential. It was not until I was well into the process of transcribing the other texts that I recognized a pattern in these remarks, which generally appeared as motifs of closure: "That's why they don't really want to do anything about drugs, too—they will do anything to keep the black race down."

In 1989, I began pointedly to ask informants if they had ever heard a connection drawn between the proliferation of illegal drugs in African-American neighborhoods and either indifference on the part of the law enforcement community or an organized conspiracy. The results were staggering. No single topic discussed in this book generated as much response as did illegal drugs. Hundreds of informants offered to share information they had heard "in the street" about the hidden reasons behind the law enforcement community's inability to halt the flow of drugs into black neighborhoods.

To investigate these rumors, I not only collected as many versions of the item I could, but I also sought to identify the information available to the American public about the sources of and policies regarding illegal drugs. Once again, I found circumstantial evidence and symbolic associations to merge in ways that spurred the circulation of the folklore. Although the conspiracy and contamination motifs reappear in the context of beliefs about illegal drugs, I feel that this category deserves a chapter of its own. For one thing, the sheer volume of versions I amassed makes drug lore a particularly fruitful cycle for exploring the paradigms of rumor development in the black community. That volume also indicates a topic of particular importance to the folk. This country's enormous drug crisis has defied almost all efforts at mitigation; examination of this cycle of beliefs may well help us to understand why the problem is so tenacious.

Overview

I have collected well over two hundred versions of rumors linking drugs in black neighborhoods with some type of conspiracy from all over the country, from various occupational groups (though some 75 percent, I must note, came from students), and from all ethnic backgrounds and ages (my oldest informant was in her late sixties, my youngest was fourteen). To my knowledge, I did not collect from anyone addicted to illegal drugs, though several prisoners I interviewed were former users. Drug-related conspiracy rumors were more familiar to white informants than had been the case with the consumer-oriented items described in previous chapters, but still not universally so. Given the diversity of backgrounds in my informant base, I would not be surprised to learn that some of the people I spoke with had used illegal drugs at some point in their lives. Yet no one rendered such a confession, and I chose not to ask. Many did volunteer that they had family members and friends who were "strung out" on drugs. I am comfortable with the generalization that close to 100 percent of my informants opposed illegal drug use and were very concerned about its devastating impact on the black community.

The following seven items are a representative sampling

of the texts I have collected. They were the first comments delivered by informants in response to the directive "Describe any theories you may have heard linking drug abuse among blacks to a white conspiracy or plot," and they contain all of the most frequently mentioned motifs.

Text #1: I have often heard that there is a conspiracy to destroy the black man. In this conspiracy this demonic system is trying to destroy black youth by using miseducation to brainwash them. Once they become miseducated, they are forced to obtain poor jobs. With poor jobs they are forced to live in poor communities. Within the poor community, drugs are placed and blacks are forced to sell or use drugs for survival or escape.

Text #2: The conspiracy of European America to practice genocide on blacks through drug abuse includes the purchase of drugs by the government and the direct transportation [of the drugs] to the areas of high black population. This practice, along with miseducation, the injection of weapons into our communities, and the constant programming of self-hate, form the parts of genocide.

Text #3: I've heard that it is the work of the government or an even more powerful group to destroy the black race with drugs, mainly powerful artificial substance today—crack cocaine. It is an effort to rid the country of an unwanted element. Crack cocaine became a major problem during the term of Ronald Reagan, as did an increase in black on black crime. Some say he is the devil in human form. The number of letters in his name = 666 [that is, each of Ronald Wilson Reagan's names contains six letters]. I have heard it talking among my friends, a discussion that had to do with the present plight of blacks. I subscribe to the theory that drug abuse is planned, because it could be done away with. Oftentimes those in power are corrupt.

Text #4: Evidence of "benign neglect" can be seen in the various police corruption scandals—selling drugs into neighborhoods where they [the police] *don't* live; the fact that while blacks are a prime consumer market for drugs, we don't seem to be in charge of much beyond low-level distribution ("Someone's getting rich —damn sure ain't us!"); the fact that the drug crisis was a crisis in the black community long before it became a national rage, but didn't become important until white teenagers came home with holes in their noses.

Text #5: Television [is] slaughtering blacks on drug abuse. They never show the whites. But in reality 80% of crack users are white. Television shows the blacks in poverty. Troop clothing and shoes are allegedly manufactured by the KKK because they know black teens and drug dealers will buy the products. I always hear drug abuse is genocide to blacks.

Text #6: I have heard on several occasions that drugs were brought into black communities by whites so that the blacks could be controlled. Blacks would die out due to the power struggle in the drug market. Death would also be caused by diseases—AIDS.

Text #7: The FBI had a plan to get rid of blacks in office. That's why they set up Marion Barry. They want to use drugs to eliminate all blacks—the poor ones—the ones in office they can't control.

Who are the Conspirators?

As texts 1, 2, 3, 6, and 7 suggest, the conspiracy motif was explicitly or implicitly present in most versions. In general, "the government," "the powers that be," or "higher ups" were identified as the conspirators, though some 10 percent of informants specified the CIA, and another 10 percent specified the Reagan administration, even well after George Bush's inauguration. According to one man incarcerated in a federal penitentiary for drug trafficking, the Reagan administration is the most common scapegoat named by federal prison inmates. When I followed up initial responses, I discovered that most informants had no real stake in defending any specific conspirators; for most, the groups were interchangeable, all equally willing to engage in such a plot. No one ever said anything like, "No, President Reagan wouldn't have done that, but the CIA would."

We have already discussed the mistrust many blacks have for the nation's major law enforcement agencies. The FBI in particular, probably because it implemented the "sting" operation that resulted in the arrest of Washington, D.C., mayor Marion Barry on drug use charges, was often indicted by informants for antiblack actions. Local law enforcement figured large as well. In texts like #4, for example, many attributed the alleged conspiracy to a group a rung or two below the federal government—namely, corrupt police departments or, in a variant, organized crime groups. Their goal is not so much the elimination of the black race but rather the profits that can be made by keeping illegal drugs flowing steadily into minority communities.

The informant for text #5 incorporates the media into the allegation, offering the genocide motif at the end of his statement. Like others who claim that the media are perpetuating a large-scale antiblack conspiracy, he feels that press coverage grossly exaggerates the extent of the drug problem in the black community while ignoring the positive achievements of African-Americans. Because the major media outlets—television, film, newspapers, magazines, and radio—are advancing the government's conspiracy by bombarding the public with images of drug-pushing and drug-abusing blacks, all blacks suffer.

In popular culture, blacks are very often portrayed in terms of negative stereotypes. Television programs and feature films consistently depict blacks as drug pushers and drug abusers; news stories often focus on black drug use and the criminal activity generated by it. In the early winter of 1989, Charles Stuart, an upwardly mobile white retailer, had no trouble convincing the world that an armed black gunman had shot him and his pregnant wife as they left a prepared childbirth class at a Boston hospital. Although Stuart's account exhibited some logical incongruities, it was not until a family member came forward with evidence that Stuart had shot himself and murdered his wife that his accusation was questioned. Informants cite this and other examples of black bashing as evidence that the media is interested only in negative stories about African-Americans.

Circumstantial Signals

No doubt an official representing the "powers that be" would look at the range of accused conspirators in these sample texts and note that many of the individuals and agencies responsible for drug enforcement policy are incriminated by the folk: the president; international, national, and local law enforcement groups; and specific government agencies, such as the Drug Enforcement Agency and U.S. Customs. In people's minds, in short, the enforcers have become conspirators—a conclusion that can be defended by referring to verifiable data about the alleged malefactors.

Presidents Reagan and Bush, in that order, were the individuals most commonly designated by informants as major participants in the alleged conspiracy. Yet during their campaigns and their terms in the White House, both men advocated strong antidrug measures; and as first lady, Mrs. Reagan was a motive force behind her "Just Say No" campaign. Why, then, do the folk perceive these leaders as drug use instigators rather than as drug law enforcers? In considering motives, most blacks interviewed did not confine themselves to these presidents' public positions on drugs alone, but pointed also to their positions on racial issues. In particular, the sweeping changes in the Justice Department under Reagan, apparent indifference to urban decay, and vocal opposition to Affirmative Action programs were construed by many as evidence of deep-seated racial hostility. Informants who maintain that George Bush continued a plot first implemented by Ronald Reagan cited the "Willie Horton incident" or Bush's 1990 veto of a civil rights bill as proof of his indifference to black well-being. Informants demonstrated an impressive command of factual information about Reagan and Bush policies and statements about blacks.

Following the arrest of Marion Barry on drug use charges, FBI and Justice Department spokespersons were clearly chagrined by the attention devoted to their reasons for pursuing the Washington, D.C., mayor. As these agencies saw things, they were merely following through on the mandate to track down drug users. In the eyes of the folk, however, the Justice Department was unfairly singling out a black elected official because the powers that be disliked seeing blacks in positions of influence. Most informants did not dispute the facts of the case or deny Barry's probable guilt; indeed, many made extraordinarily derogatory comments about Barry. But they were appalled by the energies and monies that went into the sting operation that brought Barry down. Over and over again, people speculated that similar efforts would not have been made if Barry had been white.

Much is revealed about the Justice Department's own attitude about the Barry case in its report "Toward A Safer America: The Justice Department's Record of Accomplishments in the First Two Years of the Bush Administration." In the section entitled "Combating the Drug Scourge," thirty-two cases are listed as exemplars of the department's success. The arrest and conviction of Barry on misdemeanor charges is number thirty-two. All the other cases are felony drug cases involving assorted capital crimes, numerous guilty parties, and the expenditure of millions of dollars to bring about their arrest. A newspaper synopsis on Barry reads, "Former Washington, D.C. mayor Marion Barry was sentenced in October 1990 to six months in prison following his conviction in August of illegal narcotics possession after an eight-week trial on narcotics and perjury charges. Barry was arrested in January 1990 at the Vista Hotel in Washington, D.C. by FBI agents and Washington, D.C. metropolitan officers. He is free pending the outcome of his appeal."[1]

What Drugs?

Initially, most informants would state merely that the conspirators either introduced illegal drugs or allowed them to proliferate (see texts 1, 2, 4, 5, and 6). When I asked what drugs, most specified cocaine, crack cocaine, and heroin. Many older informants recalled first hearing the rumor in the mid-1960s, when attention to a nationwide drug problem began to surface and heroin was considered the most expensive and addictive illegal drug. It is easy to see why rumors connecting heroin abuse with establishment goals to oppress blacks would have circulated at that time, for it was an era of widespread antiestablishment sentiment among both blacks and whites. "Don't trust anyone over the age of thirty" was the motto of a whole generation. It was in the sixties that police officers became "pigs" and Negroes became "blacks." The "inner city" and the battles fought there between confrontational blacks and establishment-sponsored pigs were being discovered and scrutinized by the mass media. Even during the sixties, heroin use was never romanticized as were those drugs with which young whites were experimenting, the ones glorified by rock stars and radical college professors—LSD, marijuana, mescaline, hashish. Heroin addiction was the awful end to which "dabbling" in those other drugs might lead.

My younger informants named crack and cocaine as the culpable drugs in the present incarnation of the ongoing conspiracy (see text #3). They stated that the rumors surfaced around 1985—in the middle of the Reagan years—when crack abuse began to spiral out of control. Some version of this rumor has probably existed ever since illegal drugs began to circulate in minority communities. As we shall see, the rumor resurfaces when blacks observe two phenomena. First comes the disturbing evidence that a new or notoriously satisfying drug seems to be posing a greater than normal threat to the black community's well-being. At the same time that the drug's shattering effects are being noted, blacks perceive increased white resistance to growing black access to powerful positions. Jean-Noel Kapferer states, "A rumor's eternal return thus attests to the realization, on the basis of propitious events, of an explanatory system deeply embedded in collective consciousness."[2]

Targets of the Conspiracy

My informants tended to identify virtually all blacks as the targets of this conspiracy. In some 10 percent of cases, the black *man* specifically was identified. As we have seen, many antiblack conspiracy theories pose the black man as the ultimate target, a perception that perhaps both echoes and feeds the media reports so common in the late 1980s and early 1990s on "the plight of the black male." Yet even in this 10 percent sample, the conspiracy was seen to extend beyond the realm of just the males (see text #1). Most texts propose a conspiracy designed to have a domino impact on the entire black community. In this scenario, the alleged conspirators expect a particular population, such as black underclass teenagers, to consume the drugs. Their drug habits will disrupt and erode their families; and to feed their drug habit, the teens will pursue "black on black" crime. Eventually the entire community is made to suffer for the sins of the drug abusers.

Text #7 represents an important variant within this drug lore cycle, for it emphasizes that the conspiracy is intended to bring down not only powerless blacks, but powerful ones as well. Not surprisingly, these texts were most common after Marion Barry's January 1990 arrest, his trial in August of that year, and his sentencing the following October. Some texts, however, identified Julian Bond and Andrew Young as examples of powerful black elected officials whom the conspirators were anxious to discredit by spreading accusations of illegal drug abuse.

Authentication

Three modes of authentication were offered for informants' beliefs. About 10 percent of those interviewed employed supernatural imagery, a common motif in folklore (texts 1 and 4). At first glance, text #1's passing reference to the plan as "demonic" might not suggest strongly that the devil is perceived to be behind the conspiracy, but as text #4 indicates, hell is exactly where some informants place the conspiracy's home base. That text uses a common formula for revealing satanic influences in earthly phenomena: identified in the Book of Revelations as the "sign of the Beast," the presence of three hidden sixes is often cited as evidence of the devil's handiwork.[3]

Most informants referred to the traditional rumor conduits when attempting to authenticate this item. Some cited "popular spokespersons" such as Reverend Louis Farrakhan, Dick Gregory, and Frances Cross Welsing as their source. Virtually every major news or talk show was mentioned, including associated personalities—Geraldo Rivera, Oprah Winfrey, Ted Koppel, and so forth. "In church," "in school," and "in the street" were also common refrains. Many younger informants referred to rap music in general or specific rap artists such as Ice T, Public Enemy, and NWA. Many people have heard the item from several sources and so stated simply, "I hear that every day, everywhere, in my neighborhood."

Just as many people claimed that the AIDS conspiracy had gotten out of control when heterosexual whites began to be infected, many advocates of the drug conspiracy theory argued that the powers that be never intended illegal drugs to become a problem for whites. Older informants, for example, made the case that in the sixties the drug crisis was so named only after drug abuse became rampant in middle-class white homes. The informant in text #4 makes virtually the same claim about the past decade's cocaine abuse.

Tangled with Truth

Many informants constructed a world in which drugs are just one weapon in an overall assault on black communities (texts 1, 2, 4, and 6), with "miseducation" being another weapon (texts 2 and 3). In the latter case, reference was made to overcrowded classrooms, decrepit school buildings, and overworked, inadequately trained teachers as evidence that the conspirators were determined to prevent African-American academic progress. Substandard services and "poor jobs" were also cited as undermining African-American achievement. In texts 5 and 6, other rumors were offered as components of the overall antiblack conspiracy; AIDS beliefs were most commonly cited, but some informants included references to athletic wear items as well. In these cases, the intended impact of the conspiracy is the destruction of the black race.

Malicious Intent or Benign Neglect?

The drug conspiracy rumor can be divided into two basic categories. About 80 percent of my informants reported what I call "malicious intent" texts, in which the drugs are supposedly being fueled directly into black communities in an active attempt to undermine this population. When I asked them for their own opinion, however, most professed greater belief in what I call "benign neglect" items. In these versions, the government is merely perceived as doing little, if anything, to halt the drug abuse that is destroying black communities, because African-American well-being is a low priority.

Belief

In analyzing this rumor cycle, it was difficult to determine whether informants actually believed it. Some stated categorically that they did not; others stated specifically that they did. Most informants, however, said merely that the item was "plausible," particularly given the mixed signals the government sends on the issue. A common response went something like, "I'm not sure, but you have to wonder where all these drugs come from." (One of my favorite comments was that of a young California female college student who mused, "If they can keep the medfly out of California, surely they could keep out drugs.")

Age, race, gender, and occupation did not seem to influence belief in the rumor. The only major difference I encountered relative to this issue was in the degree of conviction expressed by those informants, all black, whom I would call "hard-core believers." In 1988, a young black woman from Boston answered my question about belief by saying, "Yes, I believe R. Reagan is an unscrupulous tyrant with a profound hatred for black people." Of those whites who claimed to accept the rumor, none professed the same sort of absolute certainty. A typical response was that of a twenty-year-old Connecticut-born white woman who said simply, "Unfortunately, I think it's real."

Responses from the "Conspirators"

The powers that be are, for the most part, as anxious to deny these rumors as they were to debunk those linking the FBI with the Atlanta child killer or alleging the deliberate infection of blacks with AIDS. Of course, my training as a folklorist is not equal to the task of uncovering a massive conspiracy that, if it exists, has thus far escaped the scrutiny of investigative journalists and similar professionals. Nevertheless, I did

Thank you for your recent letter. In the coming months, I will be speaking about the important issues facing our country and I appreciate having the benefit of your views. You might also wish to write to President Bush, your Senators and your Congressmen so that they, too, can know of your thoughts.

With best wishes,

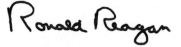

5. Form letter response from the offices of former President Ronald Reagan, received October 1990.

ask some representatives of those parties identified in my texts as conspirators to comment on the rumors. Of particular interest are the responses from the office of then ex-President Ronald Reagan and the Office of National Drug Control Policy. The former is curious simply because it in no way reflects that anyone on his staff actually read my letter (see Fig. 5). In stark contrast is the reply I received in 1990 (during the Bush administration) from the Office of National Drug Control Policy. Speaking on behalf of then "drug czar" William Bennett, the deputy chief of staff described the agency's exposure to and position on the conspiracy rumors:

We have read from time to time—in newspapers and magazines—about "rumors" that Federal, state, and local authorities are engaged in a conscious conspiracy (either by action or neglect) to maintain high rates of drug use in inner-city black neighborhoods. But interestingly enough, during dozens of visits to inner-city neighborhoods over the past year or so—and talks with black elected officials, policemen, teachers, doctors, community workers, and residents—it's an idea that (so far as I can remember, at least) had never come up directly. As a result, the short answer to the second of your questions is that, no, we do not have a strategy for combatting such suspicions—we have not really ever been required to address them.

I would nevertheless hesitate to write off the existence of such rumors (however prevalent or obscure) as "irrelevant" or "insignificant" . . . I would probably say, instead, that measured in dollars, the level of Federal anti-drug effort has almost doubled just since late last summer [1989], and that comparably intensified effort is being pursued by many state and local jurisdictions across the country. An appropriately large—and desperately needed—percentage of this work is targeted at urban communities with large black populations. So basic facts themselves contradict a conspiracy by neglect theory. And evidence to support the grotesque suggestion that drugs are being officially "planted" in inner-city areas is nonexistent.

We would naturally be distressed to learn that some significant portion of black public opinion believes otherwise; the most current national polling data I've seen suggests that a healthy majority of black Americans approves the goals and direction of recent efforts against drugs.[4]

Implicit in the numerous condemnations of former President Reagan that I heard in my interviews was the conviction that he was, at best, indifferent to and, at worst, hostile to the issues important to African-Americans. While I did not really expect a personal response to my inquiry, the fact that no one on his staff even tried to fashion a comment appropriate to the content of my letter only underscores the disinterest on the part of his administration that so upset many of my informants.

The letter from the deputy chief of staff of the Office of National Drug Control Policy offers other insights into why some African-Americans mistrust the government. In the first paragraph he carefully explains that although his agency knows that such beliefs exist in the black community, they have chosen not to deal with them. Why? Because they have read about them in newspapers and magazines but have not heard them from their black community contacts. Of course, it is not surprising that these contacts have not seen fit to share the rumors with the government representatives, for those representatives are not within this rumor's *public*. If the "black elected officials, policemen, teachers, doctors, community workers, and residents" find the theory plausible, they are not likely to tell a government official who might be party to it about the conspiracy.

The deputy chief of staff emphasizes annual increases in federal expenditures on the antidrug effort as evidence that no conspiracy either of neglect or by design exists. Other Bush administration officials also allude to the money spent on the antidrug effort, including the fact that expenditures have mounted relative to Reagan administration outlays. When informants discuss the financial aspect of the drug war, however, they don't compare one summer to another, or even one administration to another. Rather, their focus is on the monies reserved for *other* government projects—usually those outside the United States. In the sixties, informants commented, while the cities deteriorated money was being spent to send a man to the moon; more recently, vast funds have been earmarked for the Star Wars defense system, White House china, foreign aid, the savings and loan bailout, and Operation Desert Shield, while social spending continued to plummet.

In his final paragraph, the deputy chief claims that according to poll results, "a healthy majority of black Americans approves the goals and direction of recent efforts against drugs." In my fieldwork, to be sure, I encountered many informants who approve of the *stated* goals of the federal, state, and local law enforcement agencies. But that approval did not eliminate anxiety that a nefarious *unstated* agenda might be at work.

Responses from Informants

Some African-American social critics have disparaged individuals who believe drug conspiracy rumors. Commenting on a *New York Times* poll indicating that 25 percent of blacks accepted such rumors, while 35 percent found them plausible, the writer Shelby Steele said, "If you actually believe that the society in which you live is feeding AIDS and drugs to you, to eliminate you, you're not going to see your own possibilities in that society. . . . You're not going to make the effort to move into the American mainstream. It's a profoundly destructive belief."[5]

My informants focused largely on the perceived disparity between the policy statements of the powers that be and their actions in defending the idea of a conspiracy. A question that arose quite frequently was, "How do these drugs get into black neighborhoods in the first place?" It is in fact the possibility of this *unstated* agenda that caused informants to speculate on governmental misdeeds. The following case studies demonstrate how two very different informants responded to cultural cues in coming to believe the drug conspiracy rumor.

Case Study #1

When I first interviewed Lisa (not her real name), she was a senior majoring in biochemistry with a minor in Afro-American studies at the University of California, Davis. Although she eventually plans to attend medical school, her short-term goal upon graduation was to get a job as a laboratory technician. When we had our final interview eleven days after her graduation, she had just been offered an excellent professional position at a major food company in the San Francisco Bay Area, with a starting salary at just under $30,000. The daughter of a Mexican-American woman and an African-American man, Lisa has stronger ties to her black relatives than to her Latino ones.

In our first interview she told me that she had heard that "drugs were being planted in the black community by the government in order to keep black people down." I asked her if she believed the rumor, and she said, "I think it's possible, very possible." When I asked her from whom she heard it, she responded, "Lots of places, it's everywhere. I know I heard Minister Farrakhan say it in San Francisco." I then asked her if she had ever heard it prior to hearing it from Farrakhan, and she said, "Sure."

As Lisa's brief biography suggests, she is a goal-oriented individual. With one foot in the corporate world and an eye on medical school, she certainly does not fit Steele's description of someone who cannot see possibilities for herself in American society. Why, then, does she find plausible the notion that the government is introducing drugs into her community? Most of her comments on this issue reflected the enormous frustration she feels because the police seem unwilling to fight the drug trafficking in the Bay Area community in which her family lives. What used to be a solid working-class neighborhood has deteriorated into a crack-infested, crime-ridden slum. She noted that everyone on her street knows which houses are crack houses and what hours they conduct business. Yet the police do nothing. She was particularly aggravated by the lack of treatment programs. She described a cousin who "wants to get off—really wants to get off—but she can't get any help. Why can't someone help her?" She also expressed concern about a thirteen-year-old sister. Although the adolescent did not use drugs, Lisa was worried that peer pressure might entice her to try them. To combat such attractions, Lisa frequently invited her sister to visit her in Davis, hoping that she would thus be stimulated to keep her grades high and eschew the omnipresent drugs. Nevertheless, Lisa remained fearful that these visits were only brief respites from the increasingly desperate surroundings that her sister faced every day.

From Lisa's point of view, the changes in her neighborhood had all come about because of crack and the crime generated by the demand for crack. When she was an adolescent, the drug was not yet on the horizon, and she felt perfectly safe on her street. Now she always worries about whether her car will be stolen; and when she wants to go for a walk, she drives to a safer (white) neighborhood to do so. Although she acknowledged that the neighborhood pushers are all black, they must, she said, be getting the drug from somewhere. When she heard Louis Farrakhan suggest that crack was a custom-made addictive substance distributed in black communities to continue black oppression, the statement rang true. She also heard similar comments from other college students, likewise concerned about whether younger siblings would be able to "get out," and these made sense to her as well. When frustrated contemporaries of her grandmother's complained about this latest "trick" in the white man's antiblack arsenal, she could muster no evidence to the contrary. And if telling her younger sister that snorting crack only fulfills the desires of whites conspiring to sabotage her well-being would deter the young woman from trying drugs, so much the better. Lisa, in fact, is typical of a large number of informants who perceive themselves as engaged in a personal war against crack. They do not see the government as an ally in this war. As she put it, "The more politicians seem to talk about how awful it is and how much they are going to do about it, the worse it gets."

Violence per se does not figure prominently in Lisa's or any other account, though several informants noted that the government could no longer get away with lynchings or starting riots to keep blacks down, and so the drug conspiracy represented a viable alternative. Indeed, drugs are an appropriate tool to this era, in which antiblack violence is at least superficially condemned. Lisa's frustration with the lack of drug law enforcement is echoed time and again in the reports of other informants and can be verified by hard data. Boston-based informants, for instance, referred often to the endemic police corruption in that city. Lisa and other Californians, too, commented on police corruption as well as police brutality. In the winter of 1991, when the nation's attention was repeatedly called to the videotaped Rodney King beating, informants often cited that incident as verifying police contempt for black citizens.

A striking aspect of Lisa's account is that it contains little genuinely disputable information. Although I have never been to her family's neighborhood, it fits an all-too-familiar description of contemporary areas invaded by crack. The potential threat to her younger sister is no doubt quite real, for today drugs and associated crime are evident even in the best of neighborhoods. And police corruption and brutality are genuine concerns in many American locales. Lisa also placed much weight on comments her African-American father and grandmother had made regarding past racial injustices. To Shelby Steele and probably to the deputy chief of staff of the Office of National Drug Control Policy, these factors may not add up to a premeditated conspiracy. To Lisa, that theory is at least as good an explanation as any other she has heard.

Case Study #2

David is an African-American man in his early thirties presently incarcerated in a federal penitentiary in the Midwest.[6] Describing the role drugs played in his life, he stated, "My own involvement has been extensive—drugs—but primarily from an economic front. I did not use." While in prison he has worked to maximize his knowledge of African-American history; he reads voraciously, relying on outsiders such as myself to send him relevant books and articles. He also writes for a prison newsletter. His political activity behind bars, on behalf of black prisoners' rights, has gotten him into trouble with the officials on more than one occasion. At times, he seems quite pessimistic about his chances of living out his prison sentence.

It almost goes without saying that David and his fellow inmates are concerned about police brutality. He maintains that society at large sanctions police violence—that in physically assaulting blacks, police are fulfilling the desires of the white majority population.

David recalls hearing the rumors linking drugs in the black community to a conspiracy prior to his incarceration, but he paid them little attention; now, however, such talk dominates prison discussion. He reports, for instance, that "most [inmates] stated that Reagan was responsible for the conditions that led to their involvement in drug use." Invariably this perception was used to support a conspiracy theory: "I did it—drugs—to make it through another day of disappointment from job hunting, or to cope with my old lady complaining about me not working. Reagan knew that if you were out of work, you had to do something to get over the frustrations of being unemployed. So drugs were the answer. Being high made it easier to cope." In collecting texts from other prisoners, David heard such comments as, "If Reagan didn't put it up my nose or in my arm, he sure as hell made it easy for me to sell it. So in a way he is still guilty."

Equally discernible in their accounts is the idea that the system is forever conspiring against blacks. One rumor, for example, states that "white scientists in the medical field have conducted experiments to determine which drugs are the most potent to blacks or which drugs they would most likely become addicted to." Some of David's companions also believe that the media are a party to the conspiracy; he states on their behalf, "Some inmates felt that the media was playing a subtle role in getting blacks to use drugs, e.g. glamorization, just say no, when in fact they're saying 'Try it, you'll like it,' etc.—others felt that since they-blacks-were being blamed for it anyway, they may as well use it."

David and his fellow inmates justify their beliefs much as Lisa and the other students I interviewed did. In addition they state, for example, that "blacks did not have the means—planes boats, etc.—to get the drugs over here. And the United States had the means to stop it. They—government—obviously wanted it—drugs—to get through." David incorporated Reagan's parsimonious stance on drug treatment programs into his assertions about the ex-president's personal role in the conspiracy: "Reagan's policy that absolutely no federal money be spent on drug treatment programs must have come about when he realized that blacks would benefit the most from them."

David's summation reveals much about how he fits his conspiracy suspicion into his overall worldview:

What then is irrational about our fears? And if there is no proof that a conspiracy exists to destroy the Black assertive minded male, what proof is there to say none exist? Certainly it would be irresponsible to equate *all* of the social ills that face blacks as part of a gigantic conspiracy to destroy us. But it would be equally irresponsible to deny such a conspiracy does not exist. Motive, means and opportunity is usually the elements that must be overcome to either prove that a crime either existed, or was committed. These elements can be established in the case of a conspiracy to destroy "undesirables"

specifically the black male. Drugs is but a small means, in this mad-
ness. While we—Blacks—may have the power to "just say no!["]
to this menace, we are powerless to say anything about the unseen . . . the unseen power structure behind it all.

For both David and Lisa, the drug conspiracy theory not
only confirms the folk history passed on to them about blacks
and racism but also begins to explain the seemingly incon-
gruous command that illegal drugs hold over their race. Indeed, many of the black students I interviewed were hard-
pressed to explain their presence and success in college when
cousins, siblings, and even parents had succumbed to the
stranglehold of crack. Sharing these beliefs with one another
allowed them to celebrate their own savvy—"They're trying
to keep blacks down, but look at me!"—and at the same time
to mourn those less fortunate—"How could they help themselves, when the government was out to get them?" In Lisa's
case, the rumor was partially responsible for her commitment
to make things better for her community by working in the
medical profession.

The rumor plays both a positive and negative role in
David's life as well. Much more so than Lisa, he is mistrustful
and often contemptuous of the dominant society. But despite
the constraints of his situation, he is engaged in a vigorous
program of self-improvement as well as in the education of
his fellow inmates through his writing activities.

Lisa and David's accounts disclose one overall similarity
that is of critical importance: both summon up unassailable
facts to support belief in a drug conspiracy. Corruption on
local and national levels *has* contributed to the proliferation
of illegal drugs in this country. The media *have* depicted
blacks as drug pushers and drug users. Foreign policy decisions under Reagan and Bush *did* result in a deplorably casual
relationship with those countries that supply drugs to the
United States. The only component of their stories that can
be genuinely debated is the motive for this indifference on
the part of the government and law enforcement agencies.
Recall that while most of my informants initially presented
versions in which "malicious intent" directed drug policy,

they actually framed their own beliefs in terms of "benign neglect." Whatever the truth of the allegations, the mere existence of these texts serves to underscore the tenacity of metaphors linking racial disharmony with perceived attacks on individual black bodies.

Conclusion

This book began with a consideration of beliefs among Africans captured as slaves in which it was speculated that whites kept showing up on the shores of western Africa in order to obtain more black people to eat. In this manner, Africans made sense of a very real cultural assault by symbolically simplifying it into terms meaningful on a personal, physical plane. In the nineteenth-century discourse of blacks born in the New World, the cannibalism motif was eclipsed as extreme physical cruelty and sexual exploitation grew ever more severe. Unfortunately, the texts of the antebellum rumor mill proved all too often to describe the actual situation in which generations of African-Americans found themselves. In the aftermath of the Civil War, four million blacks had to face the challenges of a world in which many whites still bore them extreme malice. With no reparations offered for their enslavement, blacks were launched forth into freedom possessing little more than their bodies. As soon as they began to accumulate anything else, whites, disguised in sheets, galloped up to seize their belongings and torment their bodies. The distinction between good whites and bad was further muddied by the migration from South to North. As a consequence of these experiences, conspiracy and contamination motifs arose to identify or explain the menaces discernible in the landscape.

In the twentieth century the signals remained mixed. The identities of the good and bad whites fluctuated. Ample evidence—white supremacist violence, law enforcement brutality, dubious medical experiments—suggested that the bodies of blacks were still disputed terrain. In the 1950s and 1960s, nearly one hundred years after ratification of the Fourteenth Amendment, that article's promises were still in the process of being codified. And blacks were painfully aware that the dominant culture had not yet reached a consensus on bestowing its blessings on the descendants of slaves. Today the political climate, for the most part, condemns overt attacks on black bodies. Evidence of covert violence, however, is easy to find. Black elected officials are assassinated or drummed out of office; previously unknown diseases and devastatingly potent drugs decimate whole communities of blacks. As some African-Americans attempt to reconcile the contradictions implicit in these signs, they embrace the familiar notion that the dominant culture remains intent on destroying blacks—one body at a time.

Chapter Eight

Conclusion: From Cannibalism to Crack

In a cogent and even-handed April 1992 *Newsweek* essay, author and journalist Lorene Cary laments the obstacles that have inhibited African-American achievement: "We Americans continue to value the lives and humanity of some groups more than the lives and humanity of others. That is not paranoia. It is our historical legacy and a present fact; it influences domestic and foreign policy and the daily interaction of millions of Americans."[1] Cary offers the weekly newsmagazine readers a brief overview of the kinds of overt and covert racist animosity to which black Americans have been subjected from the slavery era until the present. *I Heard It through the Grapevine* elaborates on the antiblack practices and policies that undergird a persistent, tenacious racial mistrust that often defies the well-meaning efforts of both blacks and whites who value the lives and humanity of all Americans equally. This book seeks to delineate the connections between the realities of black oppression and the folk discourse that has been developed as blacks have sought to secure their place in America. In these final pages, I would like to retrace the path from cannibalism to crack, pointing out the detours and the shortcuts that complicated or eased my trek.

In reviewing the course of this journey, I want to acknowledge that I have not blazed this trail alone; I have not written this book in a vacuum. Real life touched my work in two ways. First, new cultural and political issues germane to material included in the book always seemed to arise—usually right after I had declared the relevant section finished. Second, like most of my colleagues I must squeeze my fieldwork, library research, and writing into a professional life that consists primarily of teaching undergraduates and, in my case, a personal life that involves a husband, young son, and a large network of relatives and friends. As I conducted my interviews and read narratives, diaries, government reports, and scholarly books from a wide range of academic disciplines, I shared the results of my research and tried out my ideas on students, colleagues, and family members. Chapters 3–7 include many of their versions of a particular rumor or legend. But these encounters with the folk gave me more than just additional versions of rumors and personal commentary that I could use in exploring the evolution and meaning of a rumor cycle. Rather, the comments, questions, and sometimes awkward silences of the people with whom I spoke, not to mention relevant developments in local, national, and international affairs, movies that I attended to "get away," and the lore itself, have all given shape to the conclusions I now want to share about this material.

Origins and Sources

Folklorists are always being asked, "Where did that legend (tale, myth, joke, song, riddle) begin? What is the source?" The question plagues us because people want to hear concrete answers, yet the actual explanations are vague and almost always impossible to verify. Nonetheless, we recognize the importance of understanding origins and so have developed various academic sleuthing strategies with which we trace contemporary items back into the recent and remote past. For example, after I accidentally ran across the Church's/ KKK legends during a course on black literature, I eventually managed to pursue all relevant versions back to the late 1970s. But after pinpointing that era for the development of the fast food fried chicken texts, a more profound question of origins emerged, one having less to do with Church's chicken per se and more with the underlying contamination and conspiracy motifs. When did African-Americans begin to share beliefs about white malice that is focused on the very bodies of black people? Who were the culprits before Church's management came to be targeted? Before the Ku Klux Klan was in existence? What did these malevolent whites want to do with black bodies before the idea of castration arose? When did beliefs about what whites were willing to do to the bodies of African-Americans first circulate? In short, the Church's chicken rumors were built on conspiracy and contamination motifs popular long before the company even existed, and it was this entire chain that mattered.

From Cannibalism to Corporal Punishment

I wrote my Ph.D. dissertation on slave narratives—a corpus of largely firsthand accounts of the circumstances surrounding their enslavement. Of the handful that recount the actual passage from Africa to the New World, a surprising proportion reveal that both in the coastal holding pens and on the slave ships rumors circulated in which the whites were described as cannibals transporting the captives in order to eat them. The sundry writings of white slave traders and explorers substantiate the beliefs evident in the slave narratives. The whole *Amistad* case would never have made its way to the U.S. Supreme Court if the Mende-born Cinque and his fellow captives had not accepted that such would be their fate as well.

While an enormous range of cultural, social, and political differences distinguished them, Africans and Europeans did have one thing in common: they shared a fundamental human impulse to characterize unfamiliar peoples whose looks and lives were unlike their own as cannibals. The Topsy/Eva phenomenon, in which nearly identical rumors circulate within white and black populations, was first manifested as whites used cannibalism accusations to justify the enslavement of Africans, even as Africans warned one another about whites who intended to eat those whom they took away on ships.

When I review this material in my African-American studies classes, many students express bewilderment and disbelief. At times, the very individuals who insist that Church's *really is* owned by the Ku Klux Klan and that the chicken *does* contain a spermicide refuse to believe that Africans ever believed their fate was to be the meal of their white captors. Some students find the cannibal rumors untenable because they reinforce stereotypes depicting African stupidity and primitiveness. How could Cinque and the others have possibly believed that whites were planning to eat them? Didn't they realize they were going to be made to work? But if Africans are to be judged "stupid" and "primitive" for concluding that whites were cannibals, what do we say about the whites and blacks who for centuries have accepted at face value the belief that cannibalism was an intrinsic component of all African tribal life? What about the whites who so readily concluded that Cinque and his fellow slaves had practiced cannibalism in their native land? Rumor and legend scholarship leaves no group unscathed. It reminds us that all folk groups may accept as fact implausible information that individuals outside that group perceive as utterly specious. Such is the nature of legends and rumor. To those removed from the concerns of the group in question, the rumor is absurd; but to group insiders, the item makes complete sense.

Many students have no problem accepting that some African captives circulated beliefs about cannibalism, particularly once they can begin to think about the slave trade from the point of view of the Africans rather than of the traders. They come to college classrooms with little knowledge of the mechanics of the slave trade; in their mental maps, a dotted line connects the ports of the New World to the ports of the Caribbean to the west coast of Africa—and that is the extent of their understanding. Few students, white or black, have ever been asked to think about the slave trade from the perspective of those individuals who were enslaved. Clearly, slave narratives and any texts that can be mined for African perspectives need to be moved to the foreground of studies of this era.

By the fall of 1991, this material was less incredible to my students. Cannibalism, after all, had taken on a new currency with the release of the hit movie *The Silence of the Lambs*, in which a pivotal character was a white 1990s cannibal. More compelling than the success of this film, however, were the horrific revelations about a real-life serial killer/cannibal, Jeffrey Dahmer. Over several months in late 1991 and early 1992, the American public faced the story of a white blond male who lured young men of color to his Milwaukee apartment in order to kill them, have sexual relations with them, dismember them, and eat them. Although his erratic behavior had captured some police attention and his black neighbors had called in numerous complaints, Dahmer's status as a white male protected him from the kind of scrutiny a black male would have received in similar circumstances.

In the second half of Chapter 2, I focus on rumors that circulated in conjunction with several twentieth-century race riots and during the two world wars. Most of my research for this section was completed in the late 1980s—before U.S. soldiers were sent to the Persian Gulf in Operation Desert Storm in 1991 and before the riots that erupted in East Los Angeles and several other cities during the spring of 1992. As these 1990s events unfolded, I had an opportunity to monitor crisis rumors firsthand. What follows is a brief overview.

Although Operation Desert Storm did not approach the magnitude of a world war, it was the first time in recent memory that young Americans faced the uncertain prospect of sustained armed conflict. Almost as soon as the first troops were dispatched to the Persian Gulf, rumors began to circulate about the "real" reason President Bush was so willing to come to the aid of the Kuwaiti people—namely, to kill off the black population. "He wouldn't be sending them so fast if there was nothing but white boys in the armed services," said one African-American male undergraduate. While most people I spoke with on the topic were less emphatic, they did express concern and uneasiness over the unfortunate fact that economic circumstances forced so many young blacks to enlist in the military rather than go to college. Those few who actively subscribed to the rumors often supported their beliefs by making reference to the racial composition of U.S. forces in the Gulf. (African-Americans make up approximately 12 percent of the population of the United States, yet 25 percent of the troops in Operation Desert Storm, and nearly half of the female troops, were black.)[2] Many informants, both those who subscribed to a war conspiracy rumor and those who did not, also introduced President Bush's vetoes of two significant pieces of civil rights legislation into our conversations. Fortunately, the Persian Gulf War lasted only six weeks, and there were relatively few American casualties. Based on those texts I did collect, as well as the nature of the rumors that emerged during the world wars, I suspect that if the Gulf War had continued, rumors alleging a connection between racism and the willingness to sacrifice American lives would have become increasingly popular in many black communities.

On the afternoon of April 29, 1992, I was working in my campus office with the radio on in the background. A news flash reported that the four Los Angeles Police Department (LAPD) officers on trial in Simi Valley, California, for the brutal beating of Rodney King had been acquitted. Knowing that my department chairman never listened to the radio while he worked, I crossed the hall to share the news. He was not surprised. He had followed the trial more closely than I had and sensed that the prosecution was not making its case. As I left his office, I commented that L.A. was going to be taken apart that night. He disagreed. He had visited the area recently and believed that there would be limited protest. When I saw him the next day, he shook my hand and said, "You called it." Needless to say, I felt no satisfaction in being right in this prediction. But based on the research reported in Chapter 2, I knew how often blacks trace their participation in a riot to a story claiming that particularly heinous abuse of a black body has occurred (e.g., East St. Louis 1917, Chicago 1919, Belle Isle 1943, Chicago 1967). If mere rumors of a white assault on a black body had moved blacks into action in the past, then the very real acquittal of whites who had been videotaped beating a black man was almost guaranteed to prompt a violent response.

In the days after the verdict was announced, rumors began to surface. Although I have not investigated these cycles thoroughly, I can report a few versions. One particularly tenacious rumor, which I heard from blacks, whites, and Latinos, alleged that Daryl Gates, then Los Angeles chief of police, had

intentionally held back police in the first few hours to allow
the rioters to gain momentum, thereby increasing the likelihood that blacks and Latinos would look bad on television.
Many informants authenticated the rumor by pointing to the
sluggish response of the LAPD to the initial outbreaks of violence.[3] In some versions, informants claimed that they knew
someone who had recognized off-duty police officers "riot-
ing" in plain clothes. These informants claimed that the police wanted to do everything they could do to make L.A.'s
black and Latino communities look bad.

Some white informants from Southern California reported
hearing that armed gangs had organized and were heading
into white neighborhoods to spread the violence to ostensibly
insulated communities. Since the officers had been acquitted
by a nearly all-white jury located in a predominantly white
community, these rumors may reflect a feeling that the black
and Latino communities planned to get even with whites for
letting Rodney King's attackers go free.

My first experience with genuine crisis rumors confirms
many of the assessments made in Chapter 2. African-Americans still often express ambivalence about fighting "for America." The belief that black bodies are valued less than whites
does exist, and, as noted above, I suspect that had the Persian
Gulf War lasted longer, cycles echoing this sentiment would
have proliferated. The Los Angeles riots also stimulated familiar rumors. For many, Rodney King's bruised body had
come to symbolize the collective body of African-Americans
in the 1990s. In this case, of course, rioters based their actions
on more than a mere rumor. The chaos and uncertainty that
followed the verdict fueled the perpetuation of rumors that
reveal the extent of suspicion and mistrust that persist between the races.

From Cannibal Lore to Klan Lore

Given that the Ku Klux Klan has always had as its foremost
goal the perpetuation of white supremacy, it is not surprising
that Klansmen are the individuals most commonly believed
to be behind antiblack conspiracies. In fieldwork and re-

search on Klan-related rumors, I was always amazed at the difference between white and black characterizations of the Ku Klux Klan and its power in contemporary American society. Many of the concerns raised by my informants are exemplified by a March 1992 story on white supremacy and the political ascendancy of former KKK grand wizard David Duke in the Sunday magazine supplement to the *San Francisco Examiner* and subsequent correspondence.[4] The article delineated the disturbing rise in racially motivated confrontations and assaults throughout Northern California and the Pacific Northwest, and it inspired numerous reader comments in the form of letters. One of these revealed a strong reluctance to take seriously a Klan presence in Northern California. After ridiculing the fashion sense of a tartan-clad Santa Rosa neo-Nazi depicted in a photo accompanying the article, and claiming that white supremacism represents ignorance more than evil, the writer insisted: "The problem is in the south, where poverty levels are the highest in the nation and where a good education is a privilege, not a right."[5]

Although the letter offers no clues about the author's race, I suspect he is white. His comments are reminiscent of those offered by my white students who cannot understand how any educated person could believe the Klan capable of fast food genocide. Presumably the letter writer was unable to accept the presence of white supremacists in a region noted for its culture and intelligentsia. The coexistence of neo-Nazis and Klan enthusiasts with the writers and artists of Marin County and University of California faculty struck a note too discordant to be endured.

Whereas this individual could not accept the existence of the Klan outside the South, I repeatedly encountered informants who assumed the Klan was everywhere. From running fast food chains to manufacturing basketball sneakers, the Klan had discarded its white sheets in favor of white shirts in order to pursue its antiblack agenda. Epitomizing white supremacy at its most threatening, the KKK retains a powerful position in the imagination of black folk. Yet white informants and colleagues persisted in making comments similar to those of the letter writer above: they could not understand how educated blacks could feel any real threat to their well-being from the Klan. As a rule, whites underestimated the Klan's reach while blacks overestimated it.

Why do blacks attribute such power to the Klan? The potential of white supremacists to hurt African-Americans in fact stems from both destructive power and symbolic power. Informants referred often to the dominant culture's willingness to tolerate blatant racist acts. Brutal beatings of randomly selected blacks are not uncommon even today, yet law enforcement agencies often do too little to find and punish the assailants. Fighting the Klan, however, necessitates more than prosecuting its members when they perform illegal acts. A prominent white supremacist like David Duke has no problem keeping his name and face in the news; when he runs for political office, the cameras follow, and enough people vote for him to ensure that he will run for another office. The lyrics of several heavy metal groups promote antiblack violence; fans buy the records. Klan groups have succeeded in securing parade permits and air time on local-access cable television networks. To many blacks, the Klan's ability to use the Constitution and the legal system to get away with these unsavory but essentially legal activities suggests that they could easily gain protection for more sinister activities carried on in private.

Because law enforcement officials have had spotty success in curtailing illegal Klan activity, independently funded civil rights groups such as the Southern Poverty Law Center and the Center for Democratic Renewal have entered the scene, monitoring Klan and other white supremacist ventures. When criminal prosecutions have failed to bring the desired results, lawyers affiliated with these organizations have launched successful civil suits aimed at forcing the Klan to make financial restitution for some of its crimes. As the list of these victories increases, the Klan's power may become demystified in the minds of African-Americans who find the rumors we have explored plausible.

Not only the KKK, but also—and more disturbingly to some—the official "powers that be" are often portrayed as promoting a concertedly prowhite agenda. The proliferation of these texts suggests that the presidents, elected officials, and law enforcement agencies of the Reagan-Bush era in part bore the burden of the transgressions of their predecessors, though through their inaction they showed themselves to be culpable on their own account. In the eyes of many African-Americans, U.S. presidents have rarely acted in the best interest of black citizens; indeed, they are often perceived as overtly hostile to the well-being of black Americans. Only Lincoln and Kennedy, presidents who made strong public commitments to black causes, have earned a place of respect in black folk history.

That history also emphasizes abuses that blacks have suffered at the hands of whites charged with preserving the status quo. The Rodney King incident, for example, was viewed by many blacks in my circle of family, friends, and students as just the latest in a long line of unjustified assaults on black men by white law enforcement officials. While some whites agreed with this assessment, others referred to the beating as an isolated incident and were quick to divorce it from historical examples of antiblack hostility.

Many individuals and agencies that fall under the general heading of "the government" maintain that these conspiratorial theories were planted in the black community by outside agitators. Thus, in answer to those blacks who believe that government scientists designed AIDS as a tool for wiping out third world peoples, whites well entrenched in the power structure will assert that communists planted the idea in black communities to perpetuate racial hatred in America. It will be interesting to see how the USIA and CIA recast this explanation in light of the dismantling of the Soviet Union. If the first belief reflects an African-American tendency to interpret contemporary threats to black well-being as just the latest attempt on the part of whites to destroy the race, then the latter betrays a white refusal to acknowledge that the dominant culture has a long history of impeding the success of black Americans. In other words, black Americans do not need communist infiltrators to spread the word that white Americans are capable of cruelty. If both beliefs are incorrect—if white scientists did not create AIDS as an agent of black genocide, and if communists did not disseminate the rumor to foster ill will between white and black Americans—then perhaps both groups need more education on these matters. Blacks need to be shown evidence that all contemporary white leaders are not in fact out to destroy them, and whites need to accept that their ancestors treated the ancestors of black Americans so harshly that the present generation still bears the scars.

Conspiracy Lore

Contamination motifs, as we saw in Chapter 5, invariably involve attention being drawn to the body's sexual and reproductive capacities. Church's and Tropical Fantasy are said to sterilize those African-American men who consume these products; the murders in Atlanta were committed so that a substance found in a young black man's penis could be used for scientific experiments; AIDS was designed to ensure that black sexuality would spread premature death among people of that race. According to this lore of the 1980s and 1990s, African-Americans' rights to control their sex lives and reproductive capacities are as constrained as they were during the era of slavery.

This pattern raises two provocative questions. First, what explains the emphasis on sexuality and procreation? Second, why do so many rumors presume black men to be at greater risk from the contamination conspiracies than black women? The anthropologist Mary Douglas's observation that rituals reflecting concern about sexuality and procreation develop among minority groups when their relationship to the dominant culture is insecure sheds some light on these contemporary legends. Relations between distinct groups forced to share a given territory are never static; members of minority groups must constantly measure the impact of the dominant culture's policies. And to adapt to ambiguous circumstances, the human imagination gravitates to a worst-case scenario. Hence, what is the worst-case explanation when a heretofore unheard-of sexually transmitted disease develops and claims a disproportionate number of black victims? That hostile members of the majority population wish to use blacks' supposedly insatiable sexual appetite against them. In other words, folklore emerges in which individuals translate their uneasiness about the fate of the group as a whole into more concrete, more personal, terms.

With the exception of new texts linking birth control implants with plans to limit the growth of America's black population (see the Epilogue), these contamination efforts focus on black men. During the early 1990s, the future of African-American men in particular has been highlighted in the media. Hardly a week goes by without a news story bemoaning the atrocious survival statistics of young African-American men—a population frequently characterized as an "endangered species." Concerned whites and African-Americans alike lament the increase in black-on-black crime. More and more of these reports include references to AIDS and drug dissemination rumor cycles as a significant component of the explanation blacks offer for their "plight."

From the days of the slave trade, when European explorers mentioned in journal entries the size of African males' "propagators," through the reconstruction era, when KKK costumes included extra padding to exaggerate the size of the white supremacists' genitals, to the 1991 jokes about Supreme Court Justice Clarence Thomas's affinity with the black male porn star known as Long Dong Silver, the white population has been preoccupied with the black male's alleged sexual superiority. African-Americans are very much aware of this aversion/fascination. Rumor and contemporary legend cycles that feature contamination motifs allow them to identify some meaning in this attention.

Cautious Consumers

My investigations into rumors connecting consumer products to antiblack conspiracies invariably resulted in the vindication of the targeted company. I am convinced that the KKK does not now and never has owned any tobacco, fast food, beverage, or athletic wear corporation. I do not believe that Al Copeland gave David Duke a campaign contribution, or that Reebok ever used its profits to support apartheid. In my fieldwork, I always share the results of my investigations with informants who want to know what I have learned; yet as a rule, few informants appear to be swayed by what I have to say. The impact of a rumor on an individual's psyche is simply more potent than any empirical evidence a researcher can supply. Even when informants seem convinced by my conclusions, they will often state that they intend to stay away from the product, "just to be on the safe side."

The *Price + Risk > Utility* formula spelled out in Chapter 6 suggests that just because the targeted companies may in fact be innocent of the charges contained in the rumors, it does not necessarily follow that black consumers should embrace their products. An exchange I had with the representative of an athletic wear company illuminates this point. After we had talked quite a while about his company's attempts to debunk the rumor, he asked me for advice on how they might restore black consumer confidence. I told him that I thought the rumor cycle reflected an increasing unwillingness on the part of some black consumers to pay inordinate amounts for name brands ostensibly designed for athletes. I told him his company might consider introducing a line of reasonably-priced athletic wear marketed at students and falling within the financial means of working-class families. He dismissed that idea, however, as in conflict with the company's overall marketing plan.

This dialogue reflects more than my unsuitability for employment within the ranks of corporate America. Corporations, it seems, are always going to place their own good ahead of the good of their customers. The companies identified with antiblack conspiracies in particular have hitched at least part of their corporate success to the desires and/or needs of black consumers. For the most part, black consumers are unaccustomed to being singled out by corporations desirous of their dollars. These rumors and contemporary legends, hence, are signals by which African-Americans remind one another that marketing perceived as "for blacks only" should be scrutinized quite thoroughly.

From Cannibalism to Crack

Rumors about the dissemination and circulation of illegal drugs in African-American communities are of two types: either the conspiracy is one of benign neglect, in which law enforcement officials simply do not do enough to fight the proliferation of drugs in black communities; or it is one of malicious intent, in which local and national government officials are actively designing and introducing drugs into black communities with genocide as the ultimate goal. Informants invoke episodes of racial hostility such as those involving Willie Horton, Yusef Hawkins, and Rodney King to explain why they find the latter rumors plausible.

Although these rumor cycles could have been discussed in the chapters on conspiracy and contamination, crack lore warrants a separate chapter. No other contemporary legends discussed in this book were as well known as these, among both blacks and whites, a fact that in itself demands investigation. Moreover, the impact of illegal drugs and the associated violence, together with the family stagnancy that ensues from addiction, are among the most critical issues facing black America in the 1990s. In a sense, the rumors about the drug conspiracy allow African-Americans to take some control of what could be considered a hopeless situation. Since I conducted those interviews, the African-American filmmaker John Singleton's highly acclaimed movie *Boyz 'N the Hood*, about coming of age in a violence-torn urban community, was released to great fanfare. In its own way, the popular film offers a case study of how a drug conspiracy rumor fit into one young African-American's worldview. Both the film's success at the box office and the critical accolades bestowed on its twenty-three-year-old director suggest that its interpretation of contemporary inner-city life rang true in the minds of its audience. Before examining the crucial scene in which one version of the rumor is told, let us review earlier scenes in which aspects of the young Tre Styles's education are depicted.

The opening scenes place Tre and his young friends walking to school through a conspicuously bad neighborhood. In the classroom, a well-meaning white teacher offers a standard lesson plan on the origins of Thanksgiving. Tre's tomfoolery disrupts the class. He accepts the teacher's challenge to teach the lesson and, pointer in hand, moves the topic from New England to Africa. His attempt to share what his father has taught him about African civilization fails to impress his apathetic classmates, and a shouting/shoving match ensues. Suspended from school for his role in the outburst, Tre is taken by his divorced mother to live with his father, Furious Styles.

The audience never again sees Tre in a formal classroom setting. But his education remains a focal point, with Tre's father now acting as the most important teacher in his life. Furious Styles, an obviously devoted father, albeit a misogynist, teaches Tre the facts of life that he thinks will equip his son for black manhood. To prevent him from being seduced by street life, Furious trains Tre to see the world in "us versus them" terms. "Us" consists of Tre, Furious, and like-minded black men; "them" are the individuals and groups who might intentionally or accidentally sabotage Tre's future. Before the film is over, this category expands to include Tre's supposedly selfish mother, young women who might misrepresent their birth control methods or freedom from venereal disease, white and black policemen, the military, and armed, drug-using "boyz 'n the hood." Furious, however, does not emerge as an unduly paranoid black parent, for the very evils to which he points—indifferent police officers, ostensibly apathetic black mothers, amorous black teenage girls, and gun-toting black teenagers—inhabit the film, giving his warnings merit. The elder Styles, in short, is engaged in a battle to save his son from the disaster that seems to await all of the other young men in the neighborhood.

One afternoon after they have taken the all-important Scholastic Aptitude Test for admission into college, Furious takes Tre and his friend Ricky to a particularly devastated area adjacent to their neighborhood. As he lapses into another of his "the world according to Furious Styles raps," other young men wander over to the empty lot. In didactic fashion, Furious tells the young men that blacks lack the political and economic clout necessary to bring drugs into a community themselves. This is evidence, he maintains, of the white man's desire to keep black men away from positions of power. In his sermonlike rendering of the rumor, he stacks several motifs described in Chapter 7 into a loosely organized call-and-response narrative, asking his audience to think about where blacks would get the money, the planes, the boats necessary to import the drugs; why television shows seem to be so preoccupied with black junkies; and why so little official attention was paid to drug abuse until it surfaced on Wall Street and in other obviously white environs.

Furious's words have a clear impact on Tre and the ill-fated Ricky. Up this point, Ricky has lacked the kind of father-to-son education that Tre has had. Ricky's overbearing single mother drinks, smokes, gambles, and clearly prefers Ricky to his overweight brother, Doughboy. Whereas Furious implores Tre always to assume personal responsibility for birth control, Ricky's mother places that burden on Ricky's girlfriend—after she has already given birth to one child. According to the filmmaker, only male parents can adequately school their sons in the ways of the world. Lacking a strong older male presence, Ricky and Doughboy are ill prepared to take control of their lives. And indeed, Ricky's one exposure to Furious's folk wisdom is not enough to save him. His senseless, violent death forces Tre to decide whether a lifetime of lessons imparted by his father is stronger than the peer pressure to succumb to the mores of street life.

The film's epilogue indicates that Furious has won: Tre's escape from the 'hood is signaled by news of his matriculation at Morehouse College, a well-known black school. The audience is clearly expected to believe that Tre's presence in college is the result of the folk schooling that Furious has imparted rather than of any formal schooling that took place within classroom walls. As one lesson plan in the Furious Styles curriculum, the rumor that drugs are intentionally disseminated in African-American neighborhoods has served its purpose, and a drug-free Tre Styles makes his way to college.

The drug conspiracy cycles show how much racial misunderstanding still exists between white and black Americans.

Four hundred years ago, Africans concluded that their white captors could only be taking them away in order to eat them. Likewise, the English reacted to the different life-style of West Africans by assuming that these uncivilized beings must be cannibals. Today, many blacks read between the lines of the policies and attitudes of white Americans and conclude that the heirs of the slave traders still intend to destroy blacks, only now it is by introducing life-threatening narcotics into their communities. Similarly, many whites hear the appalling statistics on black intraracial crime and gang violence and assume that this generation of the African slaves' progeny places a low value on human life, thus justifying the assertion that their ancestors deserved to be enslaved and the descendants deserve second-class status.

Rumor and Resistance in Black Folk Culture

Rumor and contemporary legend study lends itself to the same language that is used to study and describe illness and disease. We speak of rumors "spreading," "circulating," "infecting," and "attacking." More than once during the course of corresponding with and interviewing individuals representing the parties named as antiblack conspirators, I have been asked to offer "remedies" for individuals and groups "afflicted" or "victimized" by rumors. This language also locates the individual or organization as the innocently "wounded" party and depicts the African-Americans who share the rumors as the "carriers."

With the possible exception of professed white supremacists, including the Ku Klux Klan, most of the individuals and groups named as instigators in the antiblack conspiracies described in this book have indicated that they would welcome some kind of sweet-tasting prescription that would rid their organizations of these unwanted germs. Unfortunately, the suggestions I do have offer little in the way of pain-free rumor cure-alls; indeed, some organizations might actually find that they prefer the disease to the cure. Nor can I claim any originality regarding these suggestions—they echo those promoted by countless other individuals committed to the cause of social justice.

As I hope I have made clear, most of the rumors and contemporary legends discussed in this book are culled from readings or misreadings of real circumstances. African-Americans have been treated as second-class citizens for the entire history of this country, and then some. As a first measure in fighting the rumor "plague," therefore, it is imperative that the powers begin to send clear, unconditional signals that communicate a genuine desire and commitment to eliminating racial intolerance and inequality once and for all.

My second suggestion concerns the educational establishment in this country. I hope this book serves as a solid example of how much can be learned when folk materials are considered in conjunction with more traditional sources. Unfortunately, too few school curricula include folklore studies, and they should. All folklore genres—folktales, legends, proverbs, songs, jokes, riddles—offer some understanding of how people place themselves and others in the world. Other countries are far ahead of us in incorporating folklore and the tools of folklore analysis at all levels of school and college. Folklore is often singled out as an academic discipline that focuses on groups of people overlooked in standard history books; what such commentators neglect to consider is that the writers of the history books have folk traditions as well. The Topsy/Eva cycles, in particular, remind us that whites and blacks can be equally swayed by age-old but equally invalid assumptions.

Third, as certain as I am that folklore warrants a more visible role in the classroom, so too am I convinced that the study of black history, literature, and culture deserves to be moved from the margins to the center of academic study. As a professor of African-American studies, I am accustomed to hearing students bemoan the lack of attention black history receives in American schools. Many black and white students state that prior to taking ethnic studies classes at the college level, their familiarity with black history was limited to superficial knowledge about Martin Luther King, Jr., and Rosa Parks—period. In order for most of the rumors and legends discussed in this book to have gained any momentum, they had to ring true to a large number of people. Blacks had to believe that whites would remorselessly throw a black woman and her infant from a bridge. Whites had to believe that blacks would maliciously do the same to a white woman and her child. Such beliefs emerge out of ignorance and uncertainty, not knowledge and confidence. Black-white relations are at the very core of American history. Until both sides have complete access to the content of this relationship, the historical ignorances that have generated these rumors and contemporary legends will only be perpetuated, and the texts reinvented to fit the circumstances of the time.

Attention to the content of the rumors, however unsettling, merely detracts attention from the function those rumors serve for those who believe them. The rumors themselves do not cause the wounds from which African-Americans suffer—racism, inequality, and prejudice do. Like a scab that forms over a sore, the rumors are an unattractive but vital mechanism by which the cultural body attempts to protect itself from subsequent infection.

Epilogue:
Continuing Concerns

"Aren't you ever going to finish that book?" is a question that colleagues and family members have asked me politely (and not so politely) for the past three years. I usually reply by grumbling that every time I think I have finished work on a given rumor, a new motif—or whole new cycle—emerges. More than once I have announced to my students that a moratorium on African-American rumors must be implemented so I could get this book into print. No such luck. Since I first mailed a full draft of this manuscript to an editor late in the summer of 1991, the following rumors and contemporary legends have come to my attention. Rather than try to incorporate them fully into the book, I have opted simply to identify them here and acknowledge that I have not probed them as thoroughly as I might have. I will also identify those aspects of these new rumors that warrant further study.

Forced Birth Control

Most of the contamination rumor cycles depict African-American men as the primary target of a certain conspiracy. But at least one early-1990s cycle posits African-American women as the intended instrument for perpetrating black genocide. Norplant is the trade name for a birth control product consisting of six thin capsules that, upon being implanted in a woman's arm, release an ovulation-inhibiting hormone. Fol-

lowing the legalization of the Norplant contraceptive device
in 1990, rumors began to circulate which suggested that minority women, particularly African-Americans in the inner
city, were being forced to use the highly touted contraceptive.
Half of the dozen or so informants from whom I have collected
this item said they had heard that women who refused to have
the device implanted would lose their welfare benefits; the
other half offered an additional motif, asserting the existence
of a conspiracy by the "powers that be."

What little research I have been able to do suggests that
there was a great deal of truth in half of these texts. I first
collected versions of this rumor in the fall of 1991, almost a
year after several editorial writers and public policymakers
began to suggest that "welfare mothers" be required to have
the devices implanted as a condition of further benefits.[1] A
particularly notorious editorial spelling out just how advanta-
geous such a plan might be appeared in the *Philadelphia Inquirer* on December 12, 1990.[2] After citing the bleak future
that awaits so many inner-city black children, the editors pro-
posed that welfare mothers be offered financial incentives to
use the device. Critics responded swiftly and decisively.[3]

Advocates of the incentive plans never stated racial genocide as their goal. Instead they focused on spiraling welfare
costs. After proposing that $500 be given to any welfare
mother who agrees to having the device implanted, Kansas
representative Kerry Patrick said,

> By any set of objective criteria, the creation of this program has the
> potential to save the taxpayers millions of their hard-earned dollars.
> Something must be done to reduce the number of unwanted preg-
> nancies, and this type of voluntary program, where the public wel-
> fare recipient is given a strong financial incentive to use a safe,
> reversible contraceptive device that has a useful life of five years,
> represents the best way to prevent them.[4]

In all probability, the rumors that began to circulate about
these devices were heavily influenced by media attention.
Since policymakers *have* suggested that welfare mothers be
urged to have the devices implanted, some might argue that
this constitutes "real news" as opposed to "mere rumor."

The first version I collected was typical of those containing a genocide motif. An African-American college student reported she had heard that "*they* were trying to make black women have the device implanted in order to keep these women from having babies in order to slowly kill off the black race." Such statements are quite reminiscent of those described earlier that call crack and AIDS inventions designed to inhibit the growth of the black population. But now, rather than focus the attack on the beleaguered black man, the powers that be have singled out the black woman.

Throughout my research, I was confounded by the fact that African-American *men* tend to be foregrounded in the rumor cycles. Yet try as I might, I could not determine any real differences between the ways men circulate these texts and the ways women share them. To date, I have collected the Norplant item only from women. So, at first glance anyway, it appears that while African-American women share and circulate rumors that target men as the object of a conspiracy, African-American men are less likely to perpetuate those texts that locate women as the target. This tendency is suggestive, but more work needs to be done to support the assertion.

While collecting Norplant texts, I was told by several female informants over the age of thirty-five about rumors they recall from the mid-1970s and 1980s. In these texts, the "powers that be" were named as conspirators who placed family planning clinics in African-American neighborhoods to encourage black women to have abortions. According to these informants, young black women were being told by parents and peers in the black community that this was all part of a genocide plot. My informant base for this rumor is small, however, consisting of ten or so women in Northern California and Washington, D.C.

The connections between these two cycles are clear. In pursuing conspiracy/contamination theories as they relate to African-American women's contraception and reproduction options, I would need to explore several avenues. First, I would need to collect many more texts, and collect them from all over the United States from a diverse group of people. I would also explore the enormous literature on reproductive rights that has emerged, as well as reportage on the forced sterilizations that took place earlier in the twentieth century. I would then interview individuals engaged in pregnancy counseling and policymakers who support family planning. Finally, I would look closely at the ways in which abortion and contraception are advertised to determine if some women are perceiving a hidden message that adds circumstantial evidence to their notions about genocide.

Designer Lore

In the fall of 1991, a reporter asked me about a rumor she had heard concerning the popular Liz Claiborne line of women's clothing. In New York, she said, stories were circulating that the designer, appearing on the "Oprah Winfrey Show," had admitted to channeling her profits into a satanist organization. The next day, naming no names, I asked my California students in a large introductory class to jot down anything unusual they had heard about a well-known women's clothing designer. A few white students wrote down texts linking Liz Claiborne with satanism and Oprah Winfrey. The response of one African-American female student, however, was quite different. In a later interview she claimed that while shopping for back-to-school clothes she had admired a Liz Claiborne shirt. Her companion, another young black woman, snatched the shirt out of her hand and warned her that "Claiborne did not like seeing her clothes on the backs of black women." Her "proof" was that the clothes were sized small so that they would not fit the proportions—in particular the hips—of black females. During the next few weeks I collected the same item from several other African-American women in California and in Maryland. One student reported a related version, in which her mother recalled a similar charge being linked to Gloria Vanderbilt after her line of designer blue jeans was introduced "back in my day."

A public relations official for the Liz Claiborne company acknowledged that unfounded rumors were a problem. A fax transmitted on December 20, 1991, maintained:

As you are now aware there is absolutely no truth to these rumors. In fact Liz Claiborne has never even been on the Oprah Winfrey Show. Even though it is not true, we are taking the rumor very seriously because of its potential to confuse and upset our consumers. In dealing with this unfortunate situation in some other communities, we have found that citizens who take the trouble to call our company, or the local television station where the appearance is supposed to have occurred, or the talk show itself, have been satisfied that the rumor was groundless. But some people, believing their own sources to be credible, do not call.[5]

Several patterns familiar to contemporary legend enthusiasts are evident in the Claiborne cycle. The talk show/satanism motifs were first associated with the McDonald's fast food chain and the Colgate-Palmolive corporation in the late 1970s and early 1980s.[6] Here, too, a company owner or representative supposedly acknowledged on a national talk show that profits were being used to support a devil-worshipping cult. These cycles, according to Gary Alan Fine, reflect what he calls the "Goliath effect": as consumers develop an ambivalence about patronizing particularly large or well-known companies, they may try to dissociate themselves from the companies by perpetuating these rumors.[7]

The Liz Claiborne cycle seems particularly well suited to the *Price + Risk > Utility* explanatory formula delineated in Chapter 6. Many of my students reported that while they are fond of Claiborne designs, the prices are beyond the realm of most middle-class student budgets. The risk inherent in the product, therefore, is that they will overspend their limited clothing allowances. I intend to look into the Claiborne marketing strategy to see how (and if) black women are depicted in the company's advertisements. I did, however, go to several local department stores to get a sense of the price range of the clothing relative to similar merchandise, the ways in which it was featured in the stores, and just what it looked like. There I discovered that the Liz Claiborne company also markets a line of fashionable clothing called "Elizabeth," designed for plus-sized women. The next week I mentioned to a student that I didn't really think the rumor would have a significant impact because, after all, large-hipped women could buy from the Elizabeth line. She very patiently explained to me that those clothes were made for women who were "fat all over" and did not satisfy the fashion dilemmas of women who merely had "big butts."

In an interview for the October 1992 issue of *Esquire*, filmmaker Spike Lee repeated the rumor saying, "Last week, Oprah Winfrey had Liz Claiborne on the show. I guess she wears Liz Claiborne's clothes all the time. Claiborne got on and said she didn't make clothes for black people to wear. Oprah stopped the show and told her to get her ass off the set. How you gonna get on Oprah's show and say you don't make clothes for black women? It definitely happened. Get the tape. Every black woman in America needs to go to her closet, throw that shit out, and never buy another stitch of clothes from Liz Claiborne."[8]

I had earlier written to Oprah Winfrey's staff to ask about how the talk show emerges in rumor cycles, but received no response. Following the *Esquire* article I sent another letter, focusing on the Claiborne cycle, and this time a representative did respond, with a phone call, in December 1992. Like many corporations and media outlets, the production staff of the "Oprah Winfrey Show" takes the position that any reaction to rumors, even one of dismissal, only perpetuates them. Having clarified that point, the spokesperson did respond to one of my questions: Liz Claiborne has never appeared on the "Oprah Winfrey Show." The rumor is stronger than ever.

Liquor Lore

After an interview about African-American rumors and legends, a reporter once asked me if I could predict what companies might find themselves targeted by erroneous accusations in the future. I suggested breweries specializing in malt liquors or distilleries specializing in high-priced liqueurs. Since at least the late 1980s, these tony alcoholic beverages have been heavily promoted on billboards in black communities and in advertisements in African-American publications. Community leaders have lamented this attention and tried to develop counter-campaigns to discourage blacks from being seduced by the advertising.

At the time of that interview, I had not yet collected any rumors about such products. A few weeks ago, however, I was talking to two male African-American students from the Sacramento area, and they claimed that in the late 1980s they had heard that St. Ides, a popular malt liquor, contained a special sterilizing ingredient aimed at black men. Both young men claimed to have believed the rumors when they first heard them in high school. Although I have not yet begun to research this text in earnest, I suspect that while I may find many young African-Americans who have at least heard the rumor, I won't find many who believe it. The high number of teenage births in inner-city communities will probably stand as proof to most that these malt liquors contain no prophylactic properties.

To do this rumor justice, I need to collect from young men and women beyond the Sacramento area. I would also like to find out more about the company, its advertising philosophy, and what percentage of its market consists of African-Americans.

As noted in the introduction to this epilogue, these cycles all came to my attention after I considered the present volume "finished." Perhaps if *I Heard It through the Grapevine* is a success, I will be able to include full investigations of them in a future book on the topic.

Notes

Preface

1. Jan Harold Brunvand, *The Vanishing Hitchhiker: American Urban Legends and Their Meanings* (New York: W. W. Norton, 1981), xi.

Introduction

1. For more on World War II and sixties rumors, see Gordon W. Allport and Leo Postman, *The Psychology of Rumor* (New York: Henry Holt, 1947); D. J. Jacobson, *The Affairs of Dame Rumor* (New York: Rinehart, 1948); and Terry Ann Knopf, *Rumors, Race, and Riots* (New Brunswick, N.J.: Transaction Books, 1975).

2. These and other accounts are verbatim transcriptions of interviews conducted by the author with informants.

3. Patrick B. Mullen, "Modern Legend and Rumor Theory," *Journal of the Folklore Institute* 9 (1972): 95–109.

4. Allport and Postman, *Psychology of Rumor*, ix.

5. See Gary Alan Fine, "The Kentucky Fried Rat: Legends and Modern Society," *Journal of the Folklore Institute* 17 (1980): 232–33.

6. Allport and Postman, *Psychology of Rumor*, 167.

7. Mullen, "Modern Legend and Rumor Theory," 96.

1. Cannibalism

1. For more on cannibalism practices, see Peter Farb and George Amelagos, *Consuming Passions: The Anthropology of Eating* (New York: Pocket Books, 1980); Peggy Reeves Sanday, *Divine Hunger: Cannibalism as a Cultural System* (Cambridge: Cambridge Univer-

sity Press, 1986); and Reay Tannahill, *Flesh and Blood: A History of the Cannibal Complex* (New York: Dorset Press, 1975).

2. Robert Langbaum, "Introduction" to William Shakespeare, *The Tempest* (New York: New American Library, 1964), xxiv.

3. William Arens, *The Man-Eating Myth: Anthropology and Anthropophagy* (New York: Oxford University Press, 1979), 44.

4. Pliny the Elder, *Natural History, Vol. II, Books III–VII*, ed. H. Rackham (Cambridge, Mass.: Harvard University Press, 1942), 251, 483.

5. Basil Davidson, *The African Slave Trade* (Boston: Little, Brown, 1980), 115.

6. Winthrop D. Jordan, *White over Black: American Attitudes Toward the Negro, 1550–1812* (Baltimore: Penguin Books, 1969), 25.

7. Olaudah Equiano, "Early Travels of Olaudah Equiano," in *Africa Remembered*, ed. Philip D. Curtin (Madison: University of Wisconsin Press, 1967), 97.

8. For several years after the British abolished slavery in 1807, they forcibly intercepted slavers from other countries and escorted the Africans they liberated (such as Eisami) to the territorial colony in Sierra Leone. Such individuals, though fortunate not to be enslaved in the New World, would probably have preferred to be returned to their own homelands; thus the term *recaptive*.

9. Ali Eisami, "Narrative of the Travels of Ali Eisami" in Curtin (ed.), *Africa Remembered*, 215.

10. Samuel Ajayi Crowther, "The Narrative of Samuel Ajayi Crowther," in ibid., 313.

11. Joseph Wright, "The Narrative of Joseph Wright," in ibid., 331.

12. John Newton, "Thoughts upon the African Slave Trade," in *The Journals of a Slave Trader, 1750–1754*, ed. Bernard Martin and Mark Spurrell (London: Epworth Press, 1962), 103.

13. Tannahill, *Flesh and Blood*, 154.

14. James Pope-Hennessy, *Sins of the Fathers* (London: Cassell, 1967), 79.

15. Mary Cable, *Black Odyssey: The Case of the Slave Ship "Amistad"* (New York: Penguin Books, 1971), 53.

16. Arens, *Man-Eating Myth*, 93, citing the anthropologist Kenneth Little on the pervasive fear of cannibals among the Mende of Sierra Leone.

17. Katherine George, "The Civilized West Looks At Primitive Africa, 1400–1800: A Study in Ethnocentrism," in *Every Man His Way: Readings in Cultural Anthropology*, ed. Alan Dundes (Englewood Cliffs, N.J.: Prentice-Hall, 1968), 28–29.

18. Jordan (*White over Black*, 29, 458) notes that Englishmen frequently referred to any tailless apes as orangutans. In all likelihood, it was chimpanzees that the explorers assumed were related to West Africans; the confusion, however, remained. Thomas Jefferson's *Notes on the State of Virginia* develops the connection between "oran-ootans" and black women. For a pictorial nineteenth-century equation between black women and orangutans, see Stephen Jay Gould, *The Mismeasure of Man* (New York: W. W. Norton, 1981), 36–37.

19. Jordan, *White over Black*, 28.

20. Jan Nederveen Pieterse, *White over Black: Images of Africa and Blacks in Western Popular Culture* (New Haven: Yale University Press, 1992), 114.

21. Quoted in Pope-Hennessy, *Sins of the Fathers*, 31.

22. Thomas Winterbottom, *An Account of the Native Africans of Sierra Leone, to Which Is Added an Account of the Present State of Medicine Among Them* (London: Frank Cass, 1969), 161.

23. Ibid., xviii.

24. Ibid., 161.

25. Ibid., 162, 164, 167.

26. John Gunther, *Inside Africa* (New York: Harper & Brothers, 1955), 292.

27. Arens, *Man-Eating Myth*, 139.

28. Ibid., 12.

29. Pieterse, *White over Black*, 109–22.

30. See Claude Lévi-Strauss, *The Savage Mind* (Chicago: University of Chicago Press, 1966); Mary Douglas, *Purity and Danger: An Analysis of the Concepts of Pollution and Taboo* (London: Ark Paperbacks, 1985).

31. See, for example, Lévi-Strauss, *Savage Mind*, 105, on the propensity of cultures to link copulation and eating.

32. Joel Kovel, *White Racism: A Psychohistory* (New York: Columbia University Press, 1984), 66.

33. Arens, *Man-Eating Myth*, 160.

34. Douglas, *Purity and Danger*, 124.

35. Frederick Douglass, *Narrative of the Life of Frederick Douglass, an American Slave* (New York: Signet, 1968), 126.

36. Jordan, *White over Black*, 6.

37. Joseph Boskin, *Sambo: The Rise and Demise of an American Jester* (New York: Oxford University Press, 1986), 144.

38. Allport and Postman, *Psychology of Rumor*, 2.

39. Tamotsu Shibutani, *Improvised News: A Sociological Study of Rumor* (Indianapolis: Bobbs-Merrill, 1966), 175.

2. Corporal Control

1. Henry Bibb, "Narrative of the Life and Adventures of Henry Bibb, an American Slave," in *Puttin' on Ole Massa*, ed. Gilbert Osofsky (New York: Harper Torchbooks, 1969), 85.

2. William W. Brown, "Narrative of William Wells Brown, a Fugitive Slave," in Osofsky (ed.), *Puttin' on Ole Massa*, 219–20.

3. Douglass, *Narrative of Frederick Douglass*, 56.

4. Harriet A. Jacobs, *Incidents in the Life of a Slave Girl, Written By Herself* (Cambridge, Mass.: Harvard University Press, 1987), 45.

5. Ibid., 64.

6. Trudier Harris, *Exorcising Blackness: Historical and Literary Lynching and Burning Rituals* (Bloomington: Indiana University Press, 1984), 8.

7. Gladys-Marie Fry, *Night Riders in Black Folk History* (Knoxville: University of Tennessee Press, 1975), 44.

8. Charles L. Perdue, Jr., Thomas E. Barden, and Robert K. Phillips, eds., *Weevils in Wheat: Interviews with Virginia Ex-Slaves* (Bloomington: Indiana University Press, 1980), 79.

9. Jacobs, *Incidents in the Life of a Slave Girl*, 43.

10. Fry, *Night Riders*, 88.

11. Perdue, Barden, and Phillips (eds.), *Weevils in Wheat*, 208.

12. Ibid., 93.

13. Two particularly useful studies of tricksters in African-American tradition are Lawrence W. Levine, *Black Culture and Black Consciousness: Afro-American Folk Thought from Slavery to Freedom* (New York: Oxford University Press, 1978); and John W. Roberts, *From Trickster to Badman: The Black Folk Hero in Slavery and Freedom* (Philadelphia: University of Pennsylvania Press, 1989).

14. Leon F. Litwack, *Been So Long in the Storm: The Aftermath of Slavery* (New York: Vintage Books, 1980), 401–2.

15. Ibid., 399.

16. Prominent among the full-length studies of rumors published during the 1940s are Allport and Postman, *Psychology of Rumor*; Jacobson, *Affairs of Dame Rumor*; and Howard W. Odum, *Race and Rumors of Race: Challenge to American Crisis* (Chapel Hill: University of North Carolina Press, 1943).

17. See Knopf, *Rumors, Race, and Riots*; and Shibutani, *Improvised News*.

18. Jacobson, *Affairs of Dame Rumor*, 77.

19. Ibid., 82.

20. Allport and Postman, *Psychology of Rumor,* 175–76.

21. Roger D. Abrahams, "The Negro Stereotype: Negro Folklore and the Riots," in *The Urban Experience and Folk Tradition,* ed. Americo Paredes and Ellen Stekert (Austin: University of Texas Press, 1971), 89.

22. Jan Harold Brunvand refers to this as the "foaf" (friend of a friend) motif; see *Vanishing Hitchhiker,* 4.

23. Odum, *Race and Rumors of Race,* 136–42.

24. See Thomas J. Davis, *A Rumor of Revolt: The "Great Negro Plot" in Colonial New York* (New York: Free Press, 1985).

25. Odum, *Race and Rumors of Race,* 136.

26. Shibutani, *Improvised News,* 58.

27. For a full discussion of the East St. Louis race riot, see Elliot Rudwick, *Race Riot at East St. Louis, July 2, 1917* (Chicago: University of Illinois Press, 1982).

28. Ibid., 27–28.

29. Ibid., 28.

30. Ibid., 31.

31. Ibid., 46–47.

32. Janet L. Langlois, "The Belle Isle Bridge Incident: Legend Dialectic and Semiotic System in the 1943 Detroit Race Riots," *Journal of American Folklore* 96 (1983): 183–98.

33. Knopf, *Rumors, Race, and Riots,* 45–46.

34. Ibid., 181.

35. Ibid., 216.

36. Ibid., 209.

37. An earlier race riot had actually begun on the Fourth of July; see Jacobson, *Affairs of Dame Rumor,* 69.

38. Quoted in Lawrence H. Fuchs, *The American Kaleidoscope: Race, Ethnicity, and the Civic Culture* (Hanover, N.H.: University Press of New England, 1990), 87.

39. William H. Wiggins, *O Freedom! Afro-American Emancipation Celebrations* (Knoxville: University of Tennessee Press, 1987), xii.

40. Knopf, *Rumors, Race, and Riots,* 53.

3. Conspiracy I

1. For a comprehensive examination of African-American legends about white supremacy, see Fry, *Night Riders.*

2. Personal correspondence with Janet Caldwell, Program Associate, Center for Democratic Renewal, October 25, 1989.

3. Wyn Craig Wade, *The Fiery Cross: The Ku Klux Klan in America* (New York: Touchstone Books, 1987), 33–35.

4. Ibid., 51.

5. Report of the Committees of the House of Representatives for the Second Session of the Forty-second Congress, South Carolina, 1872 (hereafter cited as KKK Report), 5:1749.

6. See H. Grady McWhiney and Francis B. Simkins, "The Ghostly Legend of the Ku-Klux Klan," in *Mother Wit from the Laughing Barrel: Readings in the Interpretation of African-American Folklore*, ed. Alan Dundes (Englewood Cliffs, N.J.: Prentice-Hall, 1973), 586–94.

7. An excellent discussion of folklore dealing with "genital superiority" is contained in Neil A. Eddington, "Genital Superiority in Oakland Negro Folklore: A Theme," in Dundes (ed.), *Mother Wit*, 642–48.

8. Harris, *Exorcising Blackness*, 22.

9. Quoted in Herbert Shapiro, *White Violence and Black Response: From Reconstruction to Montgomery* (Amherst: University of Massachusetts Press, 1988), 219.

10. Quoted in Kenneth O'Reilly, *"Racial Matters": The FBI's Secret File on Black America, 1960–1972* (New York: Free Press, 1989), 2.

11. Harris, *Exorcising Blackness*, 23.

12. KKK Report, 3:521.

13. According to at least one former Klansman, ex–Grand Wizard David Duke is alleged to possess a collection of pornography featuring white women performing oral sex on black men. His authorship of a sex manual is a matter of record; see Ros Davidson, "The Politics of Evil," *San Francisco Examiner*, "Image" sec., March 8, 1992, 11.

14. Wade, *Fiery Cross*, 78–79.

15. Ibid., 69–72.

16. KKK Report, 5:1745.

17. Herbert Aptheker, *A Documentary History of the Negro People in the United States from the Reconstruction Years to the Founding of N.A.A.C.P. in 1910* (New York: Citadel Press, 1966), 607.

18. Booker T. Washington, *Up From Slavery* (New York: Penguin Books, 1986), 79.

19. Wade, *Fiery Cross*, 114–15.

20. Ida B. Wells-Barnett, "A Red Record," in *Black Women in White America: A Documentary History*, ed. Gerda Lerner (New York: Vintage Books, 1973), 205.

21. Perdue, Barden, and Phillips (eds.), *Weevils in Wheat*, 104.

22. Fry, *Night Riders*, 171.

23. Levine, *Black Culture and Black Consciousness*, 397.

24. Ibid.

25. Fry, *Night Riders*, 178.

26. Wade, *Fiery Cross*, 138.

27. Ibid., 151.

28. A. Philip Randolph, "The Human Hand Threat," in Dundes (ed.), *Mother Wit*, 398.

29. Wade, *Fiery Cross*, 247.

30. Ibid., 285.

31. Ibid., 303.

32. Quoted in David J. Garrow, *The FBI and Martin Luther King, Jr.* (New York: Penguin Books, 1983), 124.

33. Ralph L. Rosnow and Gary Alan Fine, *Rumor and Gossip: The Social Psychology of Hearsay* (New York: Elsevier Scientific Publishing Co., 1976), 43.

34. Martin Luther King, Jr., *Why We Can't Wait* (New York: New American Library, 1968), 144.

35. James Baldwin, *The Evidence of Things Not Seen* (New York: Henry Holt, 1985), xiii.

36. Ibid., 2.

37. Shibutani, *Improvised News*, 56–58.

38. "New Trial Sought in Atlanta Murders," *Los Angeles Times*, February 18, 1992, A10.

39. Mary A. Fisher, "Was Wayne Williams Framed?" *Gentlemen's Quarterly*, April 1991, 228–35, 264–66.

40. Fine, "Kentucky Fried Rat," 222.

41. Fredrick Koenig, *Rumor in the Marketplace: The Social Psychology of Commercial Hearsay* (Dover, Mass.: Auburn House, 1985), 39.

42. Fry, *Night Riders*, 159.

43. "Church's Fried Chicken: Cutting Loose from Its Penny-pinching Past," *Business Week*, February 27, 1984, 72.

44. "Church's: A Fast Food Recipe Is Light on Marketing," *Business Week*, February 20, 1978, 110–12.

45. Correspondence with J. David Bamberger, CEO, Church's, Inc., August 8, 1986.

46. Personal correspondence with Kathryn More Wohl, Public Relations, Church's Fried Chicken, July 17, 1989.

47. Personal correspondence with Wohl, August 24, 1989.

48. Personal interview with Wohl, November 2, 1990.

49. Marj Charlier, "Spicy Cajun," *Wall Street Journal*, March 22, 1989, A1.

50. "Athletic-Shoes Business Victim of Urban Rumor," *Chicago Tribune*, July 13, 1989, 2.

51. Ibid.

52. Marc Sandalow, "Klan Rumor Helped Ruin Sport Clothing Firm," *San Francisco Chronicle*, July 22, 1989, A3.

53. Ibid.

54. Fine, "Kentucky Fried Rat," 232.

55. "Your Sneakers or Your Life," *Sports Illustrated*, May 14, 1990, 36.

56. Sandalow, "Klan Rumor."

57. "Athletic-Shoes Business Victim," 2.

58. Personal correspondence with Thomas Lauria, The Tobacco Institute, March 12, 1990.

59. Personal correspondence with Janet Caldwell, November 20, 1989.

60. Personal correspondence with Jan Harold Brunvand, legend specialist, January 29, 1990.

61. Personal correspondence with Susan A. Strausser, Corporate Affairs, Philip Morris U.S.A., February 8, 1990.

62. Robert K. Heimann, *Tobacco and Americans* (New York: McGraw-Hill, 1960), 205.

63. Personal correspondence with John W. Singleton, Jr., Manager, Special Public Relations Programs, R. J. Reynolds, Inc., April 17, 1991.

64. Sam Hunter, *Art in Business: The Philip Morris Story* (New York: Harry N. Abrams, 1979).

65. Arlene Levinson, "Rumor Almost Ruins Small Soda Firm," *Los Angeles Times*, July 14, 1991, A2.

66. Ibid., A12.

67. This rhetorical analysis is based on the types of performance models explicated by Kenneth Burke in *A Grammar of Motives and A Rhetoric of Motives* (Cleveland: Meridian Books, 1962).

4. Conspiracy II

1. Richard Hofstadter, "The Folklore of Populism," in *Conspiracy: The Fear of Subversion in American History*, ed. Richard O. Curry and Thomas M. Brown (New York: Holt, Rinehart & Winston, 1972), 101.

2. Winthrop D. Jordan et al., *The United States: Conquering a*

Continent, 5th ed., vol. 1 (Englewood Cliffs, N.J.: Prentice-Hall, 1982), 333.

3. A. Leon Higginbotham, Jr., *In the Matter of Color: Race and the American Legal Process—The Colonial Period* (Oxford: Oxford University Press, 1980), 36.

4. To their credit, the black soldiers refused to accept any salary less than that received by white soldiers. Eventually their combat prowess, combined with negative publicity in the northern press, convinced the War Department to alter this policy. See Franklin and Moss, *From Slavery to Freedom,* 196.

5. James H. Jones, *Bad Blood: The Tuskegee Syphilis Experiment—A Tragedy of Race and Medicine* (New York: Free Press, 1982).

6. Loch K. Johnson, *America's Secret Power: The CIA in a Democratic Society* (New York: Oxford University Press, 1989), 27.

7. Shibutani, *Improvised News,* 37.

8. Ibid., 56–57.

9. O'Reilly, *"Racial Matters,"* 55.

10. Ibid., 9.

11. Philip Shenon, "Black Agent to Lead Probe of FBI Racism," *San Francisco Chronicle,* August 22, 1990, A9.

12. Garrow, *FBI and Martin Luther King,* 229–30.

13. Ibid., 126.

14. "Justice in Alabama," *Boston Globe,* February 23, 1986, A26.

15. Shibutani, *Improvised News,* 108.

16. Ibid., 62.

17. Walter Leavy, "The Case of the Disappearing Blacks," *Ebony,* December 1980, 136–38.

18. Personal correspondence with Milt Ahlerich, Acting Assistant Director, Office of Congressional and Public Affairs, Federal Bureau of Investigation, August 28, 1987.

19. Repeated attempts to correspond with Dick Gregory on this matter met with no success.

20. Personal correspondence with Jan Douglass, Director, Community Relations Commission, City of Atlanta, September 22, 1987.

21. Personal correspondence with Arthur S. Hulnick, Coordinator for Academic Affairs, Central Intelligence Agency, August 23, 1987.

22. "New Trial Sought," *Los Angeles Times,* February 18, 1992, A10.

23. Knopf, *Rumors, Race, and Riots,* 164.

24. Sun City was a popular whites-only entertainment arena in

South Africa. An international group of rock performers banded together to boycott this establishment. It is now open to blacks.

25. Personal interview with Kenneth R. Lightcap, Vice-President for Corporate Communications, Reebok International, Ltd., Stoughton, Mass., May 14, 1990.

26. Thomas Palmer, "Will Mandela Make Reebok Look Better?" *Boston Globe*, June 20, 1990, 69, 73.

27. Personal interview with Lightcap.

28. Palmer, "Will Mandela Make Reebok Look Better?" 73.

29. "Reebok: On Record with Human Rights," pamphlet available from Reebok International, Ltd., ca. 1990.

30. Personal interview with Lightcap.

31. Rick Telander, "Senseless," *Sports Illustrated*, May 14, 1990, 37.

5. Contamination

1. Koenig, *Rumor in the Marketplace*, 84.

2. "Soviet Active Measures in the Era of Glasnost," report prepared at the request of the U.S. House of Representatives Committee on Appropriations (Washington, D.C., 1988), 14.

3. Roger D. Abrahams, "Equal Opportunity Eating: A Structural Excursus on Things of the Mouth," in *Ethnic and Regional Foodways in the United States: The Performance of Group Identity*, ed. Linda Keller Brown and Kay Mussell (Knoxville: University of Tennessee Press, 1984), 24.

4. Douglas, *Purity and Danger*, 126.

5. Martin J. Blaser et al., "Epidemiologic Analysis of a Cluster of Homicides of Children in Atlanta," *Journal of the American Medical Association* 251 (1984): 3255–58.

6. For more information on the relationship between the CDC and the Public Health Service, see Elizabeth W. Etheridge, *Sentinel for Health: A History of the Centers for Disease Control* (Berkeley and Los Angeles: University of California Press, 1992), xv–xviii.

7. Jones, *Bad Blood*, 5.

8. Allan M. Brandt, *No Magic Bullet: A Social History of Venereal Disease in the United States Since 1880* (New York: Oxford University Press, 1987), 158.

9. Quoted in Jones, *Bad Blood*, 8.

10. Particularly important in this scenario is the media attention that interferon had garnered; it was, indeed, the best-known legal drug of the early 1980s era. Gary Alan Fine, in what he calls his

theory of corporate dominance, suggests that contemporary legends are most frequently associated with the largest, most visible company in a given industry. For example, McDonald's is more frequently implicated than other fast food chains, and Coca-Cola has been identified in more texts than any other soft drink. Thus, dominance within the marketplace is matched by dominance in legend cycles. See Fine's "The Goliath Effect: Corporate Dominance and Mercantile Legends," *Journal of American Folklore* 98 (1985): 63–84.

11. Baldwin, *Evidence of Things Not Seen*, 87.

12. Véronique Campion-Vincent, "The Baby-Parts Story: A New Latin American Legend," paper presented at the American Folklore Society meetings, Philadelphia, October 1989.

13. "Soviet Active Measures," 43.

14. For a comprehensive discussion of these cycles, see Alan Dundes, *The Blood Libel Legend: A Casebook in Anti-Semitic Folklore* (Madison: University of Wisconsin Press, 1991).

15. Florence Ridley, "A Tale Too Often Told," *Western Folklore* 26 (1967): 153–56; Barre Toelken, *The Dynamics of Folklore* (Boston: Houghton Mifflin, 1979), 176–79; Jan Harold Brunvand, *The Choking Doberman and Other "New" Urban Legends* (New York: W. W. Norton, 1984), 82–86; Michael P. Carroll, "The Castrated Boy: Another Contribution to the Psychoanalytic Study of Urban Legends," *Folklore* 98 (1987): 216–25.

16. Campion-Vincent, "Baby-Parts Story," 9.

17. Douglas, *Purity and Danger*, 124.

18. Randy Shilts, *And the Band Played On: Politics, People, and the AIDS Epidemic* (New York: Penguin Books, 1987), 90.

19. Shibutani, *Improvised News*, 60.

20. Gary Alan Fine, "Welcome to the World of AIDS: Fantasies of Female Revenge," *Western Folklore* 46 (1987): 192–97.

21. Susan Sontag, *AIDS and Its Metaphors* (New York: Farrar, Strauss & Giroux, 1988), 51–52.

22. Personal correspondence with Arthur S. Hulnick, Coordinator for Academic Affairs, Central Intelligence Agency, August 23, 1988.

23. "Soviet Active Measures," 12.

24. Ibid.

25. See Karen Grigsby Bates, "Is It Genocide?" *Essence*, September 1990, 76–79.

26. Ibid., 78.

27. Sontag, *AIDS and Its Metaphors*, 52.

28. Cindy Patton, *Sex and Germs: The Politics of AIDS* (Boston: South End Press, 1985), 7.

6. Consumer/Corporate Conflict

1. Xeroxlore refers to anonymous, often humorous texts that are reproduced on copy machines and circulated widely; see Alan Dundes and Carl R. Pagter, *Work Hard and You Shall Be Rewarded: Urban Folklore from the Paperwork Empire* (Austin: American Folklore Society, 1975).

2. Koenig, *Rumor in the Marketplace*, v. Most folklorists would argue with Koenig's use of the tall tale label to describe rumors and legends.

3. Fine, "Kentucky Fried Rat," 222–43; Brunvand, *Vanishing Hitchhiker*, 81–84; Koenig, *Rumor in the Marketplace*, 86–87.

4. Patricia A. Turner, "Church's Fried Chicken and the Klan: A Rhetorical Analysis of Rumor in the Black Community," *Western Folklore* 46 (1987): 297–98.

5. Gary Alan Fine, "Among Those Dark Satanic Mills: Rumors of Kooks, Cults, and Corporations," *Southern Folklore* 47 (1990): 140–41.

6. Alix M. Freedman, "Rumor Turns Fantasy into Bad Dream," *Wall Street Journal*, May 10, 1991, B4.

7. "A Storm over Tropical Fantasy," *Newsweek*, April 22, 1991, 34.

8. David Herzog, "Rumor Attacks Sales of Allentown Soda Company," *Morning Call* (Allentown, Pa.), July 4, 1991, A1.

9. Levinson, "Rumor Almost Ruins Small Soda Firm," A12.

10. Herzog, "Rumor Attacks Sales," A1.

11. Koenig, *Rumor in the Marketplace*, 45.

12. Herzog, "Rumor Attacks Sales," A1.

13. Freedman, "Rumor Turns Fantasy into Bad Dream," B4.

14. Herzog, "Rumor Attacks Sales," A1.

15. Daniel Crowley encountered a similar item while doing anthropological fieldwork in Zaire in 1960. A colleague gave him several cartons of American-made cigarettes that Africans were refusing to smoke because they believed them to contain an ingredient that sterilized blacks (personal conversation, April 27, 1991). As for the misspelling of *cool*, it is interesting that the phoneme *K* often sparks concern, among both blacks and whites. Gary Alan Fine ("Among Those Dark Satanic Mills") and Jan Harold Brunvand (*Choking*

Doberman), for example, have speculated that the *K* in the name Kroc may have been partly responsible for the emergence of rumors linking the founder of McDonald's with Satanic cults.

16. But see discussion in Chapter 3, where I detail how the first such rumors I heard originated in Europe. These overseas informants all reported having heard the Marlboro items from friends "in the States." I did not collect these rumors in America until I began to seek out informants who were present or former smokers.

17. Although industry reports vary, according to one estimate by a tobacco company, 69 percent of black smokers choose menthol cigarettes ("Tobacco and Black Americans," *Blackbook*, 1991, 65).

18. Turner, "Church's Fried Chicken," 298.

19. Fine, "Among Those Dark Satanic Mills," 140.

20. Freedman, "Rumor Turns Fantasy into Bad Dream," B1.

21. Telander, "Senseless," 43–44.

22. "Jackson Promotes Boycott," *Brockton Daily Reporter*, August 17, 1990, D1.

23. John Robinson, "The Secretary's Story," *Boston Globe*, May 20, 1990, 42–43.

24. Gary Alan Fine, "Redemption Rumors: Mercantile Legends and Corporate Beneficence," *Journal of American Folklore* 99 (1986): 214.

7. Crack

1. Frances Murphy, "Justice Department Lists Barry Case Among Top 32," *Washington Afro-American*, May 4, 1991, A6.

2. Jean-Noel Kapferer, *Rumors: Uses, Interpretations, and Images* (New Brunswick, N.J.: Transaction Books, 1990), 116.

3. The "triple sixes" were identified as evidence of Procter & Gamble's alleged connection with devil worship too; see Koenig, *Rumor in the Marketplace*, 42.

4. Personal correspondence with David Tell, Deputy Chief of Staff, Office of National Drug Control Policy, Washington, D.C., June 4, 1990.

5. Jason DeParle, "Talk of Government Being Out to Get Blacks Falls on More Attentive Ears," *New York Times*, October 29, 1990, A12.

6. I have never met David (a pseudonym), who explains only that he was convicted for being on the supply side of the drug trade. After he read a wire service article about my research on negative

stereotypes of blacks in the media, he wrote to me at my academic address. Other prisoners also wrote to me from various facilities in the United States. I asked several of them about inmates' attitudes regarding drugs. Their comments were surprisingly similar to those I collected from college students and others. I have chosen to focus on David's remarks for two reasons: first, he seemed to take great care in distinguishing his own beliefs from those of his fellow inmates; second, his letters were the most articulate. I realize that this is a rather unconventional method of folklore collecting, but I suspect this correspondence provided me with data to which I otherwise would not have been privy.

8. Conclusion

1. Lorene Cary, "Why It's Not Just Paranoia," *Newsweek*, April 6, 1992, 23.

2. Tom Johnson, "War and Race: Black Perspectives on the Gulf," *Sacramento News and Review*, February 14, 1991, 16.

3. It is easy to see how published reports of Gates's activity contributed to the popularity of these rumors. Although the verdict was announced at approximately 3:30 P.M., Gates was not in his office. At 6:30, he was in the L.A. suburb of Brentwood attending a fundraiser; although Police Commission president Stanley Scheinbaum had asked him where he was going, the chief never told him. Gates returned to the LAPD offices at 9:00 P.M. By this time the riot was in full swing. For a report of his schedule, see "The Siege of L.A.," *Newsweek*, May 11, 1992, 35.

4. R. Davidson, "Politics of Evil."

5. "Free Speech," *San Francisco Examiner*, "Image" sec., April 5, 1992, 3.

Epilogue

1. "One Well-read Editorial," *Newsweek*, December 31, 1990, 65–66.

2. "Poverty and Norplant," *Philadelphia Inquirer*, December 12, 1990, A18.

3. See, for example, Faye Wattleton, "Using Birth Control as Coercion," *Los Angeles Times*, December 30, 1990, M7; Virginia Ellis, "Witnesses Criticize Norplant Proposals," *Los Angeles Times*, October 17, 1991, A3; Cal Thomas, "It's A Short Step to the Next Horror of Eugenics," *Los Angeles Times*, December 30, 1990, M7;

Tamar Lewin, "A Plan to Pay Welfare Mothers for Birth Control," *New York Times*, February 9, 1991, 8; Stephanie Denmark, "Birth Control Tyranny," *New York Times*, October 19, 1991, 15.

4. Lewin, "A Plan to Pay," 8.

5. Personal correspondence with Sarah Patterson, Public Relations, Liz Claiborne, Inc., December 20, 1991.

6. For thorough discussions of the satanism charges faced by modern corporations, see Brunvand, *Choking Doberman*, 169–86; and Koenig, *Rumor in the Marketplace*, 9–13, 39–54.

7. Fine, "Goliath Effect," 63.

8. Barbara Grizzuti Harrison, "Spike Lee Hates Your Cracker Ass," *Esquire*, October 1992, 137.

Bibliography

Books and Articles

Abrahams, Roger D. "Equal Opportunity Eating: A Structural Excursus on Things of the Mouth." In *Ethnic and Regional Foodways in the United States: The Performance of Group Identity*, edited by Linda Keller Brown and Kay Mussell, 19–36. Knoxville: University of Tennessee Press, 1984.

———. "The Negro Stereotype: Negro Folklore and the Riots." In *The Urban Experience and Folk Tradition*, edited by Americo Paredes and Ellen Stekert, 65–94. Austin: University of Texas Press, 1971.

Allport, Gordon W., and Leo Postman. *The Psychology of Rumor*. New York: Henry Holt, 1947.

Aptheker, Herbert. *A Documentary History of the Negro People in the United States from the Reconstruction Years to the Founding of the N.A.A.C.P. in 1910*. New York: Citadel Press, 1966.

Arens, William. *The Man-Eating Myth: Anthropology and Anthropophagy*. New York: Oxford University Press, 1979.

"Athletic-Shoes Business Victim of Urban Rumor." *Chicago Tribune*, July 13, 1989, 2.

Baldwin, James. *The Evidence of Things Not Seen*. New York: Henry Holt, 1985.

Bates, Karen Grigsby. "Is It Genocide?" *Essence*, September 1990, 76–79.

Bibb, Henry. "Narrative of the Life and Adventures of Henry Bibb, an American Slave." In *Puttin' on Ole Massa*, edited by Gilbert Osofsky, 51–171. New York: Harper Torchbooks, 1969.

Blaser, Martin J., Janine M. Jason, Bruce G. Weniger, William R. Elsea, Robert J. Finton, Roy A. Hanson, and Roger A. Feldman.

"Epidemiologic Analysis of a Cluster of Homicides of Children in Atlanta." *Journal of the American Medical Association* 251 (1984): 3255–58.

Boskin, Joseph. *Sambo: The Rise and Demise of an American Jester.* New York: Oxford University Press, 1986.

Brandt, Allan M. *No Magic Bullet: A Social History of Venereal Disease in the United States Since 1880.* New York: Oxford University Press, 1987.

Brown, William W. "Narrative of William Wells Brown, a Fugitive Slave." In *Puttin' on Ole Massa,* edited by Gilbert Osofsky, 173–223. New York: Harper Torchbooks, 1969.

Brunvand, Jan Harold. *The Choking Doberman and Other "New" Urban Legends.* New York: W. W. Norton, 1984.

————. *The Vanishing Hitchhiker: American Urban Legends and Their Meanings.* New York: W. W. Norton, 1981.

Burke, Kenneth. *A Grammar of Motives and A Rhetoric of Motives.* Cleveland: Meridian Books, 1962.

Cable, Mary. *Black Odyssey: The Case of the Slave Ship "Amistad."* New York: Penguin Books, 1971.

Carroll, Michael. "The Castrated Boy: Another Contribution to the Psychoanalytic Study of Urban Legends." *Folklore* 28 (1987): 216–25.

Cary, Lorene. "Why It's Not Just Paranoia." *Newsweek,* April 6, 1992, 23.

Charlier, Marj. "Spicy Cajun." *Wall Street Journal,* March 22, 1989, A1.

"Church's: A Fast Food Recipe Is Light on Marketing." *Business Week,* February 20, 1978, 110–12.

"Church's Fried Chicken: Cutting Loose from its Penny-pinching Past." *Business Week,* February 27, 1984, 72.

Crowther, Samuel Ajayi. "The Narrative of Samuel Ajayi Crowther." In *Africa Remembered,* edited by Philip D. Curtin, 289–316. Madison: University of Wisconsin Press, 1967.

Davidson, Basil. *The African Slave Trade.* Boston: Little, Brown, 1980.

Davidson, Ros. "The Politics of Evil." *San Francisco Examiner,* "Image" sec., March 8, 1992.

Davis, Thomas J. *A Rumor of Revolt: The "Great Negro Plot" in Colonial New York.* New York: Free Press, 1985.

Denmark, Stephanie. "Birth Control Tyranny." *New York Times,* October 19, 1991, 15.

De Parle, Jason. "Talk of Government Being Out to Get Blacks Falls on More Attentive Ears." *New York Times,* October 29, 1991, A12.

Douglas, Mary. *Purity and Danger: An Analysis of the Concepts of Pollution and Taboo.* London: Ark Paperbacks, 1985.

Douglass, Frederick. *Narrative of the Life of Frederick Douglass, an American Slave.* New York: Signet, 1968.

Dundes, Alan. *The Blood Libel Legend: A Casebook in Anti-Semitic Folklore.* Madison: University of Wisconsin Press, 1991.

Dundes, Alan, and Carl R. Pagter. *Work Hard and You Shall Be Rewarded: Urban Folklore from the Paperwork Empire.* Austin: American Folklore Society, 1975.

Eddington, Neil A. "Genital Superiority in Oakland Negro Folklore: A Theme." In *Mother Wit from the Laughing Barrel: Readings in the Interpretation of African-American Folklore*, edited by Alan Dundes, 642–48. Englewood Cliffs, N.J.: Prentice-Hall, 1973.

Eisami, Ali. "Narrative of the Travels of Ali Eisami." In *Africa Remembered*, edited by Philip D. Curtin, 206–16. Madison: University of Wisconsin Press, 1967.

Ellis, Virginia. "Witnesses Criticize Norplant Proposals." *Los Angeles Times*, October 17, 1991, A3.

Equiano, Olaudah. "Early Travels of Olaudah Equiano." In *Africa Remembered*, edited by Philip D. Curtin, 69–98. Madison: University of Wisconsin Press, 1967.

Etheridge, Elizabeth W. *Sentinel for Health: A History of the Centers for Disease Control.* Berkeley and Los Angeles: University of California Press, 1992.

Farb, Peter, and George Amelagos. *Consuming Passions: The Anthropology of Eating.* New York: Pocket Books, 1980.

Fine, Gary Alan. "Among Those Dark Satanic Mills: Rumors of Kooks, Cults, and Corporations." *Southern Folklore* 47 (1990): 133–146.

———. "The Goliath Effect: Corporate Dominance and Mercantile Legends." *Journal of American Folklore* 98 (1985): 63–84.

———. "The Kentucky Fried Rat: Legends and Modern Society." *Journal of the Folklore Institute* 17 (1980): 222–43.

———. "Redemption Rumors: Mercantile Legends and Corporate Beneficence." *Journal of American Folklore* 99 (1986): 208–22.

———. "Welcome to the World of AIDS: Fantasies of Female Revenge." *Western Folklore* 46 (1987): 192–97.

Fisher, Mary A. "Was Wayne Williams Framed?" *Gentlemen's Quarterly*, April 1991, 228–35, 264–66.

Franklin, John Hope, and Alfred A. Moss, Jr. *From Slavery to Freedom: A History of Negro Americans.* New York: Alfred A. Knopf, 1988.

Freedman, Alix M. "Rumor Turns Fantasy into Bad Dream." *Wall Street Journal*, May 10, 1991, B1.

"Free Speech." *San Francisco Examiner*, "Image" sec., April 5, 1992, 3.

Fry, Gladys-Marie. *Night Riders in Black Folk History*. Knoxville: University of Tennessee Press, 1975.

Fuchs, Lawrence H. *The American Kaleidoscope: Race, Ethnicity, and the Civic Culture*. Hanover, N.H.: University Press of New England, 1990.

Garrow, David J. *The FBI and Martin Luther King, Jr.* New York: Penguin Books, 1983.

George, Katherine. "The Civilized West Looks at Primitive Africa, 1400–1800: A Study in Ethnocentrism." In *Every Man His Way: Readings in Cultural Anthropology*, edited by Alan Dundes, 22–36. Englewood Cliffs, N.J.: Prentice-Hall, 1968.

Gould, Stephen Jay. *The Mismeasure of Man*. New York: W. W. Norton, 1981.

Gunther, John. *Inside Africa*. New York: Harper & Brothers, 1955.

Harris, Trudier. *Exorcising Blackness: Historical and Literary Lynching and Burning Rituals*. Bloomington: Indiana University Press, 1984.

Harrison, Barbara Grizzuti. "Spike Lee Hates Your Cracker Ass." *Esquire*, October 1992, 132–40.

Heimann, Robert K. *Tobacco and Americans*. New York: McGraw-Hill, 1960.

Herzog, David. "Rumor Attacks Sales of Allentown Soda Company." *Morning Call* (Allentown, Pa.), July 4, 1991, A1.

Higginbotham, A. Leon, Jr. *In the Matter of Color: Race and the American Legal Process—The Colonial Period*. Oxford: Oxford University Press, 1980.

Hofstadter, Richard. "The Folklore of Populism." In *Conspiracy: The Fear of Subversion in American History*, edited by Richard O. Curry and Thomas M. Brown, 100–13. New York: Holt, Rinehart & Winston, 1972.

Hunter, Sam. *Art in Business: The Philip Morris Story*. New York: Harry N. Abrams, 1979.

"Is Frank Perdue Chicken?" *Forbes*, November 1984, 224.

"Jackson Promotes Boycott." *Brockton Daily Reporter*, August 17, 1990, D1.

Jacobs, Harriet A. *Incidents in the Life of a Slave Girl, Written by Herself*. Cambridge, Mass.: Harvard University Press, 1987.

Jacobson, D. J. *The Affairs of Dame Rumor*. New York: Rinehart, 1948.

Johnson, Loch K. *America's Secret Power: The CIA in a Democratic Society.* New York: Oxford University Press, 1989.

Johnson, Tom. "War and Race: Black Perspectives on the Gulf." *Sacramento News and Review,* February 14, 1991, 16–17.

Jones, James H. *Bad Blood: The Tuskegee Syphilis Experiment—A Tragedy of Race and Medicine.* New York: Free Press, 1982.

Jordan, Winthrop D. *White over Black: American Attitudes Toward the Negro, 1550–1812.* Baltimore: Penguin Books, 1969.

Jordan, Winthrop, Leon F. Litwack, Richard Hofstadter, William Miller, and Daniel Aaron. *The United States: Conquering a Continent.* 5th ed. Vol. 1. Englewood Cliffs, N.J.: Prentice-Hall, 1982.

"Justice in Alabama." *Boston Globe,* February 24, 1986.

Kapferer, Jean-Noel. *Rumors: Uses, Interpretations, and Images.* New Brunswick, N.J.: Transaction Books, 1990.

King, Martin L., Jr. *Why We Can't Wait.* New York: New American Library, 1968.

Knopf, Terry Ann. *Rumors, Race, and Riots.* New Brunswick, N.J.: Transaction Books, 1975.

Koenig, Fredrick. *Rumor in the Marketplace: The Social Psychology of Commercial Hearsay.* Dover, Mass.: Auburn House, 1985.

Kovel, Joel. *White Racism: A Psychohistory.* New York: Columbia University Press, 1984.

Langbaum, Robert. "Introduction" to William Shakespeare, *The Tempest,* xxi–xxxiv. New York: New American Library, 1964.

Langlois, Janet L. "The Belle Isle Bridge Incident: Legend Dialectic and Semiotic System in the 1943 Detroit Race Riots." *Journal of American Folklore* 96 (1983): 183–98.

Leavy, Walter. "The Case of the Disappearing Blacks." *Ebony,* December 1980, 136–40.

Levine, Lawrence W. *Black Culture and Black Consciousness: Afro-American Folk Thought from Slavery to Freedom.* New York: Oxford University Press, 1978.

Levinson, Arlene. "Rumor Almost Ruins Small Soda Firm." *Los Angeles Times,* July 14, 1991, A2.

Lewin, Tamar. "A Plan to Pay Welfare Mothers for Birth Control." *New York Times,* February 9, 1991, 18.

Litwack, Leon F. *Been So Long in the Storm: The Aftermath of Slavery.* New York: Vintage Books, 1980.

McWhiney, H. Grady, and Francis B. Simkins. "The Ghostly Legend of the Ku-Klux Klan." In *Mother Wit from the Laughing Barrel: Readings in the Interpretation of African-American*

Folklore, edited by Alan Dundes, 586–94. Englewood Cliffs, N.J.: Prentice-Hall, 1973.

Mullen, Patrick. "Modern Legend and Rumor Theory." *Journal of the Folklore Institute* 9 (1972): 95–109.

Murphy, Frances. "Justice Department Lists Barry Case Among Top 32." *Washington Afro-American*, May 4, 1991.

Newton, John. "Thoughts upon the African Slave Trade." In *The Journals of a Slave Trader, 1750–1754*, edited by Bernard Martin and Mark Spurrell. London: Epworth Press, 1962.

"New Trial Sought in Atlanta Murders." *Los Angeles Times*, February 18, 1992, A10.

Odum, Howard W. *Race and Rumors of Race: Challenge to American Crisis*. Chapel Hill: University of North Carolina Press, 1943.

"One Well-read Editorial." *Newsweek*, December 31, 1990, 65–66.

O'Reilly, Kenneth. *"Racial Matters": The FBI's Secret File on Black America, 1960–1972*. New York: Free Press, 1989.

Palmer, Thomas. "Will Mandela Make Reebok Look Better?" *Boston Globe*, June 20, 1990, 69, 73.

Patton, Cindy. *Sex and Germs: The Politics of AIDS*. Boston: South End Press, 1985.

Perdue, Charles L., Jr., Thomas E. Barden, and Robert K. Phillips, eds. *Weevils in Wheat: Interviews with Virginia Ex-Slaves*. Bloomington: Indiana University Press, 1980.

Pieterse, Jan Nederveen. *White over Black: Images of Africa and Blacks in Western Popular Culture*. New Haven: Yale University Press, 1992.

Pliny the Elder. *Natural History, Vol. II, Books III–VII*. Edited by H. Rackham. Cambridge, Mass.: Harvard University Press, 1942.

Pope-Hennessy, James. *Sins of the Fathers*. London: Cassell, 1967.

"Poverty and Norplant." *Philadelphia Inquirer*, December 12, 1990, A18.

Randolph, Philip A. "The Human Hand Threat." In *Mother Wit from the Laughing Barrel: Readings in the Interpretation of African-American Folklore*, edited by Alan Dundes, 642–48. Englewood Cliffs, N.J.: Prentice-Hall, 1973.

Report of the Committees of the House of Representatives for the Second Session of the Forty-second Congress, South Carolina, 1872.

Ridley, Florence. "A Tale Too Often Told." *Western Folklore* 26 (1967): 153–56.

Roberts, John W. *From Trickster to Badman: The Black Folk Hero in Slavery and Freedom*. Philadelphia: University of Pennsylvania Press, 1989.

Robinson, John. "The Secretary's Story." *Boston Globe*, May 20, 1990, 42–43.

Rosnow, Ralph L., and Gary Alan Fine. *Rumor and Gossip: The Social Psychology of Hearsay*. New York: Elsevier Scientific Publishing Co., 1976.

Rudwick, Elliot. *Race Riot at East St. Louis, July 2, 1917*. Chicago: University of Illinois Press, 1982.

Sandalow, Marc. "Klan Rumor Helped Ruin Sport Clothing Firm." *San Francisco Chronicle*, July 22, 1989, A3.

Sanday, Peggy Reeves. *Divine Hunger: Cannibalism as a Cultural System*. Cambridge: Cambridge University Press, 1986.

Shenon, Philip. "Black Agent to Lead Probe of FBI Racism." *San Francisco Chronicle*, August 22, 1990, A9.

Shibutani, Tamotsu. *Improvised News: A Sociological Study of Rumor*. Indianapolis: Bobbs-Merrill, 1966.

Shilts, Randy. *And the Band Played On: Politics, People, and the AIDS Epidemic*. New York: Penguin Books, 1987.

"The Siege of L.A." *Newsweek*, May 11, 1992, 35.

Sontag, Susan. *AIDS and Its Metaphors*. New York: Farrar, Strauss & Giroux, 1988.

"Soviet Active Measures in the Era of Glasnost." Report prepared at the request of the U.S. House of Representatives Committee on Appropriations. Washington, D.C., 1988.

"A Storm over Tropical Fantasy." *Newsweek*, April 22, 1991, 34.

Tannahill, Reay. *Flesh and Blood: A History of the Cannibal Complex*. New York: Dorset Press, 1975.

Telander, Rick. "Senseless." *Sports Illustrated*, May 14, 1990, 37.

Thomas, Cal. "It's a Short Step to the Next Horror of Eugenics." *Los Angeles Times*, December 30, 1990, M7.

"Tobacco and Black Americans." *Blackbook*, 1991, 65.

Toelken, Barre. *The Dynamics of Folklore*. Boston: Houghton Mifflin, 1979.

Turner, Patricia A. "Ambivalent Patrons: The Role of Rumor and Contemporary Legend in African American Consumer Decisions." *Journal of American Folklore* 105 (Fall 1992): 424–41.

———. "Church's Fried Chicken and the Klan: A Rhetorical Analysis of Rumor in the Black Community." *Western Folklore* 46 (1987): 294–306.

Vassell, Olive. "Are Sportswear Owners Linked to KKK?" *Washington Afro-American*, May 17, 1988, A1.

Wade, Wyn Craig. *The Fiery Cross: The Ku Klux Klan in America*. New York: Touchstone Books, 1987.

Washington, Booker T. *Up From Slavery*. New York: Penguin
Books, 1986.
Wattleton, Faye. "Using Birth Control as Coercion." *Los Angeles
Times*, December 30, 1990, M7.
Wells-Barnett, Ida B. "A Red Record." In *Black Women in White
America: A Documentary History*, edited by Gerda Lerner,
199–205. New York: Vintage Books, 1973.
Wiggins, William H. *O Freedom! Afro-American Emancipation
Celebrations*. Knoxville: University of Tennessee Press, 1987.
"Will Mandela Make Reebok Look Better?" *Boston Globe*, June 20,
1990.
Winterbottom, Thomas. *An Account of the Native Africans of Sierra
Leone, to Which Is Added an Account of the Present State of
Medicine Among Them*. London: Frank Cass, 1969.
Wright, Joseph. "The Narrative of Joseph Wright." In *Africa Re-
membered*, edited by Philip D. Curtin, 317–33. Madison: Univer-
sity of Wisconsin Press, 1967.
"Your Sneakers or Your Life." *Sports Illustrated*, May 14, 1990, 36.

Interviews and Correspondence

Ahlerich, Milt. Acting Assistant Director, Office of Congressional
and Public Affairs, Federal Bureau of Investigation. August 28,
1987.
Bamberger, David J. CEO, Church's Fried Chicken, Inc. August 8,
1986.
Brunvand, Jan Harold. Professor of Folklore, University of Utah.
January 29, 1990.
Caldwell, Janet. Center for Democratic Renewal. October 25, No-
vember 20, 1989.
Douglass, Jan. Director, Community Relations Commission, City of
Atlanta. September 22, 1987.
Hulnick, Arthur S. Coordinator for Academic Affairs, Central Intelli-
gence Agency. August 23, 1987.
Lauria, Thomas. The Tobacco Institute. March 12, 1990.
Lightcap, Kenneth R. Vice-President for Corporate Communica-
tions, Reebok International, Ltd., Stoughton, Massachusetts. May
14, 1990.
Patterson, Sarah. Public Relations, Liz Claiborne, Inc. December
20, 1991.
Singleton, John W. Manager, Special Public Relations Programs,
R. J. Reynolds, Inc. April 17, 1991.

Strausser, Susan A. Corporate Affairs, Philip Morris. February 8, 1990.

Tell, David. Deputy Chief of Staff, Office of National Drug Control Policy. June 4, 1990.

Wohl, Kathryn More. Public Relations, Church's Fried Chicken. July 17, August 24, 1989; November 2, 1990.

Index

255